P9-BJM-338

AUGUSTANA UNIVERSITY COLLEGE
LIBRARY

Men of the Steel Rails

James H. Ducker

Workers
on the Atchison,
Topeka &
Santa Fe Railroad,
1869–1900

Men
of the Steel
Rails

University of Nebraska Press

Lincoln and London

Copyright 1983 by the
University of Nebraska Press
All rights reserved

Manufactured in the
United States of America

The paper in this book
meets the guidelines for
permanence and durability
of the Committee on
Production Guidelines for
Book Longevity of the Council
on Library Resources.

Library of Congress
Cataloging in
Publication Data

Ducker, James H., 1950–
Men of the steel rails.

Bibliography: p.
Includes index.
1. Atchison, Topeka and
Santa Fe Railway–
Employees—History.
2. Trade-unions–Rail-
roads–United States–
History. I. Title.
HD8039.R12U625 1983   73697
331.7′61385′0978 82-17541
ISBN 0-8032-1662-9

ꟸ

To Mom and Dad

AUGUSTANA UNIVERSITY COLLEGE
LIBRARY

CONTENTS

ILLUSTRATIONS

Preface

In the industrialized America of the late nineteenth century the rules, rhythms, and remuneration of a man's job touched all facets of his life. The employer, at least in theory, could determine every aspect of his workday—how exhaustive, how dirty, how dangerous, and how long. The worker's employment helped determine where he resided, how frequently he moved, how much time he had for his family, how comfortable a lifestyle he could afford, and how long he might live. And even when the worker tried to seize greater control and security for himself, his success in using politics or unions was influenced by his position on his employer's payroll.

The railroad, more than any other enterprise, exemplified the growing size and complexity of business operations. In 1880, when there were just over 300,000 textile mill workers and about 230,000 miners in the United States, there were well over 400,000 railroaders. Moreover, while many miners and textile workers labored for relatively small firms, nearly three-quarters of all railroaders worked for roads employing a thousand or more. Nor did public enterprises match the scale of railroads. In the 1890s the Pennsylvania Railroad employed 15,000 more workers than the post office, the largest federal agency, while several other roads each engaged about as many men as were enlisted in all the United States armed forces.[1]

This book portrays the lives of railroaders who labored on the Atchison, Topeka & Santa Fe. It does not give equal emphasis to all portions of the Santa Fe, but concentrates on the oldest and most central section. While the company's Kansas City to

Chicago route and its Texas, Oklahoma, Arizona, and California subsidiaries are not excluded from consideration, the greatest emphasis is on the operating line from Atchison and Kansas City, Kansas, to Deming, New Mexico, and El Paso, Texas. This was the heart of the system and was the part of the line where most Santa Fe employees worked. Moreover, the historical record is most complete for this area.

In undertaking this study, I have incurred many debts. During the earliest stages Philip Van Der Meer and Walter Licht helped me to define its scope. John Tilsch of the Santa Fe's Public Relations Office led me to the company payrolls, which are the most thorough for any western railroad. The company has since deposited its treasure house of payroll records in the Kansas State Historical Society. The Lyon County Commissioners' Office in Emporia, Kansas, helped make the tax rolls available. Charles "Bud" Goebel of Burlingame, Kansas, shared valuable documents, his more than sixty years of experience with the Santa Fe, and the hospitality of his home. Many libraries and other depositories of historical data provided help directly or through interlibrary loan. Foremost among these were the Kansas State Historical Society and the University of Illinois. A group of graduate students at the University of Illinois, composed of Melvin Adelman, Jeffrey Brown, David Dunning, James Farrell, John Ruoff, and Gregory Schmidt, rendered advice, criticism, and encouragement throughout the dissertation stage of this study. The manuscript also benefited from the criticisms of Carl Graves, O. Vernon Burton, Thomas A. Krueger, and Robert M. Sutton.

Particular recognition goes to relatives and fellow graduate students, who provided intellectual, moral, and other assistance. My parents contributed in every way they could. Their patience and understanding during the years of my graduate study bear the mark of their love. Last, Professor Clark C. Spence's steady concern and gentle coaching through the doctoral program, his calm prodding in directing the author toward a worthwhile historical investigation, and his careful editing of the manuscript largely account for whatever merit lies in this story of the common men of a great American railway.

Men of the Steel Rails

CHAPTER 1

Workin' on the Atchison,
Topeka & Santa Fe

On a bright Kansas spring afternoon in 1869 engineer George Beach pulled back the throttle, sending the Cyrus K. Holliday creaking forward on its excursion trip to the end-of-track. Beach guided the second-hand 4-4-0 engine over the gently rolling hills that stretched south from Topeka. Between proud waves to the curious farmers, fireman Britton Craft shoveled in the coal as a sooty trail traced the path of the train past Pauline and on into the Wakarusa Valley. Conductor William W. Fagan spent the trip fielding questions from the press when he was not soothing the nerves of those who found the fifteen miles per hour speed to be a bit more excitement than they had anticipated. He could state authoritatively that the roadbed and track were of the highest quality and that in time the passengers would find such a speed as salubrious as the picnic weather of the day. At any rate, the excursionists' excitement would soon be relieved. As the train approached Cottonwood Falls, William Bartling and Al Dugan scampered onto the tops of the cars and set the brakes. Screeching and shivering, the train came to rest. Seven miles from its starting point, the ceremonial first passenger run of the Atchison, Topeka & Santa Fe Railroad came to an end.[1]

That trip and a subsequent picnic celebrated the initial triumph and the prospects of a venture launched a decade earlier. The story of the Santa Fe began in 1859, when Cyrus K. Holliday won a charter from the Kansas legislature for the Atchison & Topeka Railroad Company. The following year a board of thirteen businessmen from the two towns put up four hundred dollars and named Holliday president, hoping he could win a land grant, without which the infant firm would become no more than a mere fantasy of steaming engines on the Kansas prairie. Holliday got the land grant but, hindered by the Civil War and attending financial problems, the Atchison & Topeka achieved little more in the next nine years except to add to its title the name of the fabled center of the southwestern trade. Only in late 1868 were Holliday's persistent efforts rewarded, as rails began to reach south from Topeka.

After the excursionists debarked and enjoyed their lunch, Holliday delivered a stirring speech dwelling on the promise of the new road, which, he predicted, would soon not only reach Santa Fe but go on to California. Yet, only men with more capital than the Kansans could realize his grandiose schemes. And so, within a year and a half of Holliday's speech at Cottonwood Falls, Boston financiers gained a dominance in the road that they did not yield for nearly twenty-five years. In that time the Bay Staters oversaw the road's finances and chose strong-willed and experienced men to supervise its expansion. Thomas J. Peter, a Cincinnati civil engineer already associated with the Santa Fe's early construction, became general manager. In two and a half years in that position he succeeded in pushing the line across Kansas, thus securing the company's land grant. Without a general manager in the depression era of the mid 1870s, the Santa Fe made modest expansions that brought the line into Kansas City and Pueblo, Colorado. In 1877 the firm's financial leaders named William B. Strong, a man with twenty-two years of railroading experience, as general manager. Beginning with the economic upswing in 1878 Strong started a virtually unceasing expansion program. By 1881 construction crews had laid steel rails from La Junta, Colorado, through the Raton and Glorietta passes of northern New Mexico and thence south along the Rio Grande to Rincon, New Mexico, where the road forked; one line ended in El Paso, Texas, and the other made a junction with the Southern Pacific at Deming, New Mexico. In the meantime Strong, who became president in 1881, fleshed out the road's Kansas system; and by 1885 he had pushed the Santa Fe's Atlantic & Pacific subsidiary across northern Arizona to San Diego. In the following year he bought the Gulf, Colorado & Santa Fe, an important Texas line, and in 1887 Strong completed an extension from Kansas City to Chicago.

Strong fully realized the most ambitious dreams Holliday had put before his listeners in 1869. But growth meant an enormous fixed debt, and the new trackage brought little income. By the late 1880s the annual losses of the A & P, the G C & SF and the Chicago branch totaled more than $3.3 million. Allen Manvel was lured away from James J. Hill's Great Northern in 1889 to replace Strong as president. But even though he worked himself into an early grave, Manvel could not scramble out from under the crushing debt Strong's construction had placed on his shoulders, and two days before Christmas 1893 the Santa Fe went into receivership. Two years later the road emerged from receivership and its brilliant new president, Edward P. Ripley, set to work redeeming Cyrus Holliday's dream; in his twenty-five-year tenure as head of the Santa Fe, he succeeded in establishing it as one of the most prosperous railroads in the American West.

The achievements of men such as Holliday, Strong, and Ripley have long been acclaimed in railroad histories. But if these corporate leaders played key roles in the development of the Santa Fe, so too did the company's force of skilled and unskilled workers. At the time of its run to Cottonwood Falls, the Santa Fe had just one train and engine crew. Any more would have been superfluous: the company owned only one engine. The office staff consisted of a paymaster and a clerk, and the shop employed only a blacksmith. A station agent, express messenger, and watchman raised the payroll to eleven, in addition to those laying track. By 1874, the work force had risen to seven hundred. And after the Santa Fe forged into New Mexico, the payroll expanded to nearly three thousand workers. This growth also brought on a greater dispersion of the work force, particularly among shopmen. With New Mexico six hundred miles from the Topeka facilities, it became imperative that rolling stock repair work be available at division shops. The train and engine crews had long been scattered in towns at one-hundred-mile intervals, the distance that could be covered in a day. Now considerable shop operations were established at Emporia, Nickerson, Dodge City, and Coolidge, Kansas; La Junta, Colorado; and Raton, Las Vegas, Wallace, and San Marcial, New Mexico. Though in the next twenty years the company shifted some of its division points to other towns, most Santa Fe workers continued to live in division centers. This labor force burgeoned so that by 1886 it numbered seven thousand to eight thousand and by the end of the century the number employed, exclusive of the Texas, Arizona, and California lines, reached twenty thousand.[2]

The Santa Fe's railroaders can be divided into five groups, each of which maintained a roughly stable percentage of the work force throughout the road's first three decades. Shop and roundhouse men made up about one-quarter of the company's employees, of whom 30 percent labored in the Topeka shops. The shop workers handled major repairs to both engines and rolling stock. All the division points had repair crews of boiler-makers, machinists, blacksmiths, car repairers, and painters and their helpers and apprentices. At Raton and Topeka, major shops took on periodic overhauls of engines, while Topeka's massive complex manufactured both cars and locomotives and made furnishings for the line's stations and offices. Roundhouses were located at all division towns and some towns of lesser importance. Roundhouse employees were charged with maintaining the company's locomotives daily and preparing them for service. Shopmen were often called into the roundhouse to handle "running repairs" on engines that needed only minor adjustments. The most numerous roundhouse workers were the hostlers, who guided the locomotives into and out of the roundhouse, and the wipers, who cleaned excess oil and grit from the engines.[3]

Trackmen and their section bosses constituted the largest segment of Santa Fe employees. Although their numbers varied dramatically from summer to winter, they averaged approximately 30 percent of the work force. However, they were so dispersed that, except in the case of special trouble-shooting track repair crews, seldom were more than eight seen at any one place. Track crews lived along and maintained each of the six- to eight-mile sections into which the Santa Fe divided its line. The crew would spend most of its day reinforcing weak roadbeds, tapping down loose pins, replacing worn ties, and clearing the right-of-way of weeds, grass, and debris. The foreman was also responsible for daily inspection of the entire section, meaning that every day, every mile on the system was examined. The section foreman had to be a man of some experience and common sense, but the track laborer needed little skill beyond being able to hit a spike with a hammer. It was universally considered a most inferior and arduous form of labor.[4]

A third group, composing 15 percent of the Santa Fe's employees, spent their days in or about the station. The size of this force varied greatly, depending on the importance of the town. In 1895 the Santa Fe division city of Emporia had thirteen clerks, six station laborers, five train dispatchers, and twenty-three switchmen, as well as flagmen, baggagemen, and miscellaneous others for a total of sixty-three. Nearby Plymouth was manned solely by Warren Stover. But the railroad expected Stover to perform for his village much the same services as the sixty-three men did in Emporia. He sold tickets, helped passengers with their baggage, checked freight shipments, received and sent telegraph messages, relayed dispatchers' orders to trainmen, took responsibility for the local mail, lent a hand in switching cars on his side track, and made at least a passing effort to keep his station tidy enough for the most fastidious visiting grandmother.[5]

Enginemen, engineers and firemen, and trainmen, conductors and brakemen, made up another 15 percent of the Santa Fe's laborers. The typical train was manned by an engineer, a fireman, a conductor, and two brakemen. The engineer controlled the locomotive, maintaining vigilance over the steam pressure, boiler water level, fire-box temperature, and the other workings of the machinery even as he watched for obstructions on the rails ahead. Under the engineer's eye, the fireman kept the fire evenly fueled with coal, shoveling at least five tons a day through the small firebox door as the engine rumbled along. Freight conductors were responsible for the contents of all their cars, while passenger conductors sold and collected tickets and dealt with sick, drunk, and obnoxious travelers. Until the adoption of air brakes, the brakemen's primary duty was to pick their way along the tops of the cars setting and releasing the brakes, but they also had to do the even more dangerous work of switching at many of the smaller way stations.[6]

The remaining 15 percent of the work force was split up among various groups. Many were secretaries and other functionaries at the general office at Topeka. A couple of hundred more labored at the tie-pickling factory near Las Vegas. The company built this plant in 1885 to treat its ties with pine tar and chloride of zinc to protect them from insects and the weather. Numerous bridge and building gangs, each composed of a score or more men, built and maintained the Santa Fe structures in their areas. Since most bridges were of wood and washouts and floods were common, these gangs were generally active.[7]

Most employees' days were uneventful, but for many there were days that brought hardships and hazards. In the three years ending June 1888, forty-two Santa Fe employees were killed and 1,858 injured in Kansas alone. Trainmen, enginemen, and switchmen were the victims of at least 70 percent of these accidents; one out of every 108 was killed and one in 2.4 was injured every year. These figures reflected a national problem, which prompted Congressman Henry Cabot Lodge to point out that yearly railroad casualties exceeded the losses suffered by Wellington at Waterloo and Meade at Gettysburg and fell just short of matching the losses of the French and German forces at Sedan.[8]

Station agents, clerks, and telegraph operators, like their nonrailroading white collar counterparts, met few dangers. An 1897 study of Kansas workers revealed that only 5 percent of these workers considered their jobs hazardous. Occasionally some of the West's badmen encroached on their peaceful existences, since it was these employees who stood between the outside world and the company's money. Some proved heroic, including night operator Andrew Kincade of the Kinsley station east of Dodge City, who in 1878 outwitted six armed men and warned an incoming passenger train in time to help thwart a robbery. Others, such as a night operator at Glorieta, New Mexico, followed the dictum that discretion was the better part of valor and handed over the money, much to the disgust of the rough and ready local editor, who declared that "any man who cannot defend himself from two assailants ought to be robbed."[9]

The working conditions of sectionmen and shopmen were more dangerous. Over 40 percent of track crews felt themselves in danger on their jobs. They labored with heavy tools and materials, and slips were possible. Moreover, ethnic differences and the poverty and isolation of section crews helped make friction within the gang inevitable. Shopmen's working conditions were similar to those of many factory laborers. A journalist visiting the Topeka shops in 1883 commented, "The hum of industry is considerably more than a 'hum' when you are close to it. It sounds something like the infernal regions are presumed to sound." A visitor two years later reported that many years of work in the boiler shops were literally deafening. In the summer, outside temperatures of over one hundred degrees were magnified to such an extent in the boiler and blacksmith shops that men had to quit working early and machinists rigged up fans to cool themselves off and keep the ever-present flies at a distance. Beyond these discomforts there were real dangers. Stray pieces of flying metal and heavy machinery that occasionally slipped from its blocks accounted for some maimings and deaths. But a special terror, and the most dangerous job in the shops, was reserved for the boilermakers on running repairs. Because leaks could be detected only when the boiler was under pressure, these men climbed inside the firebox while there was still steam in the boiler. Should a flue plug pop loose, steam would rush into the firebox, resulting in ghastly scaldings, singed lungs, and deaths.[10]

The greatest discomforts and dangers rested on those men who moved the trains. All but 3 percent of Kansas trainmen and enginemen considered their jobs hazardous. Among major groups of nonrailroaders, only coal miners matched this percentage. Early work on the Santa Fe yielded both the romance of pioneering and the added problems brought by crude technology, substandard roadbeds, and the rowdy environment of the western frontier. In the first years of the road, when the wood-burning locomotive General A. E. Burnside ran short of fuel, firemen gathered cow and buffalo chips to help make it to the next station. The "Calamity branch" from Topeka to Kansas City ran too close to the Kansas River. A heavy rain frequently flooded over the roadbed and compelled the crew to swim the river to contact headquarters via the Kansas Pacific telegraph, because the Santa Fe's own line commonly went down in a severe storm. Those on the western end of the road occasionally spotted Indians but faced more danger from the buffalo herds, which overturned engines, and cowboys who considered shooting out train lanterns and headlights to be a major entertainment offered by Dodge City.[11]

A great hazard was involved in taking trains through the New Mexico mountains in the early 1880s. The *Las Vegas Daily Optic* probably exaggerated when it reported that eighteen engines were demolished in a four-week period. But it pointed to real dangers. Although the new roadbed and bridges were inadequate, the most spectacular accidents were caused by a lack of air brakes. In 1881 engineer Jake Brown told how, in taking an engine up a hill out of Lamy, he spotted a train coming down at him at more that ordinary speed. Brown reversed his engine, but the other train's crew, feeling themselves doomed, all jumped—except conductor Cooley, who made his way to the engine along the tops of the cars, setting the brakes as he went. The trains stopped just short of collision. Runaways were so common on Glorieta Pass that the local paper expressed relief and some surprise when a whole month went by without one. And in 1885 the *Daily Optic* rejoiced when air brakes on trains traveling over the mountains became standard, putting an end to this special peril.[12]

Some dangers did not fade with time. Track washouts continued to make trainmen and enginemen skeptical of the integrity of the road ahead. Blizzards stranded crews and posed an added danger because cattle congregated on the track between plow-built embankments. Passenger conductors throughout the century were called on to eject inebriated roughs, too many of whom came aboard with their pistols strapped to their sides. The problem with train robberies actually became more severe in the 1890s and did not start to taper off until the early twentieth century. At least six on the Santa Fe were noted by the national press in 1898, three involving the fatal shooting of engineers or firemen. But in the majority of hold-ups there was no gunfire.[13]

Tramps proved more numerous, more persistent, and at least as dangerous. This class of drifters burgeoned during the depression of the 1870s and grew to even larger proportions by the end of the century. In 1898 a remarkable Santa Fe train came into Newton, Kansas, with nearly two hundred freeloaders clinging to it, the crew totally intimidated. Few trains were entirely free of them. Trainmen were kindly toward crippled tramps and unemployed railroaders on the move in search of work. But, especially in the early years, they gave no quarter to the "Knights of the Steel Rail," and their resolve was matched by the tramps' determination to ride regardless. Bloody battles sometimes ensued. Tramps who showed fight were thrown from moving trains, beaten with lanterns and clubs, or shot. In 1885, railroaders in Winslow, Arizona, looped a rope around a tramp's neck, led him to the edge of town, and "choked him until his tongue stuck out like that of a bull calf's." Tramps were, if anything, less gentlemanly, some beating and shooting first if they got the chance. By the 1890s, the tramps were further frustrating trainmen by using the law to bring indictments against railroaders who too vigorously ejected them. However, like the train robbers, tramps boarded the trains to get something free and generally avoided trouble with railroad employees.[14]

The greatest dangers came in braking and switching. Although the Santa Fe experimented with air brakes in the mid-1870s and began installing them on many of their cars ten years later, it was not until 1898 that they had completely eliminated the need for brakemen to clamber atop the cars. Foul weather, rough and sharply curving track, bridges that only allowed a few feet of clearance, and the lack of uniformity in car design jeopardized the brakeman's precarious perch. But by far the most common accident—accounting for 35 to 45 percent of all mishaps—came as brakemen or switchmen tried to couple or uncouple cars. The link and pin coupler, which was nearly universal until the last years of the century, required men to dodge in and out between moving cars to make couplings. Sooner or later a brakeman was bound to crush his fingers. The results were far more disastrous if the worker got pinned between the cars or fell under the wheels, which could easily slice a man in two. An Emporia paper noted that switching was associated "with a strange fatality" after three successively employed night switchmen were injured in the yards, the last one being lucky to get away from a collision of two cars with only his right arm "mash[ed] . . . into jelly."[15]

Just as the working conditions were diverse, so too were the wages paid by the company. With the exception of the juvenile shop apprentices who worked for less than a dollar a day, the lowest wage went to the track laborers, who normally received $1.10 to $1.25 a day and possibly $.20 to $.30 more for special projects like laying new steel. In approximately the same pay bracket were the more menial positions in the station, shops, and roundhouse. In the 1895 payroll, station laborers, callboys, engine wipers, and numerous others were being paid in the $1.15 to $1.30 range. Somewhat higher paid but rarely getting more than two dollars a day were track foremen, flagmen, baggagemen, bridge and building laborers, station clerks, car repairers, coach cleaners, and the helpers of boilermakers, blacksmiths, and machinists. Also at this level were the vast majority of station agents, who received a flat rate depending on the importance and size of their station plus, from 1891 on, a commission of up to 5 percent of the business generated from their town. Plymouth's Warren Stover was typical of flag station agents in being paid $43 plus 5 percent a month. A man who had worked himself into a position of agent at a larger station regularly could clear twice that amount. At the $2 level or slightly higher came brakemen, firemen, hostlers, and bridge and building carpenters. In the $2.50 to $3 range were the switchmen and skilled shopmen. Pay of $3 a day and up was reserved for engineers, conductors, dispatchers, yardmasters, shop foremen, bridge and building foremen, and corporate officials.[16]

Wages were not the only income of many railroad employees. In the 1880s train baggagemen were permitted to charge passengers and persons along the line a fee for looking after their dogs or guns in the baggage car. Baggagemen could also carry on a small merchandizing business. Ed Parson in the 1880s bought fish at an Indian reservation near Watrous, New Mexico, at ten cents a pound, transported them to Santa Fe in his baggage car, and sold them to a hotel for twenty cents. Many section bosses' wives materially added to their families' incomes by rooming and boarding the men in their husbands' gangs for a charge of about fifteen dollars a month each, while telegraph operators in some towns could pick up extra cash by handling Western Union messages.[17]

The company took a dimmer view of the ways trainmen

added to their incomes. The Santa Fe had a perennial problem with passenger conductors who were "color blind," unable to distinguish between their own and the company's money. On their own or in collusion with equally corrupt ticket agents, conductors took passengers' money without turning it over to the company. Freight crews made extra cash when they let those tramps ride who greeted them with the standard bribe of a dollar. Sometimes such freight crew practices had a noticeable effect on revenues. When the Santa Fe in 1888 detected abnormally poor passenger business on its Purcell, Oklahoma, to Arkansas City, Kansas, run it investigated and discovered an elaborate passenger business run by two of their freight conductors. The two made their own tickets and had others working for them as agents selling rides for $2 apiece, compared to the Santa Fe's regular $4.50 price. Undoubtedly most trainmen at some time in their careers yielded to the temptation of the illicit dollar.[18]

The Santa Fe tried to pay its employees monthly. However, as was common with other lines in their early development, the company at times in the 1870s fell several months behind in its payroll. The road again fell badly behind in its wage payments in 1893 as it slid toward receivership. La Junta, Colorado, employees complained that the company was placing them and their families on the verge of starvation. Strikes were threatened, and one brief wildcat strike of switchmen erupted in Argentine, Kansas, and Kansas City, Missouri, on December 22. The next day the Santa Fe went into receivership, and workers all along the line were relieved to learn that the court had ordered that money previously set aside to pay creditors be expended on wages.[19]

Generally the road paid a month's wages by the third week in the following month. In the first years of the railroad, treasurer Ed Wilder would take a passenger car to the end-of-track, paying as he went. By 1872, paymaster Jim Moore took over the task in a specially constructed car and, in the following year, checks replaced cash payments. The arrival of the pay train brought men running. Even when the more mundane method of sending checks to the local agents on a regular passenger train was adopted in 1889, the accompanying celebration was not diminished.[20]

The workers' glee was possibly matched only by that of the

local merchants who supported many of them on credit. Accounts with local shopkeepers were settled the day after payday; then for many credit buying might start all over again. Some employees complained that buying on credit raised their costs 8 to 15 percent. Realizing the tremendous strain weekly payment would place on the company, most of the higher-salaried workers did not grumble. It was the employees on the lower rungs of the wage scale who complained that they could not escape the never-ending round of debt. One Kansas railroader felt the pinch especially hard during the depression of the nineties. He wrote to the state's labor bureau, "With a family dependent upon us, with no chance to accumulate enough to enable us to quit long enough to look for a better job, . . . what are we but slaves?"[21]

Santa Fe men's pay was comparable to that received by employees of other railroads and by similarly skilled workers in other industries. Wage rates differed less from road to road than from one region to another and depended on the local labor supply and cost of living. Predictably, wages were lowest in the South, especially in those positions open to blacks. Pacific coast railroaders received the highest pay, and those in the mountain states were not far behind. Outside these areas, pay levels varied little from the national norm. The Santa Fe compensation rate reflected the higher levels paid in the western third of the country. Throughout the century most of those working on the road's western end got wages 5 to 35 percent higher than employees in Kansas and on the eastern extension to Chicago.[22]

The depression of the 1870s prompted wage reductions in 1877. Some groups of railroad employees suffered specific wage cuts and nearly all were hit with a general 5 percent decrease. For example, on May 1 conductors who had been earning over a hundred dollars a month and brakemen who had been getting up to two dollars a day dropped to seventy-five dollars and forty-five dollars a month, respectively. In August the trainmen lost another 5 percent in the general reduction, so that by the end of the year their wages had plummeted at least 25 percent from what they had been at the beginning of the year.[23]

The company recovered in the early 1880s, but most employees did not regain the wage rates lost in the seventies. Then during the company's financial embarrassment of 1888–89 there was a 20 percent decrease in trackmen's hours and pay and a 10 percent cut in wages of those earning fifty dollars a month or more. But the company emerged from this setback in the early 1890s, restored the wages of the 1880s, and further increased the pay of a number of groups. These wage rates persisted throughout the depression and receivership; hours and the total number of employees were cut instead.[24]

Geographic mobility while employed by a single company set railroad workers apart from employees in other industries. On the Santa Fe, some of this mobility was almost inevitable when the company expanded from a jerkwater line linking Topeka and Emporia in 1870 to the gigantic transcontinental of 1900. But, more importantly, most classes of railroad workers had to relocate in order to climb the promotional ladder. Two regular columns focusing on old-time employees in the *Santa Fe Magazine* furnished information on employees who worked for the company for at least ten years in the nineteenth century (see Table 1).[25] Those in the standard promotion track from telegraph operator to station agent were the most mobile—40 percent moved four or more times in their Santa Fe careers. The *Sterling [Kansas] Bulletin* noted that a night operator "scarcely has time to unpack his trunk until he [had] orders to go to some other station." While townsmen might have found these frequent turnovers frustrating, their former night operator may have been delighted to be moving, especially to a day shift, after which he could hope to start his advance from agent at a flag stop to agent of a division headquarters. F.M. Shick was hired by the Santa Fe as the night operator at Winfield, Kansas, in February 1887. Two weeks later he became the day operator at Kiowa. By September he was the agent at Argonia and the following six years would find him working as an agent or clerk in three other stations in Kansas. Because of his wife's illness he obtained a transfer to Colorado, first Colorado Springs, then Denver. In 1900 he headed farther west, to California, and in the next five years labored in three more towns. In all he was transferred ten times in eighteen years.[26]

Trackmen moved for much the same reasons as operators and agents. Once promoted to section foremen, they had no way to advance without moving. Some section foremanships carried

more pay than others. Also, in preparing a man for greater
responsibility as a roadmaster, the company wished him to have
experience in various places on the line. All trackmen recorded
in the *Santa Fe Magazine* columns who retired in the same
section in which they started also retired with the same job; this
contrasts with advancements for five of the six men who moved
more than once.[27]

Similarly, trainmen and enginemen often moved to be promoted a grade in service or to get a preferred run. Some young
brakemen and firemen transferred from jobs on the eastern end
of the Santa Fe to take similar positions on the western portion
because promotion there was more rapid. Since seniority was
well established on the line among trainmen and enginemen by
the late nineteenth century, when one old-timer retired a series
of men might shift about to get promotions or slightly better
runs. Such advancement steps were more plentiful in train and
engine service than in any other branch of railroading, with the
possible exception of those in the operator-agent promotion
track. The major reason that trainmen and enginemen did not
have as high a rate of mobility (see Table 1) is that, unlike station
and track work, train and engine service jobs were concentrated
at division points and the heads of branch lines, where men
could more frequently gain promotion without having to move.

A similar concentration of shop jobs at division centers helps
to account for the very marked stability of shopmen. Moreover,
there were far fewer incremental advancements available to
these workers. The next promotion steps after an apprentice
became a full-fledged boilermaker or machinist were head
boilermaker or head machinist and then foreman. These positions were rare and when they did become vacant, men in the
local shop often could fill them. Of the shopmen who did take
transfers, many did so without gaining advancement. California
had an especial attraction, as it did for shop carpenter John Holt,
who departed the Topeka shop for a comparable position in
Richmond, California. But of all railroaders, shopmen were most
like nonrailroaders in their permanence in a community.[28]

Business necessities as well as personal ambition could
compel large numbers of men to move. A change in train
schedules might require that the train and engine crews transfer

Table 1: Geographic Mobility of Santa Fe Employees

Occupational Groups	Number of Employees	(A) Percent who moved	(B) Percent of (A) moving more than once
Operators/agents	15	87	69
Trackmen	17	65	55
Enginemen	21	81	41
Trainmen	14	79	9
Shopmen	46	22	0

Source: Pension lists and "Employes Long in the Service" columns in *SFM* 1–10 (1906–16).

to a town at the other end of the run. Sometimes almost all of the railroad's employees were required to leave one town for another. In 1897, finding that new lines had left the division center of Nickerson a backwater, the Santa Fe tore down its shops and roundhouse and moved them to Newton. Nearly all of the three hundred employees were compelled to move the forty miles to the new division center. Old-time employees no doubt wished the company would make up its mind: eighteen years earlier the extension of the Santa Fe south into New Mexico had prompted the move of the division center from Newton to Nickerson.[29]

Less drastic, but more frequent, were the temporary transfers of trainmen and enginemen shifted about to help handle seasonal rushes. When cattle and crops from one region headed to market, the Santa Fe called on men from other areas where business was slack. The New Mexico cattle rush was so large in the 1890s that every spring dozens of Kansas employees went west to lend a hand until the rush ended in June. The movement was sometimes reversed in the late fall, when New Mexico crews went to Kansas to help move the wheat harvest.[30]

Many transfers entailed hardships. In 1886 passenger brakeman Dave Moore had just gotten himself a nice home in Las Vegas and his new wife was coming from Wisconsin when a shake-up of the schedule required that he move to Albuquerque. When the Nickerson shops shut down, many men felt they could not afford to give up their nearby farms and therefore they were only able to visit their families on weekend absences from Newton. Las Vegas engineers and firemen working west of Albuquerque on the Santa Fe's Atlantic & Pacific line had ambivalent feelings toward temporary transfers. After more than a month away from home, some were anxious to return, but many delighted in the big money they were making.[31]

Indeed, many railroaders were eager for transfers. Management did not have to force promotion-connected moves. Some requested transfers to the western part of the line for their own or a member of their family's health and many Santa Fe employees on the eastern end of the road jumped at the opportunity to work in California when the company expanded its operations in the Golden State. In all, Santa Fe employees transferred for much the same reasons that other American workers moved. But the Santa Fe men could do so while retaining their jobs.[32]

Hours of labor varied by occupation and season. As in most other callings, a six-day week of ten hours a day was standard for shopmen, trackmen, and most of the workers about the station during all but the slack winter months, when nine hours was the norm. Shopmen usually got Saturday afternoon off as well as Sunday. In the 1880s switchmen normally worked twelve hours, but this had been cut to ten by the nineties. The hours of agents and operators depended on the size of their stations. Those at large facilities had ten or even eight hour days, but those in charge of small stations commonly worked twelve hours and often had to be on hand beyond these hours if there was necessary business to transact.[33]

Most employees did not labor with the same intensity throughout the day. Stationmen's days were marked by spurts of activity when trains arrived, with somewhat calmer periods in between; then, small-town agents could do their other chores and switchmen could take time out to congregate about the switchmen's shack. Trackmen and bridge and building men spent part of each day moving to and from their areas of work and the distance traveled put them far enough from the scrutiny of company officials to allow time to lean on shovels and lay down hammers. Those running the trains also escaped constant supervision and could rest whenever shunted to a side track. Some trainmen even found time during their runs to read and play cards. Only those in the shops had days unbroken by the rhythms of the train schedule and were constantly in close proximity to company officials.[34]

The trainmen and enginemen worked the longest hours; they averaged eleven hours a day and frequently ran two to four weeks without taking a day's leave. Senior men could count on the same hours day after day, but others worked whenever the callboy notified them that it was their turn to go out. Depending on the train they drew, the heaviness of traffic of a higher priority, the amount of switching to be done along the way, the condition of the equipment, and the weather, a run could take between four and sixteen hours, though the greatest number fell in the seven- to fourteen-hour range.[35]

Although the company only paid the men for their time on the run, departure and arrival schedules were poor indicators of the actual hours involved in these jobs. Workers were not paid for the hours they spent at one end of a run waiting for the scheduled return home. Conductors and brakemen were required to be on hand to check the rolling stock and receive specific train orders well before their train pulled out. Engineers and firemen had to arrive early to make a last-minute inspection of the locomotive, oil its machinery, and then connect it to the cars. And when the run was over, engineers regularly spent an hour or more in checking and repairing minor problems with their engines.[36]

Hours for shopmen, trainmen, and enginemen were even longer when a rush began. The master mechanic refused requests for leaves, sometimes even for sickness, and allowed nothing but the barest minimum of rest. At the beginning of the cattle rush of 1897, Las Vegas boilermakers and Wellington, Kansas, roundhouse workers put in fifteen-hour days. At Wellington, car repairer Ed Huffman averaged nearly thirteen hours a day in May, including Sundays. For trainmen and enginemen, twenty hours at a stretch on the road was not unusual. Often the callboy met the men as they pulled into town to notify them that they would shortly have to take another train out. New Mexico conductors' wives probably exaggerated little when they complained that they had not seen their husbands in a week because the men no sooner got in than they were turned around to head out again.[37]

Even in normal times those who moved the commerce of the Santa Fe led disrupted lives. Children could have only sporadic contact with a father who arrived home at all times of the day or night. Too often the callboy rapped on the door just as supper was being served. An unexpected call or delay could ruin even the short-range plans the railroaders could make. Shopmen, office workers, track laborers, and all but a skeleton crew in the roundhouse and yards normally had Sundays off. But commerce could not come to a standstill, so the engines ran. Sabbath work was required despite the pleas of churchmen and the charges by some Santa Fe employees that it overworked them, took employees away from families, and was counter to the "sacred commandment of the Deity."[38]

Although railroaders complained about extremely long hours, they were even less happy about working fewer hours than usual. Less time translated into smaller paychecks. A survey of Kansas railroaders in the 1890s showed that trainmen, enginemen, and trackmen overwhelmingly considered ten hours the proper workday. Agents and operators felt the twelve hours they normally worked was about right. Only among the skilled shopmen, who labored more consistently through the day, did the majority favor an eight-hour day. An Emporia bridgeman said it made "a feller feel more natural and like himself to put in 10 hours a day" instead of the eight or nine he had recently worked. Others expressed themselves more forcefully. Track workers quit en masse in 1888 when they were reduced from a ten- to an eight-hour day, resulting in daily pay of only eighty-eight cents. Shopmen all along the line in the late nineties quit rather than try to live on the wages they received when cuts in hours were initiated. Angered with the imposition of a five-day, forty-hour work week, Newton shopmen sarcastically called Saturday "Santa Fe Sunday," "blue day," and "meditation season." When their weekly hours were again upped to fifty-five "the boys were . . . full of joy."[39]

The uncertainty about work prospects helped muffle discontent with long hours. Railroad employment fluctuated for a number of reasons. Corporate fiscal and general economic problems could bring distress. Even an incident as relatively minor as the burning of the company's Fairview Tunnel in Arizona in 1898 threw the Santa Fe's finances into such a state that the Topeka and Newton shops were cut back from fifty-four to forty hours a week for a month. When the 1874 grasshopper plague dealt a blow to Santa Fe earnings, the company slashed payroll expenses 20 percent by dismissing employees or shortening hours. The Santa Fe's economic embarrassment of 1888–89 brought a 10 percent wage rate reduction, eight- or nine-hour days, and unemployment. When the nation plummeted into depression in 1893, the Santa Fe was especially vulnerable because of past corporate mismanagement and the effects of the repeal of the Silver Purchase Act on the traffic of its Colorado lines. Hours and employees were cut while the Santa Fe struggled to meet interest payments. Nonessential trackwalkers, brick masons, bridge carpenters, and painters were discharged in May. On June 9 all shop workers went to an eight-hour day. In early July, shop forces were reduced 20 percent, except those on the Colorado Midland subsidiary, which were chopped in half. Track and bridge gangs were sliced 40 percent at the very time of year when employment should have been at its peak. Regular switchmen were transferred to the extra list and by 1894 shop workers were at times employed only thirty-two hours a week. Engine and train crews were not as drastically affected at the outset, but as the nation's economy slowed, so did the demand for transportation, and layoffs followed.[40]

Machine breakdowns, illness, and the weather also had an impact on a Santa Fe employee's earnings. In 1892, when the stationary engine in the Topeka car shop blew out its cylinder head, the workers in that department were sent home for a week until replacement parts could come from the east. But the locomotives were the most fragile of the company's equipment. Major repairs were required every three or four months, particularly on those subject to the corroding effects of western alkaline water. Engine crews sometimes ran as extras or got other locomotives while theirs were in the shop. However, more often they simply did not work again until their engine was repaired. Most enginemen lost about two months a year for this reason.[41]

Sickness also cut unevenly into railroad employment. All railroaders were equally susceptible to self-inflicted "illnesses" such as "too much Fourth" or the "circus fever" that decimated the Newton roundhouse force the morning after the annual picnic in 1898. No occupational group was immune from common ailments. But Kansas survey data makes it clear that those groups who worked outdoors lost far more time than those whose work places were sheltered. In 1899 blacksmiths, machinists, agents, and operators reported eight or fewer days lost because of illness. Trackmen and those in train and engine service reported three to four times this rate of sickness. Undoubtedly it was exposure to the bitter winds of winter that accounted for the greatest amount of their absenteeism. The brakeman perched on a snow-covered boxcar, the engineman alternately exposed to the heat of the firebox and the chilling winds that whipped through his cab, and the trackwalker who had to have his clothes peeled off of him after inspecting the section in a freezing rain inevitably lost days of work in the winter months.[42]

Mother Nature could have a more direct and dramatic impact on employment. The New Mexico part of the line was especially susceptible to washouts in the summer months. In early July 1884, the company laid off twenty Las Vegas trainmen because washouts had limited train movements. A few days later, washouts hit the branch from Rincon to El Paso so hard that it took a month to reopen. Yet while train and engine crews took enforced vacations, others experienced boom times. In relatively minor flooding situations bridge and building men donned their boots and slickers at the first sign of trouble and shuttled about the line working into the night to keep the line open. In major calamities such as that between Rincon and El Paso, the Santa Fe hired up to one thousand laborers to rebuild the right of way. Blizzards jolted railroad employment in much the same way. The severe storms of 1886 closed down so much traffic in western Kansas that three train crews in Raton made only one trip each in two weeks. On the other hand, five hundred men were shipped into the area to shovel snow from the track, and baggagemen and transfer men in La Junta found that the snow blockade required two-thirds overtime to care for all the passengers unexpectedly stuck in town.[43]

The changing of the seasons dictated the major employment trends. When the snows melted, they exposed roadbeds that had sunk in places, bolts that needed tightening, and broken ties that had to be replaced. Washouts, weeds, the expansion of the rails by the summer's heat, and the commencement of the heavy traffic months all demanded continued work into the late fall. Therefore every April brought a sharp increase of 30 to 40 percent in track personnel and the force continued to grow to a peak in October, 100 percent greater than that in the low month of February. The seasonal employment pattern in the bridge and building department was similar, but less severe, jumping 50 to 100 percent on the different divisions. The bridge and building department took advantage of the summer weather to enlarge their crews and hire special forces of men to renovate the company's property. But in November the summer help in both departments started receiving discharge checks and the force continued to dwindle until the following March.[44]

For the rest of the Santa Fe labor force, seasonality was brought on by fluctuations in traffic rather than improvement in outdoor working conditions. On the Santa Fe, autumn—particularly October—produced the greatest business, though there also was a minor rise in May. Bulging shipments of wheat, corn, and cattle, as well as passengers taking a last trip before the winter, all conspired to bring about the hectic times of the fall. Most areas along the Santa Fe followed the overall seasonal trend, but the spring cattle rush in New Mexico and the Texas Panhandle provided a major exception. May, which was the apex of the spring cattle rush in these areas, registered traffic levels 25 to 60 percent above the dullest month's activity. It was this very large aberration that called for the perennial transfers of eastern railroaders to handle the rushes.[45]

Stationmen had the most stable employment. Management might add some extra operators and switchmen to handle seasonally heavy business, but rarely did station payroll outlays vary more than 20 percent through the year. The rises that did occur came during the peak traffic periods, mimicking in more modest dimensions the fluctuations among shopmen, trainmen, and enginemen.[46]

Shop payrolls varied with the pulse of traffic. Work in most shops differed 10 to 25 percent from low to high periods. The winter cutback in hours, rather than layoffs, accounted for most of the variation. The Topeka shops may have been an exception, in that they sometimes hired large numbers of men for short periods to refurbish the company's rolling stock for the traffic of an upcoming season. The peak for this work most frequently came in the early spring or in the fall. Because the Santa Fe could put off rebuilding cars and locomotives a month or more without detriment to the company, the timing and extent of the seasonal work in the Topeka shops was not very predictable. When the peak came, however, the Santa Fe often distributed 60 percent more money to its Topeka shop workers than in slack months. Much of this increase went to unskilled and semiskilled laborers who were laid off when they completed a project.[47]

The ebb and flow of commerce had its greatest impact on those who conducted the trains. Engine and train crew employment outside of New Mexico and the Texas Panhandle oscillated 25 to 50 percent from months of low to high activity. As an extreme example, some Newton brakemen were paid over $125 for November 1894 but did not get enough runs in December to earn $30. Slow times hit hardest at the "extras"—the newer employees who had neither a regular run nor a place on the "chain gang" list to take out the unassigned freight runs. Rather, these men got work only when those with greater seniority took a layoff. The extras absorbed much of the work load fluctuations, allowing the other enginemen and trainmen more stable paychecks. Those on the extra board could earn almost as much as the regulars in good months, but a Chanute, Kansas, conductor voiced the frustrations of fellow extras in the slack season when he said, "I don't wish any of the old conductors bad luck, but would like to see them lay off enough so to give the extra men a chance to make time enough to keep groceries in the house."[48]

During its first thirty years, the Santa Fe provided a livelihood for tens of thousands of men in one of a very few large-scale western enterprises. In 1880 railroads employed more than twice as many men in Kansas as mining, the state's second largest industrial employer. More remarkable than the size of the working force, however, was the diversity of railroad jobs. To be a railroader could mean clerical duty in a division or general office, service jobs about the station, mechanical work in the shops, backbreaking toil repairing bridges and roadbeds, or the hazardous task of moving mammoth rolling stock at high speeds. Wage rates ranged across the entire spectrum, from high pay for engineers to the barely subsistence income of track laborers. Most employees were required to sell their homes and move their families from town to town to get promotions, but for shopmen persistence in a community was the norm. Some worked constantly in view of their superior, while others could escape beyond the boundaries of the yards. Most Santa Fe railroaders' workdays were dictated by the clock, yet those in train and engine service came and went according to the timetable. Regular employees were able to earn fairly consistent wages throughout the year, but the extras and the large seasonal forces often found lean times after the fall rush. Indeed, there was no typical railroad occupation. Railroading demanded a variety of skills and railroaders' collective job experience was in many ways a reflection of the entire nation's workday.

CHAPTER 2

Winning the Workers:
Recruitment, Discipline,
and Paternalistic Policies
of the Santa Fe

The creation, supervision, and motivation of its labor force posed major problems for Santa Fe management. Corporate leaders may never have formulated, and certainly never publicly enunciated, an overarching labor policy. Nevertheless, the practices Topeka leaders adopted in recruiting and dealing with their employees were consistent with the need to retain loyal and competent workers.

Decisions on hiring were really two-fold—first, how many of each skill, and second, who. Rarely would anyone below the rank of division superintendent make the first decision. The question of whom to hire, however, was generally left to the official under whose supervision the man worked. Division trainmasters hired conductors and brakemen, though conductors sometimes took a hand in selecting men for their crews. The master mechanic was responsible for employing engineers, firemen, roundhouse workers, and shopmen. But in the case of roundhouses and shops, the foremen probably had more to say about who was hired than the master mechanic. The yardmaster chose the requisite number of switchmen, the section boss had charge of track crew hiring, the station agent employed his assistants, and chief dispatchers were authorized to hire and fire dispatchers and operators on their divisions.[1]

In the early days of the Santa Fe, recruitment, especially of those for skilled positions, could not have been easy. The Santa Fe met part of this problem by hiring men already in the area from its older competitor in Kansas, the Kansas Pacific. The company obtained its first engineer, George Beach, from the KP. It also got many of its early trainmen and enginemen from the Indianapolis, Cincinnati & La Fayette Railroad through a series of personal contacts. Thomas Peter, the Santa Fe's chief engineer and first superintendent, was an executive in the Cincinnati construction company the Santa Fe engaged to lay track out of Topeka. One of Peter's superiors in the construction firm served as president of the IC&L. Undoubtedly these connections explain how William Fagan, an engineer on the IC&L, became the Santa Fe's first conductor. Within a year Fagan became superintendent, and his former fellow workers on the IC&L had enough confidence in him that they accepted his recruiting efforts to work for the new road.[2]

Favoritism and nepotism would be a major factor in hiring throughout the century. The Santa Fe grew to be a family affair. Peter's brother became a conductor, Fagan's father found a place as an engineer, and Beach's son had the privilege of being the first train news vendor. The last names on payrolls of the 1870s and 1890s suggest that as much as half the work force was related to at least one other Santa Fe employee. A further study of the 1895 payrolls shows that there was a tendency for kin to be hired into the same department and often in the same town as their relatives. Of all the related workers on the payrolls, nearly half were employed in the same department, and 40 percent worked in the same town. The eminence of a patron helped to determine the type of job open to his relatives. For example, Joseph McCandless, 1896 section boss at Alden, Kansas, employed Claude, Gaither, and William McCandless as three of the four laborers in his crew. But master mechanic Thomas Paxton had the power to set up two of his relatives with skilled shop positions and two others on the promotional track to skilled shop hand and engineer.[3]

During most of the century there was a ready supply of workers for the Santa Fe. Railroads were obvious sources of employment, especially for youths in the predominantly agricultural West. Moreover, the chance for travel and high wages in a glamorous occupation swelled the roster of job seekers. The surfeit of applicants meant that many, if not most, of those who succeeded in getting jobs with the Santa Fe had to have some connections to place them above the crowd. If a prospective employee was not related to someone already at work on the Santa Fe, it was helpful for him to know someone with the power to give jobs. Also, union men spoke up for traveling brothers looking for work. And prominent citizens, including Kansas governor George T. Anthony, who in 1878 wrote a glowing three-page recommendation for an applicant, could direct the company toward a particular man.[4]

When a new set of managers came in, favoritism could bring mass firings of old employees to make way for friends of the new officers. This was the case when, in 1885, D. B. Robinson left his post as general manager on the Mexican Central to take a similar position on the Atlantic & Pacific, the Santa Fe's subsidiary west of Albuquerque. The Albuquerque Evening Democrat noted that many trainmen and enginemen were removed and replaced by men from the Mexican Central.[5]

As unions grew more capable of enforcing seniority, these firings and hirings became more rare. Nevertheless, the influence of top officers on hiring patterns was still apparent. In 1899 the Santa Fe brought in J. M. Barr of the Norfolk & Western as third vice-president in charge of operations. He in turn replaced the Santa Fe's assistant superintendent of machinery with R. P. C. Sanderson, an old crony who had been employed as master mechanic on the N & W. This move sent chills through Santa Fe men, for they anticipated that more heads would roll in favor of N & W men. Dismissals to make way for N & W employees may have been limited to the higher echelon of officers, yet hirings to replace workers lost through attrition showed the prejudices of the new officers. Dan Cunningham and two friends all had worked in the N & W shops in Virginia. In 1900 they decided to try their luck elsewhere and traveled across the country in search of new positions. They had had mixed results until they wrote Sanderson, who gave their requests special attention and found places for them on the Santa Fe in New Mexico and California. Within a few years, Cunningham remarked that the Topeka men who once dominated the shops were now outnumbered by former N & W employees.[6]

Despite the general surfeit of prospective railroaders, extraordinary situations, such as large additions to the system, seasonal demands, and strikes, required special recruiting efforts. In 1888, when the Santa Fe started moving trains over its track to Chicago, the company hired more than a thousand new employees. Illinois and Missouri were populous states, so recruitment of unskilled workers probably was not difficult. But it was a challenge to find skilled men. Fortunately for the Santa Fe, the 1888 engineers' and firemen's strike on the Chicago, Burlington & Quincy had recently collapsed and the Santa Fe was able to recruit these strikers.[7]

Filling positions in populous Illinois and Missouri, though, was far easier than finding men to work in the sparsely populated, rugged, and uninviting Southwest. M. J. Drury, a Nickerson machinist, remembered that it was difficult to recruit a steady work force in Nickerson in the rough early days of that central Kansas town. In 1891 A & P General Manager Robinson complained that he could not get first-rate railroaders because no one who could find work anywhere else would resettle in New Mexico or Arizona. In 1900 the *Railway Gazette* still considered the Southwest to be the hardest place in the nation to get quality workers. Recruitment of skilled and semiskilled employees in this region presented a problem the Santa Fe was never able to solve fully. Even at the end of the century it found many of its workers in New Mexico and Arizona abandoning the line every summer to head for cooler climes. The difficulty of recruitment for this desert area of all but the most unskilled was reflected in much higher wages and a noticeable reluctance to deal severely with strikers.[8]

The Santa Fe encountered more success in recruiting unskilled workers as it expanded into the Southwest. In the 1870s its track crews throughout the line were manned by Irishmen. Yet few whites were willing to move into New Mexico and Arizona to take these low-paying jobs. Fortunately for the company, however, once the road crossed Raton Pass it found a plentiful supply of cheap labor: beginning as early as 1882 the Santa Fe began to hire Chicanos for its track crews. This group continued to dominate New Mexico crews through the end of the century. West of Albuquerque, the A & P turned to another indigenous group—the Pueblo, Navaho, and Mohave Indians. Contracted through local merchants whom the Indians trusted, they constituted a large percentage of the company's track force and at one time numbered nearly a hundred in the lower positions in the shop at Needles. As the century came to a close the Santa Fe found still another source of cheap labor for the Southwest in Japanese immigrants. The Japanese displaced Indians in the shops and also took places in Arizona track crews for as little as one dollar a day, less than the pay received by track workers in the much more hospitable regions at the eastern end of the Santa Fe.[9]

Two other groups supplemented the native white labor force to help supply the Santa Fe's needs for cheap regular and seasonal labor throughout the line. Blacks held unskilled jobs such as warehouseman, flagman, messenger, and janitor, as well as menial temporary jobs such as coal shoveler during the rush season. Italians took unskilled positions with the Santa Fe, most commonly as seasonal trackmen or bridge and building men. They were hired in groups out of Chicago or Kansas City and shipped to where they were needed. The Santa Fe found them to be dependable and hard-working, even willing to work seven days a week at minimal pay. Sometimes Italians were received uneventfully as men necessary to the road and potential customers of local merchants. But there were times, as in Lebo, Kansas, in 1889, when their arrival, displacing recently hired local men, brought scorching protests against "the degrading presence of such a band of ruffians, outlaws and semibarbarians."[10]

Every year the company faced the need for seasonal workers. Part of the Santa Fe's requirements were filled when the perennial pool of transient trainmen and enginemen drifted into division towns as the rush season began. In hiring these and other skilled workers, the railroad would sometimes lower its standards and even hired blacklisted men until the crisis was over. For unskilled jobs in the track and bridge and building departments it was not difficult to hire unemployed townsmen in the spring, but it was hard to keep them and get more in June and July, when wheat was ready to harvest. The railroad frequently found its efforts thwarted by farmers offering expenses and three dollars a day. In 1898 a group hired onto a Newton area section gang no sooner got a few miles out on the line than a farmer enticed the whole bunch to quit and help him bring in his crop. The only argument for staying with the railroad was that anyone who quit for a few weeks of harvesting might miss out on the four or five months of track work before the November layoffs and would certainly stand little chance of securing a permanent job.[11]

Strikes, too, posed recruitment problems. Local men could be found to take unskilled jobs and some skilled positions and apprentices sometimes stuck with the company to gain a promotion. But in every major strike-breaking effort the company had to tap the labor supplies of eastern cities. It was there that large numbers of skilled and unskilled jobless men and experienced extras could be found who were willing to head west for better positions. A strike of enginemen in 1878 was quashed with the help of forty engineers and firemen from the St. Louis area. The Santa Fe tried to counter a strike of track laborers in 1890, in northern New Mexico, by bringing in workers from Kansas City and Mexico. With the help of the General Managers' Association the company set up a pipeline directly to Philadelphia, home of the Baldwin locomotive factory, through which it siphoned hundreds of shopmen as scabs during the machinists, boilermakers, and blacksmiths' strike of 1893. And during the Pullman strike of the following year the company reached out all over the country to get replacements—the little town of Winslow, Arizona, acquired men from as far away as Richmond and Minneapolis.[12]

The hiring was usually done through employment agencies. Some of them may have been honest, but there was every incentive for deceit: the agencies received a commission for the number of workers delivered to the strike area and, once the men reached the West, few could afford to turn down the job if the terms of employment were not precisely as represented. Men recruited in Kansas City in 1890 were angered to find that they had not been hired to take good-paying positions but rather to take the places of striking New Mexico trackmen. Worse, the employment agent had neglected to mention that the strike had been ordered by a terrorist organization, the "White Caps," who threatened death to anyone who went to work on Santa Fe track crews. Similarly, in the 1893 shopmen's strike dozens of men were deceived by a Philadelphia employment agent who told them they were needed to staff newly constructed shops at Chicago and Ft. Madison. When they arrived in Topeka they learned they were being hired as strikebreakers. They were incensed and complained to anyone who would listen, including Governor Lorenzo Lewelling, pleading in vain for free transportation home.[13]

On a few rare occasions the Santa Fe broke the color line to beat strikes. Management rarely hired blacks to fill skilled jobs or to work on track crews. But, when few whites could be recruited around Emporia to break a trackmen's strike in 1888, the company hired at least one entire gang of blacks. In extreme emergencies the Santa Fe did not hesitate to hire blacks even for skilled positions. In 1893 the company recruited about a dozen to replace skilled shopmen whose strike threatened a total breakdown of the rolling stock, and in the Pullman strike of the following year the strikers were angry to see a black working in the relatively prestigious position of brakeman.[14]

Finally, some strikebreakers came from among fired strikers themselves. When the Santa Fe lost a strike or decided not to make an all-out effort to break one, they naturally took back those who had quit. But even in strikes they won, the company often took back some of the less offensive strikers. In the Pullman strike a major source of new workers was the pool of men discharged from other roads. Even in the depression times of 1894, there simply were not enough experienced railroaders to man all the thousands of positions left vacant in the wake of the strike. Many of the defeated strikers changed their names to thwart blacklisting efforts. The *Las Vegas Daily Optic* noted that it knew of strikers from the Union Pacific whom the Santa Fe had hired on and predicted that the result of the strike throughout the country would be "a general swapping of places on the different roads."[15]

Once it had recruited an employee, the Santa Fe endeavored to make him a safe and efficient servant of the company. The number of written rules the company imposed on different classes of workers and the promptness in instituting them varied in proportion to the group's importance to the safety of train movements and their relative freedom from direct supervision from company officials. Shopmen and station laborers, all of whom had a secondary impact on safety and were under close scrutiny from superiors, received no written regulations. In contrast, written rules governed trainmen and enginemen from 1868, when Superintendent Peter had the regulations printed on the back of a single sheet train schedule for easy reference. By 1889 conductors received rulebooks that they were to carry on the road. The critically important and widely dispersed telegraph operators got rulebooks in 1882 and the equally scattered trackmen and bridge and building men received them the following year. The necessity of accurate bookkeeping by those routing freight business mandated the publishing of a book of freight regulations in 1890. Besides these rulebooks, the central offices in Topeka as well as the various division heads issued additional orders that were to hold the same authority as the published rules. For example, in 1889 alone, the Topeka office issued sixteen supplements to the rules of conductors.[16]

Management revealed in its regulations a strong concern for the security of company property and the prevention of legal actions against the Santa Fe. Nearly all the paperwork required of workers involved the security of cargo, the proper filing of payroll vouchers, or the keeping of accurate inventories of company supplies. Rule eleven of the 1883 track foremen's rules emphasized the care of corporate property, and dictated that track crews collect all worn shovels, picks, links, pins, and other such materials so that they could either be made serviceable at local shops or be shipped to Topeka to be melted down and reused. The company ordered its firemen to feed the engine cautiously, aiming at "smokeless firing." This had the double benefit of saving coal and preventing engine sparks, which caused the Santa Fe great financial difficulty when they set fire to farmers' crops. And to enhance its immunity from employer liability suits, the company as early as 1874 disavowed any responsibility to compensate injured or killed workers and in later years it further clarified this legally useful protection.[17]

A second concern manifested in the regulations was the safety and comfort of passengers and cargo. Telegraphers were to exercise great care in relaying train orders, and train crews were held accountable for keeping their trains within company-mandated speed limits. Freight conductors were to ensure the security of their cargo, while passenger conductors had to guard riders from offensive persons, including drunks, gamblers, purveyors of sordid literature, and those using loud and profane language.[18]

A third object of the Santa Fe's rules was the creation of an obedient and efficient labor force. Lines of authority were clearly drawn and all infractions of rules were to be reported to higher officers. Number thirty-three of the telegraph department's 1882 regulations left no doubt that "to obey the orders of superior officers strictly and without question, is the first duty of all telegraph employes." Rulebooks aimed at greater efficiency by setting down standard modes of doing work. The Santa Fe also strove to ensure that its workers understood the rules and had training in the use of new machinery. For example, when air brakes were introduced, trainmen were told to attend lectures on their workings, and superiors were charged with regular examinations of trainmen on the time-card rules. These examinations were in addition to those given brakemen and firemen before they could win promotion to conductor or engineer.[19]

Driving workers to ever greater exertions was not easily accomplished in the railroad industry. Concern for safety and customer satisfaction relegated speed to a secondary consideration. Moreover, the dispersion of the labor force made it unrealistic to expect that men would work at a slave-driving pace. Yet this did not prevent officials from attempting to make sure they were getting a solid day's work for their wages. Track rulebooks directed foremen never to leave their gangs unsupervised and exhorted them to take pride in their sections and make greater efforts in their work. The Santa Fe issued uniforms and badges to its train crews and station agents in 1878, partly to boost the company's image, but also to bolster workers' pride in their jobs and help patrons identify the employees charged with lending assistance. Finally, in the shops where hundreds of men might be employed, the Santa Fe devised a method to keep track of the hours each man worked. Beginning in the mid-1880s shopmen had to pick up small numbered blocks when they arrived each day and surrender them when they went off to lunch or quit for the evening. This "little emblem of servility" angered shopmen, but their discontent did not prevent the company from continuing its use into the twentieth century.[20]

Another class of rules attempted to regulate railroaders' activities off the job. The Santa Fe ordered trainmen and enginemen to live within three-fourths of a mile of the roundhouse in order to be called for a run and subjected them to disciplinary action if they could not be found when called. Some local officials outlawed association with bunko players or any other gamblers, while others proscribed visits to dance halls and houses of prostitution. Of course, on-duty drinking was one of the worst violations of the rules, but there were also some attempts to prohibit off-duty drink, at least by trainmen and enginemen. After all, how much confidence would people put in a road that called their employees out of a bar to guide their trains? Yet these attempts were not uniformly and consistently enforced, and they certainly were not very successful. As a Las Vegas newspaper predicted in 1895, efforts to dictate on the subject of drink probably only caused employees to "seek saloons by the back-door route, or else . . . imitate the example of the general manager, and keep the ardent at their homes in the jug-full."[21]

To say that railroaders honored all company regulations more in the breach than in the observance would be an exaggeration. Yet the Santa Fe did have considerable difficulty in enforcing many of its edicts. A Topeka bulletin board in 1884 indicated many workers' cynicism as trainmen regularly labeled newly posted rules "poppycock." There were many schemes to avoid work and evade regulations. In 1891, when George Rake of a New Mexico bridge and building gang learned that the next day he would be assigned an especially arduous task of unloading granite for improvements at Watrous, he immediately determined to be sick and, sure enough, he was not able to get out of bed the entire following day. Company officials, when surveying the line, usually traveled in a business car at the end of a passenger train. This gave enginemen the chance to give signals and forewarn gold-bricking trackmen in time to prevent detection. In the late 1890s local officials rated engineers on their ability to conserve the lubricating oil used on their engines. As a result many engineers bought or stole oil in order to look good in the records.[22]

One rule that trainmen were especially adept at thwarting

involved the imposition of speed limits. Once a train got beyond the local yard there was little that officials could do personally to check on its speed as long as the crew did not bring it into the next station far ahead of schedule. To compensate for this lack of control, officials installed a device called a Dutch clock in each caboose. This mechanism had a paper tape, similar to telegraph tape, on which it recorded the speed of the train for later examination by superiors. However, it was widely recognized that trainmen tampered with these machines to the point that it took a rather gullible trainmaster to trust in the accuracy of the speed recorded.[23]

Railroad managers were troubled most and fought hardest against the stealing of company money and goods in transit. Padding the payroll was common in the track departments of all railroads and plagued the Santa Fe throughout its first three decades. Section bosses hired, supervised, made out the payrolls, and often distributed the paychecks to their men. Therefore, it was an easy matter to add a fictitious name to the payroll or credit an employee with more days of work than he was due.[24]

Theft of goods in transit by trainmen became so rampant that an Albuquerque paper in 1882 charged that many brakemen acted as if they were entitled to all they could steal. Most cases involved no more than a handful of cigars or several bottles of some tempting liquid. At the end of the century, eighteen Arkansas City employees suffered the indignity of losing their jobs for stealing nothing more glamorous than watermelons. To supplement local police in combatting theft, the company employed detective agencies and, in the last years of the century, the Santa Fe had its own "secret service" department. Occasionally they succeeded in uncovering large rings of thieves. The biggest came to light in 1893, when the Santa Fe charged that over a one-year period a gang between La Junta and Las Vegas stole goods worth between $70,000 and $150,000. Gang members stopped freight trains at small stations or out on the line, where accomplices met them with wagons to receive stolen goods, including whiskey, silks, furniture, stoves, and an entire consignment of sewing machines. One Las Vegas merchant complained that he had had to place seven separate orders for a case of merchandise before one came through. One paper reported that the gang failed to get away with a piano only because they had insufficient manpower to get it off the train. But largely because of a premature break in the case and the sympathy local judges and juries had for the railroaders, the best the company could manage out of about two dozen men brought to trial was a single conviction of larceny of $22 worth of freight.[25]

The greatest financial losses came when passenger conductors failed to collect fares or took money without turning it over to the company. The problem was so severe that the Santa Fe in 1886 imitated some eastern roads and hired collectors at the cost of $80,000 a year. These men joined passenger train crews and were hired to collect tickets and fares. They could give their whole attention to their task. Moreover, since officers could choose them solely for their trustworthiness while passenger conductors had to be promoted from the ranks of freight conductors, management felt that collectors would cut down on petty thievery. A few conductors got used to the change and noted approvingly that their work load was reduced while their pay was not; but most felt a loss of prestige and detested the collectors, rightly seeing them as a reflection on their honesty. The collectors were considered spies and usurpers and endured almost constant abuse from other trainmen. Whether the Santa Fe began to suspect that collectors were no more immune to the foibles of the human character than conductors, or whether the officials simply did not find them worth the money in financial hard times, management abandoned the use of collectors at the end of 1888.[26]

While collectors had a fleeting existence on the Santa Fe, spotters were a permanent part of the company's battle against corrupt conductors specifically and rule violators in general. Spotters were hired spies who rode the passenger trains and visited railroad town saloons looking for railroaders breaking company regulations. The companies that bonded conductors and agents placed some of the spotters on the road, but the railroad hired most of them either through detective agencies or by paying freelancers three dollars a day and expenses. Many spotters rode as respectable middle class types and did no more than observe. However, some tried to entrap the trainmen with hard luck stories, pleading that they be allowed to ride home free to see their handicapped children, their sickly wives, or their dying mothers. For variety the Santa Fe also was reported to have hired women and Indians as spotters. With the help of George Eastman's advances in photography, proof of wrongdoing, especially that of drinking on duty, was made easier. In 1895 a Las Vegas railroader denied vigorously that he had been drinking on duty. But a spotter with a hidden camera produced a picture of him holding a mug of beer and the embarrassed offender realized further denials would be fruitless. The result of a spotter's visit could be devastating. Sometimes spotters found old and revered employees cheating and their careers came to an abrupt end. And when the company made a general offensive against dishonest trainmen, there could be a large turnover, as in early 1882, when the company discharged seventy men throughout the length of the line.[27]

The papers of one spotter have survived and provide a glimpse of the system's workings. William O. Hubbell was a Civil War veteran and a former deputy sheriff. In 1884, Santa Fe officials hired him to do a month's investigative work for division superintendent P. F. Barr in New Mexico. Barr instructed him to be especially observant of the activities of a number of railroaders. Barr had heard that conductor Farnsworth was recommending that eastbound passengers take the Southern Pacific instead of the Santa Fe and received a commission from the SP agent. He suspected that several stationmen might be stealing freight at Deming because an exorbitant amount seemed to get lost there. Barr also was suspicious of the ticket policy of three passenger conductors who had considerable money to gamble; one of them was said to have been making investments in diamonds. Barr wanted Hubbell to visit South Pueblo, Colorado, and check up on a rumored ring of ticket brokers for passage on freight trains. Hubbell was also to keep a general watch for employees drinking too much or associating with undesirable characters.[28]

Hubbell used no disguises and rode as a typical paying customer, except when trying to procure a freight ride in South Pueblo. He relied on his own observation as well as the knowledge of certain local citizens, including law enforcement officials. In his reports he praised some employees who did good work and pointed to others who needed only a reminder to curb minor inclinations to stray from proper behavior. There were, however, some very derogatory reports. Conductor Farnsworth associated with saloonmen and was twice spotted failing to collect fares from some riders, including cattlemen who seemed to rank as especially good friends. Drinking was found to be almost universal, though Hubbell felt that only a few drank excessively. He also reported the behavior of the fireman on the passenger train out of Silver City who abandoned his engine for a third of his run so that he could help entertain two "sporting women" in the passenger car. There is no way of knowing the results of Hubbell's reports, but management probably inflicted some punishment on Farnsworth and the "sporting" fireman.[29]

Trainmen hated spotters as spies liable to disrupt a smooth-running (if not always honest) crew or inform on men who were partaking of some of the few entertainments available in many western towns. They were also charged with filing negative reports on the basis of rumor and handing in knowingly false incriminating stories lest the company suspect they had not done their job. A Newton paper reported in 1897 that a spotter had filed unfavorable reports on one conductor who was off duty because of illness and on another who had been dead for two weeks. The universal disdain for spotters among railroaders is revealed in a Dodge City conductor's description of one as

that conglomeration of nothing; that institution that recognizes neither honor nor law; that being whom his Satanic Majesty will welcome with the highest gratitude, and proclaim him king of his emissaries who were allowed to inhabit the earth, and to whom justly belongs the credit and glory of being the lowest animal that God ever created, and on whom honorable thief takers and criminal hunters look with scorn.

A Las Vegas paper referred to them as the "scum of humanity," and one Kansas railroader suggested they be singled out and branded. Suspected spotters often suffered the wrath of the workers. Threats of necktie parties and tar and feathering usually convinced them to leave town but some did so only after receiving a few bruises and losing some teeth. At any rate, the never-ending nature of the battle between the spotters and railroad workers was testimony to the continuing failure of the company to achieve compliance with its rules.[30]

Punishments for breaking the rules were most commonly meted out by local officials, who had great latitude in how they handled disciplinary problems. The disposition of individual cases depended on the company's reigning disciplinary policy, the past record of the employee, the local officials' disciplinary practices, and the personal relationship between the offending railroader and his superior. Until the late 1890s some rule violators were fined. The Santa Fe had an unevenly enforced rule in the 1870s that brakemen who set the brakes so tightly that the wheels wore flat would be charged for replacing the wheels. Railroaders could also be fined between one dollar and twenty dollars for a broad range of such offenses as not wearing badges, breaking a lantern, running a railroad crossing without stopping, or failing to transfer mail to or from a train at the proper time.[31]

Sometimes used in conjunction with fining, and far more common, were demotions, suspensions, and discharges. There was no clear line between offenses meriting firing and those deserving the less severe punishments. Generally officials limited discharges to major violations: drinking on duty, stealing from the company or its patrons, gross insubordination, or causing a collision. Demotions and suspensions came for such infractions as failing to be home when the caller knocked, neglecting a safety rule, or actions leading to a minor mishap. Of the two lesser punishments, suspension was by far the most common.[32]

On August 1, 1897, the Santa Fe adopted a discipline program that is still in effect on that road. It was a scheme of merits and demerits called the Brown system, after its originator, George R. Brown, general superintendent of the Fall Brook Railway in New York. The Brown system gained great favor in management circles in the late 1890s, receiving the endorsements of the *Railway Gazette* and the American Society of Railroad Superintendents. By 1900 nearly sixty lines had adopted it. Under the system the company could still hand out summary discharges for major offenses, but all others could be punished only by reprimands or demerits, a record of which was

kept for each employee in the offices of the division superintendent. An employee was notified of each mark entered against his
name and had the right to appeal those he considered unjus-
tified. Should too many demerits, or "brownies" as they were
commonly called, appear besides a worker's name the superintendent could call on him to explain the mistakes, and, if un-
satisfied, dismiss him. By heroism, exemplary performance, or
months of flawless work, employees could cancel demerits
charged against them.[33]

Some employees in lower positions, like brakemen and
firemen, objected to the Brown system because it reduced the
number of extras. Suspensions created a supply of temporary
openings. But with suspensions abolished, those in the lower
ranks found themselves bumped back to the edge of unemployment. For example, in Newton, Kansas, three extra engineers
were forced back to firemen. This move in turn bumped passenger firemen back to freight firemen, freight firemen went
back to the extra board, and some extra firemen were dismissed.
A few perceptive railroaders objected to the new regime because
they saw it as part of a blacklisting system in which the demerit
books were open to all future prospective employers; in 1901 the
Santa Fe admitted in a report to the U.S. Industrial Commission
that this happened. There was also some feeling that the Brown
system resulted in greater favoritism. The Brown system may
have short-circuited the appeal system won by a number of
unions. A few brownies marked against an individual seemed
less important than suspensions and the brotherhoods and individuals involved may have been less aggressive in appealing
them. At the same time, a local official, knowing this, may have
been willing to charge an offender with substantial demerits
while he might have given only a reprimand under the old
policy.[34]

However, the vast majority of railroaders supported the
Brown system. The Order of Railway Conductors praised it as
"the rational way of dealing with honorable men." The *Railroad
Trainmen's Journal* editorialized that the Brown system would
"lead to many better results than have been experienced under
the old and crude system of suspension and discharge." A
Kansas survey in 1899 revealed that 80 percent of Santa Fe

trainmen and enginemen preferred the demerit system to the old program. In virtually every case the reason for this support was that workers who had erred did not have to suffer the temporary loss of employment and income that came with suspensions.[35]

Management preferred the Brown plan because, in the words of general superintendent H. U. Mudge, "it [would] encourage and stimulate all employés to coöperate heartily with the officers of the Company." Furthermore, the services of some of its best men would not be interrupted for some minor offense. Company officials also saw the Brown system as a more effective discipline arrangement. Under the old suspension policy many railroaders felt that once they had served their ten or thirty days, they returned with a clean slate and were content with paying for future errors in the same manner. But with demerits the worker knew that the company was monitoring his performance and that should he repeat past failures he might very well lose his job. Moreover, good work was encouraged since brownies could be erased if the employee remained especially attentive in the future. Another benefit was that the Brown system could instruct employees on the proper way to handle certain situations. Division superintendents issued occasional bulletins describing actions that had earned brownies or merit points. For example, a Newton railroad column noted in 1898, "Hereafter it will be unrulable for an engineer to run through a flock of anything larger than mosquitoes," since a New Mexico engineer who stopped and shooed away a flock of sheep received thirty merit points even though he arrived at his station half an hour late.[36]

Finally, by adopting the Brown system the Santa Fe took a step toward centralizing labor management and limiting the opportunities for local officials to abuse their power. Local bosses had to document the errors of their workers, and as the number of brownies for a given mistake became standardized, their discretion narrowed. In a similar vein, higher management limited the chance for extortion from subordinates by forbidding the practice of giving gifts to superiors. Following earlier, less sweeping decrees, President E. P. Ripley in 1897 completely outlawed the practice throughout the system. Moreover, the Santa Fe at times got rid of local officers whose arbitrary methods alienated workers. For instance, in 1891 Ben Wilton, an abrasive Albuquerque yardmaster, fired a number of his crew, thereby precipitating a strike. Upon investigation by the super-intendent, the workers were reinstated and Wilton was demoted to conductor.[37]

The brotherhoods helped to systemize disciplinary proce-dures. Possibly as early as 1877, members of the Brotherhood of Locomotive Engineers won the right to be heard in their own defense in dismissal cases. Other unions later promoted this appeal process. In 1890 the Order of Railway Conductors and the Brotherhood of Railroad Trainmen received a guarantee of their right to appeal to the division superintendent and then the general superintendent or general manager for all suspensions or dismissals, except those for intoxication, insubordination, or collision. If the suspension or discharge was found to be unjust, the worker would be reinstated and compensated for the lost time. In the next three years unions for the telegraphers, machinists, blacksmiths, and boilermakers obtained compara-ble contract provisions.[38]

In the meantime engineers and firemen had achieved an even more desirable and elaborate system that virtually elimi-nated the problem of arbitrary decisions by local officials. In its 1888 accord with the enginemen, the Santa Fe agreed that, except in cases of serious collisions or intoxication, they would not suspend or discharge these workers unless their guilt was established by a board of inquiry composed of the division superintendent, the division master mechanic, and one disin-terested engineer from the division on which the complaint arose. Even should this board rule against the employee, he could appeal to the same general corporate officials as he could under the straight appeal system. By the time management introduced the Brown system, the trainmen also had achieved this trial procedure.[39]

These appeal processes did not serve merely as rubber stamps for the decisions of lower officers. Don Ventura, a Winslow, Arizona, brakeman on the Atlantic & Pacific, noted in 1892 that the men always got satisfaction on appeals to higher officers. Some successful appeals were especially noteworthy. In 1892 the dismissal case of D. W. Curtis, an A & P conductor, rose through the appeal process until the company requested that the decision be left to a board of arbitration in Chicago, which ultimately supported the worker and awarded him back pay. In 1899 general superintendent Mudge made a marked exception and reinstated four passenger conductors who were caught and admitted pocketing fares. He did this because of the extraordinarily good records these men had made over many years of service. And the reports of the Order of Railway Conductors' Grand Chief Conductor in the 1890s reveal that, through personal intervention with company officials, he or one of his top assistants gained reinstatement for at least nine, and possibly two dozen more, Santa Fe workers.[40]

The introduction of the Brown system with its fairer and more lenient treatment of employees fell in line with a long-standing drive of the Santa Fe to stimulate greater loyalty to the company. The clearest incentive to perform on the job was the knowledge that no railroader was indispensable. Even a skilled engineer had only to look at his fireman to see someone eager for his position. After all, there was nothing in the engineer's job that put it beyond the capacity of a normally intelligent youth with enough nerve and a little experience in the engine cab. Likewise, in the shops skilled men realized that many of the apprentices and helpers were quite able to do the work of a full-fledged journeyman. And on the reverse side of this relationship, the higher pay and prestige of the engineer, conductor, and skilled shopman was less a recognition of their greater talents and service per hour on duty than a lure to men in lower positions to perform faithfully and conscientiously in the hopes of eventual promotion.[41]

The company realized that more was needed to create a loyal work force and so in the last two decades of the nineteenth century the Santa Fe embarked on a number of programs to promote greater devotion to work. Shop apprentices often abandoned the Santa Fe after serving only a portion of their training period. The problem became so severe that in 1892 the company began deducting 5 percent of the wages of the first year apprentices and 10 percent, 15 percent, and 20 percent of those in their second, third, and fourth years, respectively. At the end of the fourth year all of this was paid back to the apprentices. Special rewards for exemplary service were a more openhanded incentive. In 1878 the roadmasters conducted a contest in which the foreman with the best maintained stretch of track was awarded a prize of $50. Two decades later awards of $200, $150, and $100 were handed out to the station agents who registered the largest percentage increase in locally generated business. Heroism also had its rewards. A. R. Glazier was a passenger engineer in 1879, when he stuck with his locomotive as it headed for a collision and thereby prevented injury to anyone in the train. His thankful passengers passed the hat and awarded him and his fireman $25.40. By the 1890s, the company took over the responsibility of rewarding heroism. In 1893 Glazier, now a conductor, exhibited courage in the face of robbers and was given ten days paid leave and the privilege of riding the Santa Fe anywhere he wanted during that period.[42]

Winning the loyalty of railroaders entailed helping those who were injured as a result of their occupations. There were inevitable conflicts over what compensation was owed to employees killed or injured at work. Common-law defenses presented a formidable barrier to the employee or his heirs. The fellow servant doctrine absolved the company of all liability for injuries or death to employees caused by other employees. The principle of contributory negligence freed the employer of liability if the injured was himself partly to blame. And as a third major defense, the railroad could contend that employees assumed the risks of normal railroading hazards. If this was not enough, the entire legal process could result in seemingly interminable delay. Switchman G. H. Swarts and his family discovered this in 1894 when he won a suit against the Santa Fe for a hand badly mangled in the Winfield, Kansas, yards the previous year. He was elated upon winning a judgment for twenty-five hundred dollars in a lower court. But when the company appealed to the state supreme court, he learned that with two thousand cases ahead of his, he probably could not hope to collect his money for three and a half years.[43]

Although the railroad corporation could usually win in court, there still was some incentive for the company to come to fair terms. Public opinion, the sympathy of juries for injured men, the managers' own compassionate impulses, and the need to assure other employees that the company would not abandon them if fate chose them next all dictated that the Santa Fe treat those involved in accidents more liberally than was legally necessary. The company was especially generous to some widows of veterans killed on the job. Engineer John Myers had labored faithfully through fourteen years and two strikes before he was killed in a derailment in 1889. Even though the company was not legally liable, it granted his widow five thousand dollars. Eight years later a twenty-year veteran engineer, W. W. Frisbie, died in a collision. Again there were legal defenses open to the Santa Fe but the company gave Mrs. Frisbie seven thousand dollars.[44]

For those injured workers incapable of resuming their old jobs, yet not totally disabled, the Santa Fe commonly offered a less demanding position in an out-of-court settlement. In 1888 switchman Friday Rickert lost his leg in an accident. Besides paying him thirty-five hundred dollars, the Santa Fe agreed to employ him for the rest of his life. In July 1883, Frank Willard was braking in Colorado when he too lost a leg. When he recovered, he was assigned a job in the freight office in Argentine, Kansas. John Black, a black trucker in the Atchison freight house, lost his arm at work in 1874. The Santa Fe installed him as the crossing flagman on Fifth Street, a position he held for fifty years. While some men may have wondered whether such settlements could fully compensate them for their loss, the company made an effort.[45]

The Santa Fe had no pension plan until 1907. However, old-timers too enfeebled to carry on their usual jobs were sometimes given easy tasks they could handle. The superannuated got such positions as watchman, gatekeeper, or, by the end of the century, telephone operator. When the company established employee reading rooms as alternatives to saloons, old-timers frequently were named librarians. This was the case with retired switchman Ed Eagen in 1893 and with sixty-five-year-old wiper W. T. C. Wooden in 1898. H. M. Newhall was sixty-four in 1899 when he was taken out of train service to take the post of watchman. Two years later he was given the pleasant job of telling all the young whippersnappers who wandered into the

Barstow, California, reading room how things were in the old days. Some of the old-timers may have bridled at these demotions, but considering that such moves were not forced on most men until they were well into their sixties and that the Santa Fe had no obligation to continue to employ them in any capacity, the company's policy was both reasonable and compassionate.[46]

For injured employees there were more immediate needs than compensation. Good medical care was scarce in the West. In most new railroad towns of the early 1880s there was no hospital and most of the men were single, eating at restaurants and sleeping wherever they could. When injured or seriously ill, they had no place to turn. Even in Emporia, nearly a quarter of a century old when it became a division town, many injured workers were cared for in hotels.[47]

Management was not oblivious to its responsibilities. In 1877 the paymaster granted Frank O'Dowd nearly two months' pay at the regular trackman's rate for caring for an injured section man. At least by the early 1880s the Santa Fe had company-appointed doctors in many towns on the line. In an attempt to deal more systematically with the problem of injured and ill workers, Santa Fe Vice-President A.E.Touzalin on March 1, 1884, issued a circular announcing the inception of the Atchison Railroad Employees' Association. He said that the Santa Fe was sponsoring its creation at the urging of several hundred employees on its southern division. The purpose of the organization was to build hospitals and contract with doctors throughout the line to care for sick and injured employees. Workers may have been anxious for such an association, but company officials had been talking of a hospital program and examining possible cites for facilities at least since 1881. Indeed, the A&P had established a similar organization and built a hospital in Albuquerque in 1882, before that road had even finished laying track to Needles.[48]

The Santa Fe's system was similar to those established earlier on two neighboring roads—the Missouri Pacific and the Denver & Rio Grande. Starting in April 1884, wages were deducted from employees' paychecks to support the program. These contributions were on a graduated scale, ranging from a twenty-five-cent monthly deduction from those earning thirty dollars or less a month to two dollars for those paid over two hundred dollars. Although workers were given input on the board of directors, the control of the association was lodged securely with the officers of the railroad. Most of the hospitals were built and furnished by the Santa Fe on land donated by the company. Beyond this, the association was self-supporting.[49]

Reflecting the relative need for care facilities, the first hospitals were built in 1884 in Las Vegas and La Junta. In 1888 others were opened in Ottawa, Kansas, and Ft. Madison, Iowa. By the end of the century there were additional facilities in Temple, Texas, and Needles, and a major center in Topeka. The association contracted with public hospitals in many of the towns in which it had no facilities of its own, and also had contracts with hundreds of doctors in towns along the line to respond to emergencies and handle minor injuries and illnesses. Company doctor prescriptions were filled by local druggists, whose bills were paid by the association. All employees were eligible for aid, except those sick because of venereal disease, intemperate habits, or illnesses contracted before hiring on with the Santa Fe.[50]

The compulsory deductions irked many workers. When Kansas railroaders organized to lobby the 1891 state legislature, one of their goals was to gain a law against compulsory company railroad hospital associations. Yet these complaints were directed not at the association in principle, but at its inadequacy in its early years. To receive association benefits for long term illnesses or major injuries, railroaders had to enter a company hospital. Some married men preferred to remain at home even when a hospital was nearby, and many refused to be sent hundreds of miles from their families unless it was absolutely necessary to save their lives. Consequently, an Arkansas City brakeman in 1885 thought only 30 percent of the Santa Fe's employees were aided by the association. Topeka shopmen in 1892 noted that they had to go to Ottawa or La Junta to receive treatment in serious cases. They were among twenty-three hundred Santa Fe employees from as far north as Concordia and as far south as Wellington, Kansas, who petitioned for a facility in Topeka. In 1896 the association responded with a $125,000 hospital. The company contributed $30,000 while the rest came from the accumulated surplus of the association. This silenced criticism through the end of the century. The *Locomotive Firemen's Magazine* for May 1896, in a long scathing denunciation of company hospital associations, specifically singled out the Santa Fe's as one about which it had received no complaint. That same year the journals of both the engineers' and brakemen's unions also lavished high praise on the Santa Fe's system; the *Railroad Trainmen's Journal* said that it was "everywhere acknowledged as the best hospital system of any railroad in the United States."[51]

Other corporate paternalism extended to the workers' everyday lives. In the early 1880s the company gave scrap tie wood to married employees for fires. Until 1891 San Marcial workers were supplied with free ice. In Albuquerque the A&P maintained a burial plot for those rootless men killed in the company's service who had no known relatives. The Santa Fe sponsored annual picnics, providing transportation and helping with arrangements. The 1891 Topeka shop picnic involved transporting workers and their families—a total of three thousand people—to St. Joseph, Missouri, for a day of sightseeing, baseball, and other amusements; Missouri, unlike Kansas, was wet. A Newton newspaper reported on the elaborate middle division picnic of 1898, but hesitated to give a thorough description of the doings in the dimly lit company-furnished car reserved for young couples on the return trip. The Santa Fe also rendered assistance to the various social events of the railroad brotherhoods. An 1899 firemen's dance and supper in Needles was decorated with headlights, flags, and lanterns lent by the master mechanic. Management supplied the 1885 Las Vegas brakemen's Christmas ball with music by the "AT&SF Military Band and Orchestra," which the enthusiastic local paper called "the finest band in the west." Superintendent Charles Dyer attended to encourage such activities while trainmaster Frank Rain and his wife were reported to have helped with work in the switching yards to allow as many yardmen as possible to go to the ball.[52]

The Santa Fe, like most other railroads, granted pass privileges. Representatives of the brotherhoods traveled free to and from annual conventions on the Santa Fe. Mourners of employees killed on the job also frequently were transported gratis. The company's policy toward free travel for its own workers varied over the years. In 1886 faithful employees could get passes over the entire system for themselves and their families. Later, free travel usually was limited to one's own division and families were not always able to benefit. Sometimes workers received only a discount in ticket prices rather than free passes.[53]

As a frontier railroad, the Santa Fe at times had to supply its employees with temporary or permanent homes. By 1873 the company had built fourteen section houses for crews in areas where housing was in short supply. The Santa Fe does not seem to have made any effort to provide its workers with housing in division towns in eastern and central Kansas, but did exert itself farther west, where there was no adequate pool of carpenters to quickly construct residences for the scores and even hundreds of men who came to division centers. The first residences furnished by the railroad in Raton, Las Vegas, and San Marcial were cabooses and boxcars. In 1882 most San Marcial railroaders lived in boxcars while railroaders and their families—some three hundred people—were lodging in cars in Raton. The cars were lined up near the Raton yards and railroaders of all ranks lived in them at some time. In November 1881 a Raton paper noted the unorthodox local housing in which twenty-one wives struggled to make snug homes out of side-tracked boxcars.[54]

In the meantime the company's bridge and building crews were busy constructing a variety of more permanent wood-frame housing. Raton was typical. By January 1882, some railroaders had been able to relocate from the boxcars into a compact community of Santa Fe residences. The master mechanic, trainmaster, and train dispatcher were each furnished with two-story, seven-room homes. Engineers and firemen were the first single men to be given dormitory-style housing, which consisted of a one-floor wooden structure with twenty rooms, each twelve feet by eight feet. These were extremely cramped since two men were assigned to each room. Nearby were laundry, washroom, and bathroom facilities, along with the quarters of the janitor and matron, who cared for the household's needs.

Four tenement houses for married men were completed in 1882. Each tenement had five homes, each eighteen feet by twenty-eight feet, or about half the size of the structures built for the top officers.[55]

As the years passed the tenement house came to dominate. The cost to live in one in 1882 was thirteen dollars a month, less than one-third of a low level railroader's pay, and it appears that the monthly fee dropped in later years. The homes in flat, dusty, and arid San Marcial were all painted dull Santa Fe red and were surrounded by cottonwood trees to shelter them from the summer sun. Those that lacked running water had a spigot in the yard; all had backyard privies. The kitchens had coal and wood ranges. It was the transiency of railroaders as well as the expense of building in such desolate places as San Marcial that kept railroaders from building their own houses. Company housing served San Marcial railroaders until a flood virtually destroyed the town in 1929. Corporate housing also remained in Wallace, Raton, and Albuquerque at least into the 1890s. The persistence of Santa Fe residences and the total lack of complaints add force to the conclusion that railroaders found the housing program both adequate and fair.[56]

The scarcity of alternatives to barrooms as resting places for train crews awaiting orders and for general social gatherings moved the Santa Fe by the early 1880s to establish a large number of reading rooms. The company had already constructed one in Raton while many of its employees still lived in boxcars. By 1885 there were fifteen reading rooms strung from Argentine to Deming, and six more were added in the next three years. In periods of financial stringency in 1889 and the depression of the nineties, management closed the rooms and sold some of the books. But the company believed in their worth and with improving times always reopened them.[57]

Management credited the reading rooms with making superior workers. Santa Fe President Ripley wrote in the late 1890s, "We make no pretense to unselfishness—we aim only to practice enlightened selfishness; we want better men, and we are willing to spend money to make them better, because they will do their work more intelligently and more conscientiously." To meet the competition of bars and dance halls, the reading rooms were open into the evening. Gambling and boisterous and profane talk were forbidden. The rooms were supplied with books, journals, and newspapers through the contributions of railroad officials and prominent members of local communities. Among the reading matter were mechanical reference books and journals, the more popular periodicals, and a collection of local and regional newspapers. In early 1888 the one at Argentine had several hundred books, six out-of-town daily papers, thirteen weeklies, and four monthly journals. Cards, dominoes, checkers, and a pool table were also available. In the late 1890s, under the direction of Rev. S. E. Busser, the reading rooms expanded their operations by increasingly involving wives and initiating a series of lectures that were especially directed at the culturally starved western towns. By virtually all accounts, the rooms were a success. When the railroad moved to close them in 1889, the employees at La Junta held a mass meeting and petitioned that hospital funds be diverted to keep them open. They were reported to be well patronized, some having fifty or more employees in daily attendance, and when speaking of the greater temperance and improving morals of railroaders, a Kansas fireman acknowledged, "The railroad reading rooms have been a blessing to us all."[58]

A company-sponsored Railroad Young Men's Christian Association existed alongside the reading room system. Railroaders organized the association in Cleveland in 1872 and the Santa Fe became involved about a decade later. The Santa Fe and four other roads contributed to a railroad YMCA in Kansas City in the early 1880s, but the Santa Fe's only other contribution until the late 1890s went to a Topeka facility, which replaced an early reading room. The first gospel service for railroaders in that city was held in a passenger car in April 1882. Later the YMCA moved the service into a nearby boarding house. The response was enthusiastic enough that the railroad bought the boarding house and converted it to use as a full-time YMCA. Besides providing services similar to the reading rooms, the association held socials, Bible studies, and prayer and inspirational meetings. In the early 1890s weekly noon meetings were begun in the shops with average attendance through the rest of the decade of

100 to 150. In the last few years of the century, the Santa Fe, led by President Ripley, sponsored three new branches, each costing over ten thousand dollars, at Argentine, Kansas, and Cleburne and Temple, Texas. The company footed the bill for the land, salaries, and most of the building costs of these railroad YMCA's.[59]

It is not possible to state with certainty the motivation for the Santa Fe's recruitment, disciplinary, and paternalistic policies. President Ripley's role in reforming the discipline policy and invigorating existing paternalistic policies may have reflected the importance of personality. It almost certainly reflected a general paternalistic trend among railroad leaders after the Pullman strike and the attacks on railroads by Populists and budding progressives.

But there is a unifying element that runs through all the company's labor policies. It was not a great trial for the railroad to recruit men to fill its positions. However, to hire men who would remain faithful and efficient was a challenge—a challenge the Santa Fe's labor policies worked to meet. The debased groups hired into menial jobs from which there was little or no upward mobility were often contented with their positions, since greater opportunities were not in the offing. For the most desirable occupations, friends and relatives were better known and trusted quantities than strangers. An employee, thankful for the favor and wishing not to disappoint his patron, could be counted on to render good service. Moreover, the practice of favoritism encouraged him to remain loyal in the hope that he might be able to pass along his good fortune to his friends and relatives.

Local personal discipline was nearly inevitable, given the size of the road. Those with good relations with local bosses could sometimes benefit from lenient treatment, which would increase their attachment to the job. At the same time, the company realized that unjust punishments were detrimental to worker morale. Higher officials overturned some unfair discharges and suspensions. They also instituted the Brown system to curb arbitrary discipline, shelter the Santa Fe's best employees from suspensions, and thus win the workers' gratitude.

However, the company was cognizant of its inability to supervise properly the workday of most of its employees and understood that discipline depended more on trust than on rulebooks, Dutch clocks, and spotters. The various paternalistic programs were designed to show the Santa Fe's concern with the workers' welfare. They encouraged loyalty, attempted to instill both knowledge and virtue, and offered alternative amusements to those that dissipated workers' talents and paychecks. The company's paternalism, like its recruitment and discipline policies, tended to make its workers contented; it thereby lessened turnover and kept those trustworthy and efficient railroaders who made the Santa Fe one of the premier railroads of the nineteenth century.

CHAPTER 3

Boomers, Old-Timers, and the Romance of the Rail

A railroader's occupation, like that of a miner, soldier, or sailor, was far more than a way to earn the necessities of life. Railroaders were proud of their vocation and developed an unusual degree of esprit de corps. They found unique characteristics in their work that set them apart from those who spent their lives in what many railroaders considered to be less prestigious or more routine callings.

Railroaders were far from a uniform group in their lifestyles. The transient, or boomer, element gained a deserved reputation as rowdies who cared more for drink than decorum, cards than church, and lust than love. However, many railway men, especially the more sedentary ones, led quite different lives. Responsible and steady in their employment, they occasionally voiced disdain for the boomer and tried to uplift their drifting fellow railroaders.

Santa Fe men, whether chronic drifters or workers with several decades of seniority, showed an abiding drive to improve themselves. As proud as they might be of their connection with the romance of the rail, many yearned for a chance to be their own boss and all realized that only a minority could continue railroading once they reached old age. Happily, the underdeveloped Santa Fe region held forth a multitude of opportunities for those with ambition, talent, and a little capital.

Pride in one's competence at a task, knowledge of the operations of an important business, and the fellowship that all workers commonly felt for those employed alongside them engendered among Santa Fe employees a special attachment for their labor and fellow laborers. For railroaders, particularly for the flamboyant enginemen, trainmen, and switchmen, this identification with their work was nurtured by unusual hardships and hazards, an especially mobile life style, and the excitement of working with the most dynamic and advanced technological miracle of the nineteenth century.

Santa Fe men exhibited their esprit de corps in several ways. One of their favorite pastimes was to gather on the porch of the local Harvey House restaurant or some congenial watering spot and brag of their proficiency at their work—"swapping lies," as one New Mexico newspaper called it. A Kansas City news reporter overheard a Topeka engineer declare that on one run his locomotive beat its shadow to Emporia by several minutes. Many railroaders looked down on the more humdrum lives of those outside their ranks. They referred to some of these drab unfortunates as "barn yard cadets" or "pumpkin huskers." To themselves, though, Santa Fe workers assigned nicknames conveying color and camaraderie—"Alkali Jack" Lyons, "Crazy Horse" Williamson, and "Black Jack" Leonard. Though such flamboyant names faded from the scene by 1900, one could always tell those railroaders whose years of experience had earned them special respect, for these men were invariably called "Dad."[1]

The popular press did nothing to deflate railroaders' opinion of their reputation. In an era before automobiles made train travel appear leisurely and jet aircraft made it ludicrous, the locomotive provided man with the first mechanized form of transportation with superhuman speed. The public's imagination was easily fired by the rash of short stories and novels, aimed both at children and adults, that centered on the activities of railroaders, particularly those of the West. A host of contemporary authors portrayed the railroad as offering excitement, travel, varied experiences, and opportunities to display bravery and chivalry. No wonder the *Railway Gazette* found that "the disposition among country youths to get into railroad employment [was] . . . universal."[2]

Railroaders' crucial role in moving the nation's commerce enhanced their evaluation of the importance of their jobs. Especially on the western Plains, a town without a railroad was cut off from the outside world and its future was uncertain. All knew from experience that railroad strikes could last only three to five days before a town's grocery supplies became scanty and local businessmen suffered from the inability to send their goods to outside markets. The Kansas Bureau of Labor and Industrial Statistics in 1897 acknowledged, "No other . . . body of wage-earners in the state contributes more to the welfare and prosperity of the commonwealth." Moreover, during normal operations railroaders realized that their jobs involved the safety of scores of passengers and thousands of dollars of freight. One nineteenth century railroader wrote: "Knowing that amid the darkness of night, the storms of winter, and the war of the elements, hundreds of human beings are to be kept in safety, carries with it a peculiar dignity and sense of responsibility that is felt all along the line, from the man at the switch, the man on the locomotive, the man who controls the train, up through all the various ranks."[3]

Shared dangers further cemented the sense of camaraderie among large groups of railroaders. Fear of injury or a gruesome and sudden death on the job imprinted itself deeply in the consciousness of railroad employees. In 1885 the Medical and Surgical Reporter carried an article declaring that engineers often suffered insomnia and dyspepsia after narrowly escaping death on the job, and that many found alcohol alone could provide relief from their severe tension. Some railroaders' fears invaded their dreams, much to the discomfort of their wives. In the early 1880s one brakeman striving to stop a nightmare runaway train woke up to find that he was twisting his wife's head instead of the brake wheel, while a Santa Fe engineer woke one night in 1898 with his wife screaming because he was pulling her arm out of its socket trying to reverse his engine. Loss of nerve, insanity, and suicide also were attributed to employees' narrow escapes from death on the Santa Fe. Yet for all the inner terror involved in their perilous occupations, railroaders accepted injuries as part of their jobs; indeed, some took an amount of pride in them. The Argentine Republic noted that some boys relished the hazards involved in railroading. A typical one, spending his youth playing around the moving cars in the yards, would hire on as a brakeman or switchman. Inevitably he would get a few fingers pinched, and though he might rise to prominence in the company "he will never experience the same thrill of pleasure as he did the day he got his fingers pinched coupling. . . . He will never again see as much pleasure as he did with his two crippled fingers tied up in a dirty rag." In railroading, where men accepted considerable risk daily and witnessed maimings at a more or less regular rate, such a "Red Badge of Courage" served as proof of full membership in the profession.[4]

Santa Fe railroaders, especially engineers, took pride in the technology they used to slice through the Southwest. To the engineers their locomotives became living companions with unique personalities and characteristics. The men at the throttle avoided ugly engines, which were said to portend tragedy, and those locomotives with unlucky numbers. Occasionally engineers received spiritual warnings of disaster and some Santa Fe officials complained that the men heeded these superstitions even when they involved breaking company rules. Engineers took a proprietary attitude toward the engine assigned them. At least in the 1880s they had some say in minor fitting options, and throughout nearly all of the century Santa Fe engineers watched over the necessary repairs when locomotives entered the shops.[5]

To an extent their concern was practical; an efficient and well-maintained engine made for safer, easier, steadier, and more remunerative work. But many engineers' solicitude for their machine went far beyond pragmatic considerations. Concerning one local engineer, a Las Vegas newspaper in 1891 noted, "He fancies that the big thing feels and seriously contends that the machine is capable of affection and will run twice as well for him as for any one else." When in 1886 veteran engineer Jakey Brown got a beautiful new 2-8-0 he instantly fell in love with it; the newspaper reported that he had been "fondling his monster machine nearly all day, and loafing around and bragging on it, with the affectionate solicitude of a mother petting a favorite child." Emporia's Amos "Dad" McKanna greeted a new engine as he would the arrival of a baby, by passing around cigars. Some engineers sang to their engines on the road, and virtually all boasted of the speeds their machines achieved. And when Chanute's "Dad" Tully saw his Number 402 removed to another division in 1891 he mourned the loss "as though she were one of his own children."[6]

Enginemen and many other Santa Fe railroaders took enough interest and pride in their work to invent and patent improvements. Until 1897, when President Ripley offered those men with new ideas a chance to use company machines and materials on company time, the Santa Fe employee-inventors had little official high level support for their work. Partly as a result of Ripley's encouragement, the last years of the century produced an increase in the output of novel devices by Santa Fe men. Emporia engineer McKanna in 1899 patented a contrivance to transmit train orders from stations to enginemen and trainmen without stopping the train. This or a similar device ultimately gained acceptance on railroads throughout the country. In the same year a Santa Fe section foreman at Chapman, Kansas, invented a weed killer for use along right of ways. Shopmen exceeded all others in their mechanical innovations, especially in the 1890s, when Santa Fe employees found a multitude of labor-saving adaptations of the recently introduced compressed-air machines. Shop foremen took the lead in this work, for they generally had the greatest experience and knowledge, had more freedom to spend time on such projects, and lacked any inhibitions about introducing labor-saving devices. Among inventions credited to foremen were a compressed-air bolt cutter, which reduced a day-long job to one or two hours; a flue-cutter, which converted that task from a three-day to a one-day operation; and car and building spray-painting machines, which similarly could save labor. Whether the general machinists and shop laborers greeted all these machines with enthusiasm is questionable, yet some were intrigued by them. Furthermore, the technical question-and-answer column that invariably formed an important part of engineer, fireman, and shop union journals attested to their interest in the best methods to do a job.[7]

The railway men's chance to travel, like that of the sailors of the clipper ship era, attracted many to the profession. Except in depression times, it was relatively easy to quit a job on one railroad, hitch several rides from friendly conductors, and find another railroad job wherever one wanted. Transiency caused most of the great turnover with which company officials had to deal. The Santa Fe, running so close to Mexico, found that many of its men quit for jobs south of the Rio Grande, where Americans predominated in skilled positions. Some adventurous Santa Fe men traveled as far as South America and Africa practicing their trade. Turnover in the Coolidge shops proved so severe in the late 1880s that the company had to send repairs that should have been done there one hundred miles east to Dodge City. However, railroaders took jobs with the Santa Fe at about the same pace as they abandoned them. Moreover, these floaters provided railroads with much of their essential seasonal labor.[8]

Various reasons accounted for the roving ways of some railroaders: the desire to see new places, to escape an unpleasant past, or—in the case of many Santa Fe railroaders—to enjoy New Mexico or Arizona weather in the winter and a more northerly climate in the summer. Turnover was very high among unskilled track, station, yard, shop, and bridge and building employees because many of them were local casual laborers, often hired only for a season, who when discharged returned to farming or a variety of other part-time occupations. For example, the seasonal section workers in Emporia in 1895 included a farmer, a cook, a real estate agent, and a college student. Telegraph operators, agents, switchmen, firemen, and brakemen demonstrated high turnover and geographic mobility. One switchman in 1892 noted that his fellows had "gained a national reputation for their migratory habits, and to work in one yard or stay in one town for more than three consecutive months would kill them sure."[9] Letters to union journals attempted to keep members informed of each other's whereabouts, but a Santa Fe telegraph operator confessed that the personnel at the keys on his division changed so fast that he could not keep track of them.[10]

The twin phenomena of turnover and geographic mobility also were related to age, marital status, pay level, and property holding. In the early 1880s central Kansas Santa Fe employees who were forty-five or older were twice as likely to continue working for the company in one town as younger men, while in the last years of the century fewer than a third of the employees under twenty-five stayed with the company, compared to more than half of those in older age groups. In the same periods married men exhibited at least 25 percent greater persistence than their single counterparts. Those earning the best wages in each occupation also tended to stick to their jobs. Since those who remained with the company usually further increased their pay status relative to other employees, persistence and increased earnings reinforced each other. Last, home-owning railroaders were 20 to 50 percent more likely to remain with the company. These factors largely explain why 46 percent of nontrack workers continued on the middle division payroll covering central Kansas over the last five years of the century, while only 30 percent of Santa Fe men did so in the later 1870s. The 1890s employees were older and more likely to be married and to own their homes. And analogously in the late 1890s Kansas workers were less transient than those men in bleak, uninviting southern New Mexico, whose age, marital, and home-owning profiles were similar to those of the pioneering railroaders of the 1870s.[11]

Drifting railroaders gained a reputation as a boastful, rough-speaking, hard-living, immoral lot. Such a characterization may have done an injustice to some of the boomer element, yet even apologists admitted there was much truth in the stereotype. Lorenzo S. Coffin, an Iowa railroad commissioner in the 1880s and a reformist friend of railroaders, confessed that among the ranks of brakemen were many deadbeats whose life consisted of roaming about and beating up others whenever an opportunity arose; "Rox," a station agent, in 1893 conceded that the popular notion that railroaders were "without conscience, principle or conviction" was largely correct.[12]

Bragging was especially prevalent among the roving element. A young lady of Albuquerque avoided the highly mobile brakemen, for she had been told that trainmen liked to gossip about the women they knew "and each in order to glorify himself and tell the best story, [would] not hesitate to introduce names and highly color their narrative." The drifters' bragging of their amorous triumphs as well as their abilities on the job and fearlessness before company officers often irked the more

AUGUSTANA UNIVERSITY COLLEGE
LIBRARY

sedentary workers. A Trinidad railroaders' poem dedicated to
the "Tourist Brakeman" caught the tenor of the outrageous
boastfulness of the boomers.

> From the east, the west, north and south
>   We see them "heading in,"
> All bloated up with grievances,
>   But rather short of "tin."
>
> They tell us of "those only roads,"
>   Where they could "get a train,"
> Away down south, in Hoosierdom,
>   If they'd go back again.
>
> Where they were the "swiftest people,"
>   And they "set 'em all afire,"
> Where they learned to court "by signal,"
>   And marry girls "by wire."
>
>   . . . .
>
> They used to "run a brotherhood,"
>   Before they ventured here;
> And if we will only let them,
>   They'll "put us into clear."
>
>   . . . .
>
> They'll "can the superintendent,"
>   And get us all a train;
> Then "interview the manager,"
>   And show him where "he's lame."[13]

Many of the boldest boasts were nurtured during railroaders'
all too regular visits to local taverns, numerous enough in the
rough towns along the line. In early 1885 the temperate traveling
Santa Fe machinist Ben Johnson found himself writing his
mother from a San Marcial saloon, the only suitably lighted
facility in this division point where bars outnumbered groceries
six to one. Even without alcohol's often imposing availability,
however, many railroaders displayed an uncommon attraction
to a state of inebriation. Realizing this, the Women's Christian
Temperance Union in the first five years of its existence established a permanent committee to promote temperance among
railroaders, the only occupational group targeted so early for

special work. Similarly, in the 1890s evangelical preachers, including some active Santa Fe railroaders, traveled and spoke in the interest of the Railroad Temperance Association and formed local branches in numerous towns on the Santa Fe.[14]

The efforts of the association, though, even when augmented by company rules against drinking and the dry laws of Kansas, fell short of their goal of taming the wild ways of the boomers. A steady railroader at Las Vegas complained in 1892, "The only switchmen who come here are drunken bums, who quit just as soon as they get money enough to get drunk." Kansas towns in the 1880s and 1890s periodically saw railroaders boisterously carousing in the streets for a few nights after payday, sometimes assaulting people, and ultimately leaving when their revelry was over. Occasionally their intoxication prompted outlandish behavior, such as Tom Foley's "El Paso Special." A competent machinist, Foley quit his job in the La Junta shop shortly after being paid in February 1898. For some days he spent his money "like a prince and did his best to 'corner' the liquor market." With his funds nearly gone, he decided it was time to seek the winter warmth of El Paso. Still saturated with alcohol, he boarded an idle engine, recruited three tramps as passengers, and opened the throttle wide. The engine left the yard like a shot, terrifying the tramps who were not accustomed to rides quite this dangerous. Fortunately, the locomotive had little water in the boiler and quickly ran out of steam. In the end, if Foley ever reached El Paso, it was only after a stay in the La Junta jail.[15]

If boomers liked drink, drunkenness tended to perpetuate their careers as drifters. One engineman wrote in 1890 that in the previous seven years he had been employed by five railroads, including the Santa Fe and the Atlantic & Pacific, and had lost each job through drinking. Alcohol was the prime cause of discharges from the Santa Fe. Too much drink caused others to quit their jobs impetuously. One drunken Santa Fe brakeman named Palmer signed himself into the army, something in more sober moments he might never have done. Not long after enlisting Palmer began serving a term at Leavenworth for desertion.[16]

Their affection for drink caused some workers to spend the contents of an entire month's pay envelope within a few days or hours. Common thieves and saloon gamblers found drunken railroaders attractive targets. Trainman Chauncey Del French, who in 1876 found both the whiskey and the gambling at Dodge City too tame for his tastes, may have been among a minority of railroaders who won at the gambling tables. More common were the tales of men who lost their entire month's pay in one drunken spree.[17]

Drunk or sober, railroaders could be a rough bunch. In the early years at the extreme western end of the road, crudeness prevailed even among many of the railroading elite. A New Year's dinner held in Trinidad, Colorado, by Santa Fe men of all ranks featured numerous off-color jokes and enough alcohol to send everyone home in a drunken stupor. Most notices of rowdiness, however, referred to those in the more transient occupation groups. Ben Johnson in 1884 despaired that any self-improvement plans, such as the company reading rooms, would ever uplift the brakemen, whom he dismissed as a "hard class." It is impossible to determine how common brawling and gunplay were among these railroaders, but they occurred most often in the 1870s and 1880s and in the rugged areas of New Mexico and Arizona. Not surprisingly, much of this violence was associated with the excessive use of alcohol by one or more of the participants.[18]

It also is not surprising that the boomers gave railroaders an unsavory reputation among members of the opposite sex. A letter from "Three Bachelor Trainmen" to an Albuquerque paper in 1891 bemoaned the fact that they were rejected by the local belles, who generally considered trainmen an undesirable class because "they are ignorant, ungentlemanly and inclined to dissipations . . . few among them are able to even converse reasonably upon any of the topics of the day . . . they prefer saloons to sermons and liquor to lectures [and] . . . their occupation is only selected as a makeshift until something better offers." The ways of the drifter often caused problems for those who did marry. Many wives fretted over their husbands' drinking and gambling. Others complained that their husbands met their love with cold indifference, if not outright cruelty. Train and engine crews' jobs, which took men away from home night after night, made infidelity both tempting and easy. Railroaders, single and married, were known as frequenters of houses of prostitution.

Nor did marriage cure all Santa Fe employees of their desire to travel. Some simply abandoned their wives and families, taking advantage of past experience of fending for themselves on the road. Once in a new location, their past could be put farther behind them by changing their names, an easy and common practice. Others might maintain tenuous contact with their families but continue to change employers, as they had when they were single boomers, spending months and even years at a time away from home.[19]

At the other end of the spectrum from the carefree hobo railroaders were the Santa Fe men who, having hired on with the company, loyally remained on its payrolls for the rest of their working lives. In 1907 engineer William Parr published a Santa Fe work register from 1878, noting that four of the six engineers on the list were still running for the company. Patrick Reagan began more than thirty years in the Santa Fe shops and yards in 1869. In 1897 Jonas Stafford was still track walking after working over twenty-five years in Santa Fe section crews near Dodge City. Patrick Walsh joined the Santa Fe as its first baggage master in 1875 and remained in that post for more than fifty years. As the century closed, two of the most loyal employees surely were the engineer and conductor working on the run between Newton and Jetmore, Kansas. Conductor John Bender received his first Santa Fe pay in 1870, barely a year after the first train ran on Santa Fe track. But his engineer, Peter Telline, was ahead of him in seniority, having hired on to the construction gang the second day it began building the line south of Topeka in 1868.[20]

Undoubtedly, some of the more permanent railroaders shared the vulgar ways of the drifters. Yet most tended to be more proper in their habits. At the end of the century, when railroaders were becoming more sedentary, many noted a change for the better in their character. Fairly typical was the *Chanute Tribune*'s comment in 1897: "A few years ago it was no uncommon sight to see a lot of railroad men under the influence of liquor when off duty, but that day is in the past. Railroad men now, as a rule, are sober, intelligent, thinking men."[21]

Santa Fe railroaders shared the everyday problems and joys of all working men. Some, especially those in the poorer-paying jobs, battled to make financial ends meet. An extreme example was the Topeka railroad laborer who earned $250 a year in the late 1880s. The only one working in a family of ten, he leased land for a dollar a month and in the course of two years managed to build a two-room shanty and purchase a cow. Few regular employees faced nearly as difficult a struggle. Most spent 30 to 40 percent of their incomes on food, though those in the lowest-paid positions often spent 50 percent or more to keep themselves and their families fed. Clothing and rent each consumed about 15 percent of a worker's yearly wages, while medical costs accounted for 5 to 10 percent more and fuel took about a twentieth of his earnings. The rest was divided among insurance, taxes, and the usual miscellaneous expenses of day-to-day living.[22]

Railroaders enjoyed many of the simple pleasures of life. Emporia car foreman Samuel P. Chase in 1895 was as proud of his new pair of tan "razor toe" shoes as "a little boy with his first pair of knee breeches," while Ben Johnson once wrote home that he intended to "wear boiled shirts, tight pants, high heeled boots and a cane and be generally exquisite" when he was promoted to engineer.[23] As early as 1879 a baseball club of clerks in the general offices challenged other Topeka teams. By the 1890s Topeka's office workers and shopmen throughout the line annually organized baseball teams to play each other and whatever other competition could be found. In the 1880s Topeka shop football teams engaged in contests with the local students of Washburn College. By the late 1890s some railroaders also began forming basketball teams, gun clubs, bands, and glee clubs. Enginemen and trainmen, having less regular and uniform schedules than office and shop personnel, found it difficult to participate in organized sports. They were more likely to fish or hunt.[24]

Even the irregular schedules of engine and train crews did not preclude a happy family life. Some relatives of Santa Fe men took great interest in their work. A sister of an Arkansas City fireman said that she liked "as well as the engineers or firemen to see a nice, new and bright engine come out of the shop." Wives and sweethearts listened for the unique combination of whistles that engineers adopted to announce their return to town. When a family member was sick, railroaders commonly exchanged runs to be home more regularly. Some made decisions like that of Las Vegas conductor George Hill, who gave up a passenger train to which he had recently been promoted in favor of a freight run that allowed him more time with his family. Company-sponsored picnics provided railroad families an enjoyable time together and Santa Fe pass privileges gave opportunities for wide-ranging family vacations.[25]

If many of the boom railroaders were immoral, habitual drunkards, there were some employees who took temperance and religion very seriously. In 1892 and 1893 Jennie Smith, the "railroad evangelist," won supporters to the Railroad Temperance Association on her tour over the Santa Fe. C. E. Quick, the chief dispatcher at Newton, counseled railroaders on the Christian life and was a locally prominent lay preacher. The Railroad YMCA sponsored the talks of two Santa Fe engineers. At the end of the century J. T. Blodgett spoke to a Topeka audience on the topic "Can a Railroad Man Be a Christian?," while C. W. McClure, a member of the Railroad YMCA's national executive committee, often took leaves from railroading to travel and give what all agreed to have been spellbinding, room-filling orations of his Christian experience.[26]

Santa Fe railroaders engaged in numerous ventures to win wealth or gain a more secure income. In March and April 1889, Santa Fe workers became excited by the prospect of claiming property when the Oklahoma District opened April 22. The chance for free land prompted Lew Vaughn, a Las Vegas round-house man, and others to pack up their families and all their possessions to travel to the starting point for the big rush. One Santa Fe conductor whose train was passing through the territory at the appointed hour abandoned his post at Edmond to stake a claim. J. B. Cooper, an Emporia engineer, organized a three-coach party to ride the Santa Fe into the territory. Cooper had long taken an interest in the Oklahoma District, participating as a top lieutenant to boomer David L. Payne in the early 1880s. Apparently Cooper and other Santa Fe employees succeeded, for he acquired a farm near Seward and after the rush there were complaints that Santa Fe employees, abusing their right to travel into the territory, had gotten many of the best lots.[27]

Gold rushes also attracted railroaders. In 1876 some Santa Fe employees quit to take part in the rush to the Black Hills. More than two decades later in February 1898 the *Topeka Journal* commented that the Klondike fever had struck local Santa Fe men hard and that if an inoculation was not found soon the shops would be depopulated by spring. Not only the young and poorly-paid workers departed for the frozen north; among those who set off in search of instant wealth were Winslow's train-master and division master mechanic.[28]

Other Santa Fe men pursued less spectacular alternatives to railroading. Former Santa Fe employees took up every type of employment from professional baseball player to physician. Many went into business for themselves. Although even low-paid railroad laborers started their own enterprises, a dispropor-tionate number of those who were able to become self-employed had held positions in the higher-paid ranks of railroading, where they had been able to amass sufficient capital for the undertaking. This helps to account for a reversal of a pattern noted earlier. For most railroaders home ownership and high wages rooted them to their jobs. But among middle division employees who were forty-five or older in 1895, the well-paid and the home owners were much more likely to quit than less well-to-do workers of the same age. With the approach of old age, poorer men clung to the security of their Santa Fe jobs. Those who could afford it, though, worrying that decreasing vigor would bring demotion and eventually discharge, set them-selves up in business so that no one could ever force them to retire.[29]

Former Santa Fe employees plunged into a variety of busi-ness activities, especially those catering to railroaders — man-aging a hotel, boarding house, restaurant, or tavern. These men capitalized on old friendships and their firsthand knowledge of railroaders' desires. But some business attempts failed. For those men like former conductor William Wright and former boiler-shop worker William Thomas whose meat markets went under, or former assistant station agent Peter Dorsch whose Emporia saloon closed because of Kansas prohibition, a return to the

Santa Fe's regular payrolls provided a secure income when their dreams for something better came to naught.[30]

Many railroaders sought greater economic independence without quitting the Santa Fe. In 1882, two hundred Topekans, composed largely of railroaders and led by a Santa Fe shop mechanic, formed a cooperative store that sold goods to members at cost and to other townspeople at prevailing prices. Las Vegas railroaders founded a similar enterprise a decade later, but apparently both of these efforts at economic cooperation were short-lived. The Locomotive Engineers' Cattle Company of Raton was a larger-scale and more successful venture. Formed in the midst of a cattle boom in late 1883 by local Santa Fe engineers, the company sold shares of stock through published ads. The company survived until 1891; regardless of how its ranching operations prospered, it probably proved successful as a speculative stock scheme.[31]

Workers also engaged in small business while still railroading. Track foremen, assisted by their wives, commonly earned extra income by housing and feeding their crews. Some Santa Fe employees cut the cost of living and made a small side income by planting gardens or raising chickens. And in New Mexico railroaders took time off from work to prospect in the mining districts of the territory.[32]

By far the most common occupation mix was that of ranching or farming with railroading. Some Santa Fe employees dwelt on their land and commuted to work. Jack Meierdicks, a clerk at Florence, Kansas, lived on his homestead six miles from town. Every morning he rose before the sun, did the chores, and rode to work by seven o'clock. Nearly as often, the farm or ranch was far removed from the work place and the railroader went to it only on weekends or at times when much farm work was required. Several who acquired farms in Oklahoma continued to work for the Santa Fe in Kansas while some eastern Kansans worked farms or ranches in the western part of the Sunflower State. Farming and ranching were the prime alternative employments for a number of reasons. Many railroaders of this era probably were raised in agrarian settings. To undertake farming or cattle raising, therefore, did not require much expertise they did not already possess. Second, farming and ranching were not labor-intensive businesses. Some railroaders were able to carry on their farming interests by taking time off from work to do the planting in the spring and the harvesting in the fall. Third, farm or ranch lands could turn a family from a financial liability into an asset. Frequently, a sturdy wife and a few young sons took care of the day-to-day operations. Even if the railroader could not count on a family to look after his farm, hired labor could be found to do the work. And all the while, the land served as an investment. In an era before pension plans and Social Security, owning productive land promised a secure income for a railroader's old age.[33]

Restlessness was a trait of many Santa Fe railway men. That of the boomers was displayed in boozing, brawling, and roaming ways. Old-timers also had an eye out for their big chance and some showed an eagerness to quit railroading for other work. This restlessness was a product of some discontent with railroading coupled with an awareness of the opportunities offered in an expansive, fast-developing society. Moreover, railroaders' adventurousness resulted in part from a reputation that fed on itself. Many railway jobs were known as exciting and dynamic and, therefore, they attracted young men ready to work hard, accept responsibilities, travel, take risks, and break old emotional ties. Maturity and growing families eventually made men more conscious of the need for steadier habits. However, even this did not tame all restlessness, because a process of natural selection dictated that railroading attracted more than its share of adventurous American youth.

The shop force at La Junta, Colorado, 1884. *Kansas State Historical Society*

Topeka roundhouse gang in 1885. *Santa Fe Railway*

Funeral train, provided by the company, bound from Temple to Goldthwaite, Texas, to bury a Santa Fe fireman killed in an 1898 train holdup. *Santa Fe Railway*

Track workers and hand car at station in Ponca City, Oklahoma. *Santa Fe Railway*

The Rincon, New Mexico, station in 1883. *Santa Fe Railway*

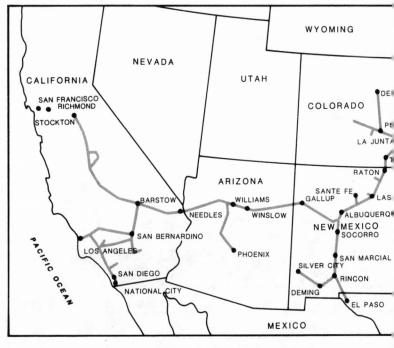

The Santa Fe system in 1900. Some branch lines have been deleted.

Engineer Jim Phillips works on his engine before pulling a passenger train out of Arkansas City, Kansas, in 1899. *Santa Fe Railway*

Part of the Topeka switch yard force with a new engine in 1886. *Santa Fe Railway*

CHAPTER 4

Railroaders and Their Neighbors:
Emporia, a Case Study

Located at the edge of the Flint Hills of eastern Kansas, Emporia in 1878 was like many towns on the fast-receding Plains frontier. Aspiring to be a commercial and industrial center, it was neither. On its north end the State Normal School, which graduated fewer than a score of students each year, added more prestige than profit to the town. William Soden had a grain mill south of town on the Cottonwood River and the Joneses ran a small iron foundry. But who could call Emporia the "Pittsburgh of the Plains" on the strength of these enterprises? Then in 1879 the Santa Fe built a thirty-six-stall roundhouse at the town's western edge and designated it a division center. The boom that followed did not alter the flow of trade in the region, nor did it generate a series of new industries, but it did give Emporia a large new population of railroaders who became a distinctive and permanent element in the community.[1]

Santa Fe employees in Emporia displayed few traits markedly different from those of neighboring nonrailroaders. Even brakemen and firemen, with their high mobility and sordid reputations, were at least as likely to marry or to have children as most classes of nonrailroad laborers. The ethnic make-up of the Santa Fe's work force in Emporia did not contrast with that of the general population. Nor were they far richer or poorer than those employed in other sectors of the economy. Indeed, the general profile of railroad workers provides an only slightly variant image of the broader working class.

One distinctive characteristic of the town's railroaders was the concentration of their residences around the station and shop. Not surprisingly, railroaders tended to find homes near their place of work; more than two-thirds lived in one quadrant of the town. However, even though they lived apart and were recognized as a distinct group, the Santa Fe men were not denied, nor did they eschew, the friendship of the rest of the community. Rather, railroaders and nonrailroaders interacted socially within class lines.

The typical Santa Fe division town was not an imposing sight. The company had made its home in some of the most underdeveloped parts of nineteenth century America. From the Missouri to the western terminuses on the Pacific, Santa Fe trains passed through an endless number of small towns. The Santa Fe placed some division centers in established towns such as Emporia, Dodge City, and Arkansas City, Kansas, and Las Vegas, New Mexico. Railroaders generally accounted for 10 to 20 percent of the working population of these towns. The desirability of spacing division shops at roughly one-hundred-mile intervals sometimes required the Santa Fe to place shops in new towns or barely existing villages. This was the case with Nickerson, Kansas, and Raton and San Marcial, New Mexico, where railroaders constituted about half of all adult male workers.[2]

Santa Fe decisions on the location of division towns were critical to the prosperity and even the viability of many communities of the Southwest. In May 1887 a newspaper of Arkansas City—a town Topeka officials had recently designated as a future division center—rejoicingly commented, "It is a well established fact that the Atchison, Topeka & Santa Fe company can make, . . . a large town, and from indications we should judge this company intends showering its favor upon Arkansas City." The construction of the large division shops at Raton in 1882 prompted townsmen to boast of their municipality as the future "Pittsburgh of New Mexico." A dozen years later the company's shops were still important to Raton, as a citizen noted in a commentary about the Santa Fe's payday: "[It is] the important epoch . . . upon which everything depends. . . . Directly or indirectly, every man, woman and child in the place has an interest in it, from the merchant with heavy obligations to meet to the little one promised a new plaything."[3]

The histories of Nickerson and Coolidge, Kansas, illustrate the critical importance of the location of division centers. In early 1878 Nickerson was an insignificant hamlet of fifty inhabitants. Then the Santa Fe announced that it would place shops in the town within the year. In the next few months nearly a hundred buildings, including two hotels, rose upon land that had been wholly devoted to farming only a year earlier. Coolidge's experience was the antithesis of that of Nickerson. In the mid-1880s Coolidge was the home for about 150 Santa Fe railroaders on its western divison. But in the fall of 1890 its shops were dismantled and virtually all the town's railroaders were transferred to La Junta. Businessmen soon began to abandon Coolidge, many following the railroaders to La Junta. One of the town's newspapers moved to neighboring Syracuse. The town's two other papers ceased publication altogether, one complaining in its last days that Coolidge did not have "the resource of one poor nickel outside the RR."[4]

Emporia was established in 1857, when it was laid out two miles square on the grasslands just north of the meandering Cottonwood River. In the next two years it grew rapidly. A large portion of the earliest settlers were the Welsh who came to dominate the southern part of the town. With the Civil War, growth stopped and the subsequent period saw only modest expansion, despite the entrance into town of both the Missouri, Kansas & Texas Railroad and the Santa Fe by the early 1870s. Almost from the beginning, though, Emporia was more than the agrarian-centered service towns nearby; the State Normal School opening in 1865 and the College of Emporia founded in 1883 made the north end of town for a time the educational center of Kansas.[5]

The Santa Fe entered Emporia in 1871. From the beginning, the town had a small number of Santa Fe workers. This included a dozen or more enginemen and trainmen, a handful more in the four-stall roundhouse, and a scattering of others in and about the station and yards. However, through the 1870s the number of railroaders was too small for their fellow townsmen to recognize or treat them as a separate and distinct portion of the population. But in 1879, when the Santa Fe established its divisional system, Emporia received major additions to its company work force and its long career as a railroad town began. Over the next two years the town's railroad population climbed to three hundred as new roundhouse, shop, station, and yard facilities were constructed. Emporia's population, which had lingered well under three thousand for much of the 1870s, shot up to more than forty-six hundred by June 1880. The town boomed. Woodframe homes were built as fast as possible as hundreds of newcomers crammed into hotels and boarding houses. Housing agencies daily turned away applicants. The June 1880 census taker found many railroaders in rooming houses, their wives still unable to join them.[6]

While a modest number of Emporia's women worked, none were employed by the Santa Fe.[7] Elsewhere on the line women constituted but a minute segment of company employees. In the 1870s a handful of women labored as coach cleaners, a position from which they appear to have been excluded later in the century. The large majority of Santa Fe women worked at clerical jobs. Their pay was uniformly low, yet the Santa Fe paid wages at least comparable to other employers of women. By the 1890s women commonly appeared on the payroll, assisting their husbands who were agents at small stations; the husband worked the day shift and the wife, the night. In the last years of the century, however, women began to take telegrapher positions on their own and held regular membership in the telegraphers' union.[8]

In 1880, while only a few years younger than the generally young nonrailroad population and nearly as likely to have children, the Santa Fe employees were dramatically less settled in Emporia. Nonrailroaders were three times more likely than railroaders to own their homes. Seventy-six of the town's 232 railroaders lived in one of two large boarding houses. While nearly nine out of every ten married nonrailroaders had their wives with them, more than a fourth of all married railroaders had not yet sufficiently established themselves in town to induce them to send for their wives. And the city directory compiled in 1884 revealed that railroaders were more likely to leave town or change residences within Emporia than were their nonrailroading neighbors (see Table 2).

The distribution of the birthplaces of 1880 Emporia workers

Table 2: Characteristics of Emporia Railroaders and Nonrailroaders

	1880		1885		1895		1900	
	RRer	N-RR	RRer	N-RR	RRer	N-RR	RRer	N-RR
Average age	30.5	33.8	32.7	37.0	34.8	40.3	35.9	40.0
Average number of children of those living with wife	1.5	2.0	1.9	2.1	2.2	2.3	1.8	2.0
Percent owning home	6.0	18.0	17.0	30.0	12.2	31.3	25.3	36.0
Percent heading household	39.2	54.1	59.5	67.7	75.0	71.3	69.5	64.2
Percent persistent next 5 years	24.1	41.6	32.8	27.7	46.0	54.3	——	——
Percent of persisters to move in next 5 years	71.1	57.7	57.5	36.8	47.8	36.7	——	——
Percent married	54.1	56.9	61.0	67.0	76.5	65.6	71.5	65.3
Percent of married not living with wife	27.0	10.9	2.1	3.6	——	——	2.1	3.5
Percent born in Kansas	.5	1.7	1.7	2.1	9.1	12.6	14.7	20.0
Percent born in Wales	.5	6.4	4.6	8.5	3.0	7.0	4.5	5.8
Percent born in South	3.5	14.9	12.2	15.9	7.6	9.3	6.8	10.6

Source: Emporia data for 1880, 1885, 1895, 1900.

reflected the relative newness of the Santa Fe employees to the town. Those born in Kansas and Wales were greatly underrepresented among railroaders. The Welsh and Kansans were the old-timers in the community who had settled down to jobs in the nonrailroading sector of Emporia's economy long before the

Santa Fe built its division facilities. To be a long-time Emporia resident virtually disqualified one from many railroad occupations, since skilled posts required experience that Emporians had no means to attain. Also, relatively few Southerners were railroaders. This was because nearly half of all Southerners and more than 10 percent of nonrailroaders in town were black, and the Santa Fe employed not a single black in Emporia. Throughout the rest of the century, blacks represented about a tenth of the town's workers but never more than a twenty-fifth of the local Santa Fe labor force.[9]

In the years after 1880 railroaders came to resemble more closely other Emporians. While their age and the size of their families did not change relative to those of nonrailroaders, Santa Fe employees did begin to find homes in Emporia. Home ownership continued to lag behind that of their neighbors, but railroaders began to match and even exceed nonrailroaders in the percentage to head households, the percent to persist in town over five years, and in measurements of marital status and cohabitation of husbands and wives. And at the same time Santa Fe workers found a home in Emporia, Emporia's older population gained jobs with the railroad. Kansans, Welsh, and Southerners remained underrepresented among railroaders, yet the gap that had existed in 1880 closed quickly.

Considering the variety of railroad occupations and the at least equally diverse occupations of other Emporians, dichotomous comparisons of railroaders and nonrailroaders conceal as much as they reveal. For closer examination, Emporia workers have been divided into twenty-two occupational classifications—twelve describing various job sectors of railroading, ten delineating work groups among the rest of the town's population (see Appendix). Two factors deserve priority in this examination because of their impact on other characteristics. First is the railroaders' tendency to move. Except during the late 1880s, railroaders were more transient than the rest of Emporia's working population (see Table 3). The low persistence of nonrailroaders from 1885 to 1890 probably was related to the collapse of the boom era of Kansas expansion, which occurred in the middle of that period. The collapse had a greater impact on the livelihood of businessmen, the self-employed, and those working for small enterprises than it did on the men employed by Kansas' major railroad. Of course, the second half of the 1890s also was marked by a bad economy. But this collapse had not followed such a dramatic expansion as that of the 1880s and was national in scope, compelling men to realize that moving could not bring relief.[10]

Santa Fe trainmen, enginemen, officials, and laborers frequently recorded persistency rates 50 percent less than those of some of the more sedentary railroaders, whose tendency to stay in Emporia was comparable to those of nonrailroader groups in the early 1880s and late 1890s. Indeed, shop workers generally equaled or exceeded white-collar railroaders and many nonrailroaders in their attachment to the community. Therefore, those who considered railroading an exceptionally mobile occupation were correct about only a limited range of workers. Even among men in the same age groups, the pattern of variation in transiency between occupation groups did not change. Instead, the cause for the differences in persistence lay in promotions that often required officials, trainmen, and enginemen to move; the casual or seasonal nature of many railroad laborer positions; and the type of men with peripetetic urgings who were attracted to jobs as railroad laborers, trainmen, and enginemen.

The second critical factor was age. Reflecting the maturation of a near-frontier society,[11] the average age for workers in each occupational classification rose gradually by one to five years from one census to the next. Relative ages between job groups within one year varied little over the two decades. Throughout, Emporia's top businessmen and professionals were the oldest groups (averaging forty years of age in 1880 to nearly forty-eight in 1900) followed by farmers, craftsmen, and those businessmen with more modest enterprises (thirty-five to forty-four). Santa Fe officials and some of their top employees—engineers, conductors, and foremen and skilled railroad craftsmen—were a little younger (thirty-three to forty-one). Still younger were the town's small craft-oriented businessmen and all types of common laborers in and out of railroading (twenty-nine to thirty-eight). The youngest group included Emporia's clerks and salesmen and the most youthful railroaders—the firemen, brakemen, telegraph operators and dispatchers, and agents and clerks (twenty-seven to thirty-four).[12]

Among men of the same age, income, but not mobility,

Table 3: Percent in Each Occupation Classification
to Persist in Emporia, 1880–1900

	1880–84		1885–90		1895–1900	
	No.	%	No.	%	No.	%
All railroaders	224	24.1	259	32.8	328	46.0
All nonrailroaders	327	41.6	313	27.7	604	54.3
Santa Fe officials	2	0.0	5	20.0	8	37.5
Conductors	33	18.2	16	12.5	26	42.3
Engineers	35	22.9	27	33.3	49	55.1
Firemen	32	15.6	18	27.8	24	41.7
Brakemen	55	18.2	13	53.8	32	25.0
Foremen and skilled	12	25.0	35	54.3	47	59.6
Agents and clerks	11	36.4	11	54.5	12	66.7
Shop laborers		*	21	52.4	17	82.4
Yard and station men		*		*	32	50.0
Railroad laborers	22	31.8	101	18.8	68	27.9
Business elite	16	62.5	44	54.0	30	77.2
Professionals	18	27.8	35	27.2	36	44.2
Small businessmen	44	52.3	100	17.9	51	51.9
Small craft businessmen		*	61	24.0	66	55.6
Craftsmen	96	38.5	229	25.9	141	51.7
Farmers	21	19.0	58	27.7	55	60.9
Government employees		*	25	29.5	20	50.0
Clerks and salesmen	26	38.5	48	33.6	60	51.8
Menial service jobs	11	18.2	24	24.6		*

Table 3 continued

	1880–84		1885–90		1895–1900	
	No.	%	No.	%	No.	%
Physical unskilled	80	48.7	189	27.3	127	53.1

* Ten or fewer cases. In no year were there more than ten in track crew or operator-dispatcher classifications. Company officials are included because of special interest, despite their small numbers. See Appendix for descriptions of job classifications.

Source: Emporia data for 1880, 1885, 1895.

affected the likelihood to marry. For example, 81 percent of the conductors and engineers between the ages of twenty-five and thirty-four were wedded, compared to 65 percent of the brakemen and firemen. Perhaps the attractiveness of their social and financial status made courtship easier for those with the best jobs. More likely, their economic well-being enabled them to afford the added responsibilities of a family while the elevated social position of a "family man" appealed to men already high on the occupational ladder. On the other hand, the mobility of some railroad occupations did not necessarily result in lower marital rates. Only the top businessmen of Emporia were more likely to be married than Santa Fe engineers and conductors, and firemen and brakemen had a marriage rate nearly as high as other classes of railroaders and higher than the great majority of nonrailroaders. Once married, men in the various occupations in the same age group displayed little difference in their number of children.[13]

Most men in every job classification headed their own households. But the distribution among the railroad groups of boarders and those living with relatives suggests some differences. Enginemen, trainmen, and railroad laborers constituted the highest percent boarding; nearly 30 percent of the last of these boarded. Certainly the disproportionately small number of railroad laborers who were married played a role in this statistic. But marital data cannot play any part in explaining why engineers and conductors between twenty-five and thirty-four were more than twice as likely to board as were foremen and skilled workers of the same age. Rather, it apparently was the former's high mobility that made their places in the community less settled. The transiency of enginemen and trainmen was also reflected in the percent who lived with relatives. Among foremen and skilled workers who were twenty-five to thirty-four, 30 percent lived with relatives, a figure roughly equivalent to that found for nonrailroading groups. In contrast only 8 percent of enginemen and trainmen of this age group lived with relatives. Since most of those who lived in relatives' homes were sons in their father's household, enginemen and trainmen were far less likely to have been recruited from local youth than were the more sedentary railroaders.[14]

As long as a man was white and not a Chicano, he could engage in any type of railroad work and aspire to advance. In the 1870s Irishmen predominated in Santa Fe track crews and in Emporia in 1880, Germans and Irish were overrepresented among the lowest level workers. But these distinctions vanished quickly. Payrolls of the 1890s found the Irish influence in track work greatly lessened and by the end of the century both an Irishman and a German had acted as a local officer at Emporia. The Topeka shops employed inordinately large contingents of Germans and Russians, yet these groups were not predominant in Emporia. The Santa Fe employed no blacks in Emporia in 1880 but by the 1890s blacks had gained a few positions. Invariably they served in a laborer's role and none could hope for better in railroading. Of course, this was not far different from the place of blacks in the rest of the town's economy, where 80 percent did menial service or common physical labor. The railroad industry reflected the values of its day. The Santa Fe held open its doors for jobs and advancement to men who offered hard work, loyalty, talent—and a white skin.[15]

The range of wealth among railroaders was not strikingly different from that of the rest of Emporia's workers. Very few railroaders employed a servant and those who did generally came from the higher ranks. Similarly, the nonrailroading business elite, small business men, and professionals employed 70 to 94 percent of all servants working in Emporia. The businessmen and professionals also regularly ranked first and second in the percent to own homes, the value of those homes, and the worth of their personal property. Although tending toward the bottom of these rankings, railroaders were spread throughout the middle range of classifications. Like the data on servants, home and personal property information indicated that few railroaders could claim wealth equivalent to the top level of Emporia society, yet below that level, railroaders and nonrailroaders were not far apart.[16]

Quite understandably, there was a strong relationship between pay rate and home ownership and real and personal estate values. Railroad laborers and shop laborers always scored near the bottom of wealth rankings while Santa Fe officials tended toward the top. Yet, because of their high mobility, and despite their excellent pay, enginemen and trainmen rarely owned homes nor were the ones they owned very opulent. In the last fifteen years of the century about a fourth of the town's engineers and conductors owned homes. This was the same proportion as among common laborers, even though the skilled railroaders made two, three, or four times the daily wages of a laborer. Santa Fe foremen and skilled workers who usually earned a dollar less a day than engineers and conductors were always more likely to own homes and those they owned were at least as expensive. Agents, railroad clerks, and yard and station laborers also owned better homes, though they earned considerably less. When age or marital status are controlled these relationships still hold true. The lower scores of engineers and conductors stemmed from their transiency, which made them reluctant to invest in a permanent home. In 1891 a woman writing to the *Railroad Trainmen's Journal* remarked that few trainmen owned their homes because their occupation so frequently required them to move. This was so despite good salaries because "even the section man working for a dollar and a quarter per day, [was] more secure in the enjoyment of a permanent home than the conductor drawing over an hundred dollars per month." In Emporia in 1900 the truth of this observation was borne out; 27 percent of trackmen and 22 percent of conductors owned their homes.[17]

If mobility meant that some railroaders were reluctant about investing in real estate, it did not mean that they failed to accumulate wealth. Men whose transiency made them unlikely land owners instead spent their money on personal estate goods, which could be transferred readily to a new home. The poorly paid, highly mobile railroad laborers came in last in both home ownership and home value, but in total personal estate value they scored considerably higher. And conductors and engineers who scored lower than foremen and skilled workers in real estate holdings far outstripped them in personal estate value.[18]

Since Emporia railroaders resembled the rest of the town's population, the question arises whether these similarities brought Santa Fe Emporians into the social life of their peers in the town or if, instead, they formed a community of their own based on common day-to-day contacts on the job and subjugation to the direction of the same bosses. Insight into this question was offered in an 1897 article published in the State Normal School's student paper and reprinted in the *Emporia Gazette*. The author, Perlee Burton, wrote:

Emporia "society" is divided into three castes—the school and resident folk, the railroaders, and the "niggers." An incoming stranger may ask the Santa Fe conductor who lives here, about President Taylor [president of the Normal School], and this blue-coated official will answer; "never heard of him. The hackman will tell you." Equally the northenders profess the utmost ignorance of any "doings" in the south end of town, where the railroad boys live. But ask a Stringtown darkum and he will give you a personal history of everyone in the whole town, for his "woman" has washed at their house.[19]

In response, a black woman protested the failure of "our learned college student" to call blacks by their proper racial name and denied that all black wives were washerwomen and incurable gossips. Most of the *Gazette*'s letters to the editor, however, came from railroad people. "A Railroader's Wife" resented that the article placed the town's Santa Fe employees just above blacks and she declared that the railroad women she met at church considered terminating their subscriptions to the *Gazette*. However, they decided the fault was not in the article, but in the town. The letter writer oserved:

The people of this town are all organized into little cliques . . . , and they show no more hospitality to strangers than they would if the strangers were black. Men who could buy and sell the whole "sassiety" crowd in this town, come here working for the railroad, with their wives and families, and are snubbed on every hand by the so-called high toned people. . . . Merchants doing business in this town expect us to buy of them, and their wives never know us on the street.

An "Engineer's Wife" agreed: "One feels the cold shoulder ever since he or she has been a brother, or sister, wife or mother of a railroad man and we have reached the limits of endurance." "A Railroad Man's Mother" expressed a different sentiment. Responding to "A Railroader's Wife," she resented the latter's bemoaning railroad wives' exclusion from "society." "A Railroad Man's Mother" wanted nothing to do with the better element. "We are as good as the professors. . . . We don't thank them for their so-called kindness. We are railroaders and proud of it and no rat-eaten aristocracy of this town." Finally, "Ex-RR Man" provided a wholly different perspective. For him the article was highly offensive for being unfair to men such as Dr. Jacobs, the railroad physician; Colonel Severy, a railroad director; H. B. Morse, yardmaster, prominent citizen, and land owner; "and many other men who do not live on Third Avenue." These men were accepted by Emporia's elite and Burton's publication sullied their names and those of their wives and daughters, many of whom held "the highest places in church, educational and society work."[20]

The institution of a division center at Emporia in 1879 led to a residential pattern that lent credence to Burton's charge. An 1877 city directory showed railroaders as too scattered and too few to have been recognized as a distinct segment of the town's population. The sympathy of Emporians for a strike staged by local enginemen in the following year supports the idea that railroaders were not seen then as separate from the rest of the townsmen. However, by June 1880, less than a year after the new division shops opened just west of the corner of Third and West streets, railroaders began to concentrate around Third Avenue and scores were crowded in a few large boarding houses. In subsequent years railroad housing gravitated even more toward the southwest corner of town.[21]

In 1880 there remained a significant amount of residential democracy, but even then each of Emporia's four wards displayed distinctive occupational characteristics. The ward boundary lines, which did not vary through the end of the century, ran south down Commercial Street and east and west on Sixth Avenue. In 1880 the northern wards—the First and Fourth—tended to house the business and professional classes. The Second Ward, which lay in the southeast quadrant of town, housed a disproportionate number of craftsmen and common manual laborers, and the Third Ward in the southwest corner had concentrations of a variety of mid-level workers. Still there was a measure of equality in the housing patterns. Of the eighty-two members of the business elite, no ward had more than twenty-two and none had fewer than nineteen.[22]

A local observer in 1898 commented on the effect of the influx of people that accompanied the Santa Fe shops: "The hobbledehoy days were passing, and the lines which money draws in social affairs became plainly marked. Some went up and some went down, and equality has only been restored on the hill northwest of town." While residential segregation by class may not have started with the institution of the shops, it clearly continued and may have accelerated from 1880 on. In 1880, 27 percent of the business elite lived in the First Ward. Five years later the figure was 33 percent and the concentration of the richest in the First Ward continued, so that over half resided there by 1900. Meanwhile, nonrailroaders in the more prestigious occupations left the Third Ward, where most railroaders lived. In 1880, disproportionate numbers of professionals, small business men, and government employees, including U.S. senator Preston B. Plumb, lived in the Third Ward. By 1885, of these three groups, only professionals remained in disproportionate numbers and in subsequent census years they were also no longer heavily represented in the railroaders' ward. By 1883 the Plumbs moved to the north end.[23]

As the upper crust found homes elsewhere, railroaders increasingly concentrated in the Third Ward. Santa Fe employees always were a negligible portion of the Fourth Ward, which lay farthest from the yards and shop. In the First and Second wards they made up 6 to 15 percent of the working population. The Third Ward was home for most railroaders and became increasingly dominated by them; their part of the working male population grew from 24.4 percent to nearly 46.2 percent in the last fifteen years of the century.[24]

Nevertheless, for all this residential segregation, Perlee Burton's description of railroaders as a group distinct and separate from the rest of Emporia is incorrect. In most years, 70 percent of the town's railroaders lived in the Third Ward, but 30 percent had homes in wards in which they were only a small minority of the population. Even in the Third Ward, nonrailroaders always outnumbered Santa Fe men. Nor does an examination of lists of officers and members in fraternal organizations in the mid-1880s and 1890s lend support to the idea of railroader exclusivity. Fraternal lodges provided important grounds for sociable interaction in the nineteenth century. Most fraternal organizations were secretive and membership rosters are rare. However, an 1883 list for the American Legion of Honor and an 1885 list for the Knights of Pythias survive. The occupation of all but a handful is clear from city directories and censuses. Of the fifty-five members of the Legion on whom information was available, six were railroaders, while two of the twenty-seven Knights came from the ranks of railroaders. In neither case did the proportion of railroader members match their percent of the population. Yet the discrepancy was not large. Moreover, railroaders were not simply limited to roles as members. Three lists of lodge officers were found for 1885 and four for 1895. Railroaders held one or more officer positions in all but one of these organizations. Railroaders, then, were neither shut out by the rest of the community, nor did they themselves shun their neighbors.[25]

Santa Fe men were not set off from all other townsmen. Yet Emporia failed to constitute a "community" as defined by Thomas Bender—"a network of social relations marked by mutuality and emotional bonds." Burton was correct that there were divisions within the town; but he defined them inadequately. "The school and resident folk" did not encompass all white nonrailroaders. In his article, Burton described the annual round of events engaged in by this caste. The girls started sewing and cooking groups, the boys instituted dancing clubs, the women organized literary societies, and their businessmen husbands went to lodge meetings where they talked politics.

Burton's "resident folk" were limited to the "northenders" in the higher strata of Emporia society. In his mind, railroaders, as the largest group of manual labor, represented all Emporia's "blue collar" work force in the southern part of town. This certainly was *Gazette* editor William Allen White's interpretation when, in an editorial defending Burton, he asked for greater social intercourse between the north and south end, rather than between railroaders and the rest of the town.[26]

There were at least two communities of whites in Emporia, based on class divisions. Although most railroaders' social relations with nonrailroading townsmen were with those in the less prestigious class, some could lay claim to a place in the community of "resident folk." It was this group that "Ex-RR Man" sought to defend from association with lower-class railroaders. Not surprisingly, none of the men he mentioned had homes in the Third Ward. Residence in the north end was neither mandatory nor sufficient to join in fellowship with the more highly esteemed ranks of Emporia. But class lines tended to be drawn by the list of railroad occupational groups most likely to make their homes in the First Ward. Santa Fe officials, agents and clerks, conductors, engineers, telegraph operators, and dispatchers were the railroading groups most heavily represented in the First Ward. They constituted the railroader elite; engineers and conductors were among the highest-paid railroaders, and the others were white-collar employees. Many such railroaders failed to develop attachments with the cliques of bankers, businessmen, and professors. Key personal friendships and family relations also doubtless played a role in determining these men's friends. Furthermore, as the *Locomotive Engineer's Journal* pointed out in 1876, some high-placed railway men did not attain the fellowship of town elites either because, as railroaders, they were "clannish" and preferred to find their friendships among other railroaders or because they lacked the cultural attainments to gain the respect of those in the best circles.[27]

Another look at the fraternal organizations' rosters of members and officers sheds more light on the class basis for railroaders' attachments to portions of the nonrailroading community of Emporia. The available lists reveal separate upper- and middle-class orders. Of the two large rosters for the mid-1880s, the

Knights of Pythias represented the middle class and the American Legion of Honor, the upper. Both enrolled businessmen of small- to moderate-size enterprises, but there the similarities ended. The top officer in the first group was a photographer. The identity of the leader of the second is not clear, but his first lieutenant was a doctor. The Knights had a number of manual laborers; the Legion did not include a single laborer. Given the class lines of these two groups, it is not surprising that both railroaders in the Knights were brakemen, while the six in the Legion included the trainmaster, a clerk, three telegraph operators, and a conductor. The lists of officers displayed the same pattern of railroaders segregated by rank. In 1895 the lodges that recruited from the middle ranks of Emporia's work force included a Santa Fe bridge builder, a hostler, a conductor, and a freight department worker, while the elite unit's officers included an architect, a professor, a dentist, the president of a bank, and, leading them all as "Eminent Commander," John Lucas, the Santa Fe agent.[28]

Emporia railroaders found a sense of community in several different overlapping groups. Rather than diminishing in the late nineteenth century, the opportunities for a sense of community were multiplying.[29] Railroaders could gain acceptance and form friendships with that class of nonrailroaders whose socioeconomic standing was closest to theirs. They also identified most closely and gave their greatest loyalty to those with whom they came in almost daily contact on their jobs. As will be seen, the measure of loyalty and fellowship they gave to other railroaders sometimes encompassed only those in whose gang they worked. Other times it extended to include railroaders of various lines of work all over the country. Railroaders' relationship to the rest of their communities and their ability to unite effectively would be tested in their efforts to further their interests through politics, unions, and strikes.

CHAPTER 5

"Damn the Railway Men":
The Politics of
Frustration

If politics was in any sense a communal activity,[1] it was one in which railroaders seldom participated as a distinct group. Rather, they generally voted much like their nonrailroading neighbors. Santa Fe division towns often elected railroaders to local political positions, but railroad candidates could not count on solid support from fellow Santa Fe employees, and few issues arose in local government that divided railroaders and nonrailroaders. Above the local level, Santa Fe employees failed to unite behind any political party, even self-proclaimed worker-oriented parties. The closest railroaders came to allowing their occupational interests to dictate their votes came during the Populist upheaval in Kansas, when fear of rate regulation edged them further into the Republican camp. In the early 1890s, railroad union leaders turned to politics, but failure in the states and territories prompted the strongest brotherhoods to send a lobbyist to the nation's capital in the late 1890s to urge federal railroad labor legislation.

Politics in small town America was normally the province of lawyers, bankers, and businessmen, but in Santa Fe towns some offices regularly fell to railroaders. Station agents in struggling young towns represented a key business link with the outside world. Consequently, they often found themselves in high local offices. A greater indication of the political clout of Santa Fe employees was the election of railroaders to division town offices. There politicians slated railroaders for numerous minor posts. This was the case in Las Vegas, where the local paper in

1892 noted, "The railroad vote seems to be fully appreciated by all the political parties, as a county commissioner on one ticket and a legislative candidate on the other fully attest." In some division towns, however, the railroaders so dominated that the most important offices went to Santa Fe men. In 1891 Raton elected passenger engineer William Tindall as its first mayor. In the following three years the engineer was succeeded in office by the yardmaster and then the division master mechanic. Nor was Raton unique among division towns. In the 1890s, active or former railroaders served in the mayor's chair in Argentine, Emporia, Coolidge, and La Junta.[2]

Railroaders did not automatically support their coworkers. In 1892 Topeka shopman William B. Swan ran as the Republican candidate for the state legislature. Although he won the election, he trailed the other major GOP candidates in the ward with the highest percent of railroaders. Similarly, Topeka's railroader ward gave a larger percentage of its votes to that year's Republican gubernatorial candidate, "Farmer" Smith, than to Emporia railroader Bruce Lynch, who stood on the same ticket as Smith. A year later Emporia Populist railroader L. H. Witte ran behind the rest of the ticket in the railroaders' Third Ward. Yet the Third Ward sometimes showed pronounced affection for Santa Fe employee candidates. In 1897 two Santa Fe dispatchers and two others who had worked for the company before the Pullman strike ran far ahead of their opposition and near the top of the Citizen's Party ticket in the Third Ward. The Republicans fought back in 1899 by nominating the popular yardmaster, H. B. Morse, for mayor. The third warders, who had given the opposition mayoral candidate over 60 percent of their support two years earlier, now backed Morse by well over a two-to-one margin.[3]

Despite their political strength, there is little evidence that Santa Fe men used it for special treatment from their local governments or that there were sharp conflicts in local politics between railroaders and nonrailroaders. It was in the interest of local government and business to propitiate the company and the workers who gave the town vitality. Only during strikes did railway men's political power clearly influence local officials. For example, during the Pullman strike an Emporia Third Ward councilman brought forward a resolution demanding the removal of federal marshals sent in the interest of the company. The sheriff at Raton displayed more forceful support. At the height of the strike he tried to disarm a deputy marshal, an act that resulted in his own arrest.[4]

Beyond the local level, a number of political groups tried to appeal especially to railroaders. In the wake of the Great Railroad Strike of 1877, which had barely touched the Santa Fe, Topeka-area Democrats saw an opportunity to gain a foothold in local government. Within two weeks of the end of the turmoil, a group of local politicians called a meeting to form a "Workingmen's Party" for the November county elections. The meeting attracted a large crowd of workers, "a majority of whom were men from the A., T. & S.F. RR shops." In this and subsequent meetings, resolutions were passed to nominate none but "honest, actually employed workingmen" and to pledge the party to a platform including a lien law, the abolition of convict labor, and equal pay for equal work for both sexes. The subsequent development of the party was farcical. The vast majority of those placed on the ticket were not workers but farmers, and some of them were quite wealthy. Moreover, of the nine-man slate, all but one of them rejected their nomination, and, whereas some of the men originally nominated were Republicans, their replacements revealed the Democratic basis for the insurgent party. Finally, in November no Democratic ticket appeared and in the resultant head-to-head confrontation the Republicans piled up large majorities throughout Topeka for a city-wide two-to-one margin and a sweep of all the contested offices.[5]

A more genuine worker political movement arose in 1886 under the auspices of the Knights of Labor. There is no way of knowing the number of Santa Fe men who joined the Knights, but many of the more than one thousand members in Topeka worked in the yards and shops and it was reported that the vast majority of Emporia switchmen belonged. The Knights in Kansas were a driving force behind the formation of the Union Labor party in 1887 and in the surprisingly strong showing of its gubernatorial candidate the following year. However, other local prolabor slates backed by the Knights proved to be more successful and more appealing to the railroaders than the Union

Labor party. On one hand, the insurgent Kansas City, Kansas, Republican, Thomas Hannan, mobilized the city's Knights, with its large railroad element, and captured control of both his party and the city's mayoralty. Similarly, the support of the Knights in 1886 was of crucial importance to Emporia's successful mayoral candidate. On the other hand, the Union Labor state ticket fared considerably worse in a number of railroad division towns than it did in the state as a whole.[6]

The Populist era brought the most significant political activity among railroaders. At the call of the local lodge of the Brotherhood of Locomotive Engineers, representatives of all the important railroad unions of Kansas met at Topeka in February 1891 to prepare bills for consideration at the six-week state legislative session. The national brotherhood's bylaws as well as its monthly journal had encouraged such activity for several years. This call by the Topeka lodge reflected a surge in political action by union legislative committees in several states and came while railroad unions were exhibiting unprecedented vitality both nationally and in Kansas. More importantly, it also was a reaction to a new political situation in the Sunflower State. By gaining control of the lower house of the legislature, the newly formed "People's Party" had punctured the GOP's traditional control of the state.[7]

The new party posed intriguing possibilities and perplexing problems for Kansas railroaders. Its attacks on corporations and its frequent linking of the interests of the laborers of the field and factory had encouraged some railway men to abandon old party loyalties in the November poll. They hoped that the Populists' control of the lower house would mean favorable labor legislation. This optimism was shared by half a dozen nonrailroad trade unions, which mobilized their own political pressure element. However, while most of the state's labor force could on economic grounds view the advent of Populist power with equanimity, if not joy, railroaders were concerned that Populist attacks on the railroads could hurt company employees. Should railway profits be raided, should traffic be strangled, railroaders reasoned that they would inevitably suffer through lower wages, fewer hours, and more layoffs. In the end, the Topeka meeting was motivated by a combination of these hopes and fears, and

possibly by an optimistic calculation that the brotherhood leaders could generate enough pressure to get the two parties to
compete for the favor of the state's railroad votes, estimated as
high as thirty-two thousand.[8]

The seventy-eight delegates represented unionized enginemen, trainmen, switchmen, boilermakers, machinists, dispatchers, and telegraph operators. For four days they met in secret
session, drawing up legislative proposals and determining their
own stands on bills already before the legislature. They called
for laws against Pinkertons, blacklisting, and compulsory deductions from pay for company hospital plans. They backed
bills mandating automatic couplers, modifying the fellow servant doctrine in employer liability cases, setting a minimum age
limit of eighteen for railway telegraph operators, and forbidding
railroads from hiring men as engineers who had not fired a
locomotive for at least three years, or employing a man as conductor who had not worked two years as a freight brakeman. The
committee also supported a child labor act endorsed by the other
Kansas unions. However, the most controversial of their stands
would be their strong attack on a bill to lower the rate railroads
could charge their traffic. Before adjourning they appointed two
engineers, William H. Hamilton of Topeka and C. C. Crouse of
Neodesha, to remain and lobby the legislature in the interest of
all railroaders. And, most significantly, they approved a resolution that railroaders' votes should "first, last and all the time" go
to candidates supporting railroad interests.[9]

Railroaders expected little sympathy for labor bills in the
Republican senate. In the previous legislature not a single
worker bill came to a vote. The record in 1891 would be similar;
three railway labor bills were placed so low on the calendar that
they did not come to a vote, while a child labor proposal lost
twenty-one to eight. Seeing their best chance in the Populist
house, railroaders initiated the majority of their bills there. There
were some early indications that the workers' hopes might be
realized. On the second day of the railroaders' meeting, the
house passed the anti-Pinkerton bill, eighty-three to two, and,
after lobbying by the workers, the Committee on Railroads reversed an earlier stance and backed a bill prohibiting wage
deductions for company hospitals. The next day, after asking the

workers their opinion, the House Committee on Labor reported favorably on a bill requiring corporations to give written reasons for discharging employees. The entire house later overwhelmingly approved this antiblacklisting legislation. And while there is no evidence that the railroaders worked hard for the bill, the house's labor committee also approved an hours bill for railroad employees, although, like the hospital bill, it never came to a vote of the entire house.[10]

At the end of the session, however, railroaders expressed their greatest frustration and anger with the Populists. Some of the most vociferous assaults on the Populists may have found root in political retribution and ambition. If the Populist party posed a threat to the GOP, it virtually obliterated the power of Kansas Democrats. Therefore, it is not surprising to find that the most vocal Kansas railroader spokesman against the Populists was Democrat W. M. Mitchell, an Order of Railway Conductors member from the Santa Fe division town of Winfield. Possibly as a reward for his attacks on Populists, Republican governor Lyman U. Humphrey appointed Mitchell to the Railroad Commission. Part of the more general prejudice against the People's Party can be accounted for by lingering party ties. Republican loyalists, especially, would be anxious to divert criticism from the poor performance of the senate by pointing out that half a dozen pieces of railroader legislation failed in the Populist house.[11]

However, railroaders' unhappiness was based primarily on the new party's support of a rate bill. The railroad employee representatives strongly protested that thousands of employees could lose their jobs while the workloads of the remainder would be greatly increased with no comparable raise in pay. When it became clear that the workers refused to withdraw their vigorous protests over the rate bill, the Committee on Railroads blocked all railroader labor reform proposals that came before it. The chairman of the committee was reported to have exclaimed, "Damn the railway men, we are not here to make laws for railroad men; we come here to make laws for farmers."[12]

Kansas railroaders made some lobbying efforts at the next meeting of the senate and house in 1893. However, this time larger partisan battles preoccupied the legislature. The Populists had clearly won the governorship and the senate, but the dispositions of some of the house races, and the control of the lower chamber, were hotly contested. In an episode declared a "war" by the press, Topeka witnessed two separately meeting "houses," each claiming to be legitimate, while the state militia tried to keep the two groups of dignified, but indignant, lawmakers from breaking open each others' heads. In the end the alignment of 1891 was reversed, with the People's Party controlling the senate and the GOP maintaining a veto power in its dominance of the house.[13]

Despite the recrimination that followed the previous session, the Populists in 1893 again proved more active than the Republicans in promoting labor measures. The senate approved bills outlawing blacklisting and the hiring of inexperienced engineers and conductors. The Populist "house" approved an anti-Pinkerton bill, but the work of that body was brought to an abrupt end and its accomplishments negated when the Republican house was recognized as legitimate. The only labor legislation accepted by the GOP-dominated house was a weekly pay bill, and from this the railroaders were explicitly excluded. The same bill was passed by the senate and became the sole piece of labor legislation to become law in 1893. Even in the debate on this enactment, a sizable segment of the senate Populists evidenced greater concern for the railway men, or, at least, less concern for the welfare of the railroads, than did the Republicans. Of the nineteen Populists voting, eight supported an amendment to include railroaders in this bill; none of the nine Republicans backed the amendment.[14]

Railroaders were not united on the need to be included in the weekly pay bill. The line of division ran between those in the moderate and high-paying jobs and those receiving the lowest unskilled wage. The latter wanted to be written into the law since they found it especially hard to escape the recurring cycle of credit buying. The primary spokesman for the inclusion of railroaders in the weekly pay bill, Populist senator Moses A. Householder, said that the legislation was needed for the shop and track workers earning less than forty dollars a month. However, the railroad labor lobbyists in Topeka, representative of relatively well-paid union members, made no effort to promote weekly pay legislation in 1893. In fact, in 1891 these railroaders had spoken out against a similar measure. Not directly affected by the chronic problem of credit buying, they saw no compelling reason to burden their employers with paying weekly wages to thousands of men scattered all across the state. The legislative agenda of unionized railroaders was narrow and self-centered; bills setting qualifications for, and thereby protecting the jobs of, conductors, engineers, and telegraph operators were featured, while legislation providing prompt payment to those living with the bill collector at the door was ignored or even opposed.[15]

The history of the weekly pay bill in 1893 also revealed the Santa Fe intimidating railroaders to lend it political support. Persistent public activity by Santa Fe employees in all political parties indicated that the Santa Fe did not follow a policy of meddling with the politics of its workers. However, the Santa Fe management decided that a petition from the Topeka shopmen against the weekly pay bill would assist company efforts to exclude the railroads from this legislation. The result was a memorial variously reported to have been signed by 30 to 60 percent of Topeka shopmen. It is unlikely that this number would have signed had there not been at least strong implied support from above. This was the charge of Senator Householder, and a number of layoffs ordered shortly after the petition was circulated were rumored to be related to the failure by some to sign the document. This management power, even if rarely used, was not something most workers could ignore. The possibility for intimidation could cause some employees to accomodate the company on political issues and to assume cautious policy on legislation affecting the worker-employer relationship.[16]

The most significant pieces of legislation in 1893 were the separate, and finally irreconcilable, rate regulation proposals passed in the house and senate. Swaying with the temper of the time, the Republican lower chamber put forward a bill strong enough to attract the unanimous acceptance of house Populists, but too weak for the more radical senate. The result was no law at all. More interesting, though, was the reasoning for negative votes given by several house members from railroading communities. A. C. Sherman of Topeka noted that he represented "a constituency, . . . composed of about one-half railroad people" and felt compelled to vote against the measure. The influence the Santa Fe employees could have is seen most vividly in the stands of the two Republican members from Reno County. J. F. Greenlee, the representative from the southern part of the county, which included the important shipping center of Hutchinson, introduced the rate-cutting bill. Less than forty miles north of Hutchinson was the division town of Nickerson, whose voice in Topeka was J. W. Dix. Dix opposed his neighboring representative's measure: "I have, in my district, a railroad division with roundhouse and machine shops, that gives employment to about three hundred men, . . . and I cannot vote for any bill I think would injure them as to holding their employment, or as to wages paid."[17]

Some of the railroad brotherhoods presented their wishes to the lawmakers in a low-keyed manner in the remaining years of the century. Populists continued to work for a rate bill while the Republicans stiffened their resistance. Republicans remained less enthusiastic about labor legislation than the Populists. However, by the 1897 seating, the Populists were also at best lukewarm toward the railroaders. A Kansas engineer's comment that year that the Populists broke campaign promises, that a rate bill would mean the firing of up to five thousand of the state's railroaders, and that Populist leaders were blocking railroaders' legislation in retaliation for the workers' opposition to the rate bill were all clear echoes of the disappointing campaigns of the preceding six years. At most the Kansas railroaders could claim some responsibility for thwarting the efforts to set railroad rates. Beyond this, they came away from their legislative efforts empty-handed.[18]

Both union and Populist leadership failed in Topeka. Union leaders failed partly because their hold over members' votes was unproven and railroaders, though numerous, were not in a position to dictate to politicians. Moreover, union leaders displayed their lack of political skill. With the possible exception of 1893 the GOP always stood ready to stop any severe rate bill. The workers need not have agitated so strongly against it. By placing their emphasis on the rate bill, they gave neither party any incentive to promote labor reform. Populist leaders showed similar political immaturity. The farmers' dominance of the party required that its politicians push for a rate bill. But the Populists' policy of restraining railroader legislation in retaliation for worker opposition to the rate bill was nonsensical. Such a policy would not move the railroaders away from their position. Moreover, had the Populists passed most or all the railroaders' desired legislation, they would have forced the Republicans dominating the other house to either pass the legislation or open the GOP to charges of blocking a host of labor reforms. This certainly would have won some labor votes for the new party and may have set the groundwork for a wider farmer-worker coalition. As it was, the Populists bungled an opportunity when they failed to realize that, in a two-party political system, parties had a responsibility to represent more than a single interest group.

Railroaders achieved no breakthroughs in New Mexico, which was the only other political entity in which Santa Fe employees could play a significant role. The Republican party and, more specifically, its "Santa Fe Ring," dominated territorial government. The ring's power in the late 1880s extended to controlling not only the GOP, but the head of the territory's Democratic party as well. What political competition existed was based far less on party and philosophy than on personal, factional, and local ambitions.[19]

In 1893 New Mexico railroaders called for employer liability legislation and an act similar to that proposed in Kansas requiring that only experienced men be hired as engineers and conductors. In January, three Santa Fe employees came to the capital as the spokesmen for these measures. They succeeded in getting both bills introduced into the house and a duplicate employer liability measure in the council. The house discussed both measures on February 22, passing employer liability but rejecting the hiring requirements. When it passed the liability bill, though, the house must have recognized the futility of such action. The council had debated the measure early in the month and had emasculated it by leaving the company free from responsibility as long as it exercised "reasonable care and diligence" in choosing competent employees. The council, led by

Albert B. Fall, who in the 1920s would serve as Warren Harding's secretary of the interior, had made it clear that any more forceful legislation would not be passed. The house itself had acquiesced in the watered-down council version by a unanimous vote on the eleventh. Although a lone diehard Albuquerque council member would attempt to get the council to accept the house version, it was a foregone conclusion that railroaders would have to satisfy themselves with the modified proposal.[20]

Votes on the railroaders' legislation could not be drawn on party lines in New Mexico, for none existed. Rather, the majority of those who backed the railroaders' efforts were from those districts with division centers, but these towns elected no more than a quarter of the council and house. In addition, the friends of railroad company interests held the powerful argument that whatever progress the territory had made was the result of the coming of the rail lines. New Mexico was still too backward to be in a position to anger corporations who were its lifeblood and who could quicken or slow further development. Fall noted that New Mexico "was a new country that [could] be developed only by the aid of railroads" and Councilman Joseph E. Saint of Albuquerque warned that if the territory enacted the legislation the railroaders wanted "the world [would] say New Mexico antagonizes railroads." Defeated and discouraged, the railroaders refrained from legislative efforts for the rest of the decade. But, if their failure was disappointing, it was also inevitable. In underdeveloped New Mexico, politics was too immature, the railroads too important, and labor too weak for any other result.[21]

Without meaningful party labels and finding their own representatives sympathetic, New Mexico railroaders had nothing and no one on which to vent their unhappiness at the polls. This was decidedly not the case in Kansas. Kansas railroaders began to politicize their grievances after the failure of their 1891 legislative offensive. William Hamilton, the chairman of the employees' legislative board, found both the GOP and the Populists failing. But both he and other spokesmen for Kansas railroaders made the farmer-dominated party bear the brunt of their attacks. This was done against the advice of some of the railroad brotherhoods; the Railway Conductor chastized the Kansas railroaders, saying that "the employes and farmers are natural allies."[22]

Such reasoning was accepted by a minority of Santa Fe men during the 1890s. Some not only voted for the Populists, but also ran for office on the People's Party ticket. There was an especially pronounced affinity for the Populists among the activists in Eugene V. Debs' class-oriented American Railway Union. These men were attracted by the party's talk of working-class unity, repelled by the association of the GOP with the railroad corporations, and gratified by the material and moral support organized by the Populists for the Pullman strikers. Conductors R. J. Sloat and J. W. Lyon, leaders in the union's lodges at Topeka and Emporia, were enthusiastic Populist supporters even before Pullman. Recognizing these men as symbols for all frustrated laborers, the Populists nominated both for the state legislature in November 1894. Other Santa Fe men who belonged to the union ran on local Populist tickets. Despite condemnation by many railway men, the Populists had not forsaken the railroad vote. Moreover, a number of Santa Fe men remained steadfast in their belief in a common cause of farmers and workers against corporations.[23]

The prevailing sentiment expressed by Kansas railroaders, however, was hostile toward the People's Party. When letters lambasting the farmer party appeared in the brotherhood journals, not a single Santa Fe railroader responded in its defense. C. C. Crouse, the secretary of the 1891 legislative board, found a sizable following around the state when he returned home to Neodesha and began contributing editorials to the local weekly paper. Far from being a sycophant for management, he scathingly criticized the Santa Fe hospital association and promoted united and expanding unionism. But a large proportion of his writing attacked the Populists, whom he felt had turned their backs on railway men and were endangering the interests of workers. His columns became a regular feature, growing to fill nearly half the paper. Soon each issue included letters to the editor from railroaders throughout much of Kansas. The popularity of Crouse's views was further attested by the decisions of two Kansas-centered unions—the Brotherhood of Stationmen and the Brotherhood of Bridge and Building Men—to make his paper their official organ.[24]

Most Santa Fe employees took their stand on the issue of self-interest. They saw themselves as railroaders first and members of the "toiling masses" second. The *Monthly Balance*, the original and short-lived journal for the Brotherhood of Stationmen, classed the farmer Populists among those demagogic souls who, failing in their own business affairs, insisted on meddling in those of others. In October 1891 it argued that it was the "bounden duty" of each railroad man "to combat the wave of unreason, repudiation and anarchy which so recently swept over Kansas . . . for the reason that [a Populist] success would result in blighting his own interests and irreparable injury to his state."[25] Whatever his motives, W. M. Mitchell stated more clearly than anyone else the rationale for the antagonistic concerns of farmers and railroaders. He noted that the railway men wanted to sell their labor at the highest amount, while agriculturalists thought the men were already getting too much in wages, partly accounting for traffic rates that the farmers felt were exorbitant. Mitchell also enunciated the case for the mutuality of interests of employer and employee. He reasoned, "The railway company and its employes were, . . . joint stockholders in the property, the company furnishes the money to build and equip the road, while the employés furnish the brain and muscle to operate it. Without one the other can't exist." Mitchell concluded, "for one of the stockholders to work against the common interest of the other shows a lack of principal and business sense."[26]

Partisan politics was outlawed from union lodge rooms. Therefore, it was during a recess of the Newton Order of Railway Conductors meeting in early October 1891 that the membership passed resolutions stating that "capital and labor are inseparable," that "all railroad legislation shall be mutually in the interest of the corporations and employés," and pledging that their votes would go to any political party whose platform incorporated these sentiments. About a week later the men who had led this movement called for a meeting in Newton to form a statewide Railway Employes Club. In the next three years local clubs were established in many Kansas Santa Fe towns, with as many as fifty lodges sprouting up in railroad centers across the state.[27]

The club's avowed purpose was to function as a nonpartisan association to unite railroad employees against government actions prejudicial to the railroad industry. It was active in Kansas into the fall of 1894 and enjoyed a brief revival in 1896. Although

the club's activities included lobbying and even the establish-
ment of a reading room and an insurance program, its primary
function was to attack antirailroad politicians. It was part of a
similar national organization initiated in March 1888 in Minneapolis to oppose anticipated antirailroad decisions by the
Minnesota railroad commission. Company interests gave at least
informal encouragement to both the national and state organizations. Santa Fe workers were instrumental in the Kansas club.
While the Santa Fe controlled about 30 percent of the state's
railroad property, its employees held all but one of the club's
state-wide offices in its first year of existence. The Kansas organization received assistance from the state's Republican party,
but some of its leaders were Democrats. Conductor A.R.Glazier,
the president, went to the Democratic convention in 1892 and
ran for local office in Newton as a Democrat in 1894. Democrats
in the club, however, were probably neither double-dealing nor
dupes. The club did not assault Democrats. Moreover, Democratic members shared with their Republican coworkers a bitter
dislike for the railroad legislation promoted by the Populists.
The clubs provided a vehicle to speak out against these measures. The Republican party saw it as an advantage to give
support to the clubs because in Kansas the Democrats alone
posed no threat. Only when they fused with the Populists, as
they did in 1892, 1896, and 1898, could Republican dominance
be endangered. And it was in just such instances that the anti-
Populist propaganda of the Railway Employes Club could promise to peel Democrats away from their traditional party loyalties.[28]

Surveys of electoral returns in four towns help explain how
closely Kansas Santa Fe railroaders' voting reflected the dominant anti-Populist sentiment of their leaders. In Emporia's Third
Ward and Arkansas City's Fourth about one-third of the voters
were railroaders, while the other three wards in each town
ranged between 2 and 17 percent railroader. Nickerson and
Peabody were fifty-five miles apart and of similar size and ethnic
make-up. But while half the employed men in Nickerson
worked for the Santa Fe, Peabody had only a handful of track
workers, a small station force, and no large industry.[29]

In the gubernatorial elections from 1888 through 1896 the

similarities between the railroader and nonrailroader voting patterns in these districts were particularly noticeable. Emporia's railroader-dominated Third Ward voted similarly to the Second Ward, its working-class neighbor. Arkansas City's Fourth cast a majority of its votes for the candidate who won the nonrailroading wards in 1888, 1892, and 1894. And not only were Nickerson and Peabody consistent Republican supporters, but the average percent of their votes to go to the GOP over the decade was virtually identical.[30]

Still, it is possible to deduce some conclusions about Santa Fe employees' response to the rise of Populism. First, W. M. Mitchell erred in declaring that the vast majority of Kansas railroaders had voted for the Populists in 1890. All three railroader voting units gave either a majority or a plurality of their support to the Republicans. The highest proportion gained by the Populists was a sixth of all votes in Emporia's Third Ward. Indeed, in comparing railroader and nonrailroader responses in 1890, the former showed themselves especially reluctant to back the new party. The railroader wards of Emporia and Arkansas City scored lower percent support for the Populists than did at least some of the other wards in these towns, and Nickerson's backing for the new party was barely half of that in Peabody.[31]

But support should be measured in change of votes from 1888 rather than static percentages. A study of Kansas politics has noted a strong relation between Union Labor party support in 1888 and Populist backing in 1890. If Union Labor men generally voted Populist, how many more votes did the People's Party attract than its predecessor? In Arkansas City's railroader ward there was no increase. In Emporia's Third Ward and in Nickerson the Populists did do 44 and 118 percent better, respectively, than had the Union Labor party. But more significantly, in Peabody and Emporia's nonrailroading wards the Populists attracted between 333 and 921 percent more voters than the Union Laborites. Nonrailroaders, then, were more likely than railroaders to express their discontent with the economic slump of the late 1880s by voting Populist.[32]

Declaring that the Populists were irresponsible and would bring economic ruin to the state, the Republicans in 1892 staged a comeback. The GOP's upturn was reflected in an increased percentage for the Republicans in every ward and town studied. Yet the railroaders, possibly responding to disappointment with the 1891 legislature, were especially reluctant to support Populists. In each railroader voting unit, the fusion of Populists and Democrats received a smaller proportion of the vote than did the Democrats alone in 1890. In contrast, Peabody and two of the six nonrailroader wards cast more votes for the fusionists than for the Democrats.[33]

Election returns from railroader areas for 1894 and 1896 are more ambiguous on Populist support than those for 1890 and 1892. This was partly a reflection of vacillation and little cumulative change in the voting of all Kansans. No clear-cut trends emerge from the 1894 totals, despite Populist governor Lewelling's expressed sympathy for Santa Fe shop strikers in 1893 and his party's backing for Pullman strikers only three months prior to the election. In the election of 1896 William Jennings Bryan's candidacy reversed the drift of the last four years and led the Democratic-Populist gubernatorial ticket to victory. As it did among most nonrailroading units, this 1896 fusion won a larger proportion of railroaders than did the Democrats and Populists combined in 1894. Yet, Santa Fe employees' movement toward the watered-down version of the People's Party represented by the Democratic Bryan, who emphasized free silver rather than an attack on railroads, must be measured against their previous opposition. Thus the railroader voting units of Emporia and Nickerson registered greater loyalty to the GOP in 1896, relative to their stance in 1888, than did the nonrailroader areas.[34]

Historians have long recognized Bryan's failure to win the urban industrial masses as a cause for his defeat. Such a failure should not have come as a surprise to observers of Kansas politics. Kansas railroaders as early as 1890 had made it clear that an ideology and a rhetoric that threatened or that political opponents easily could make appear as threatening, the prosperity of American corporations could not hope to win the support of workers dependent on corporate America for their livelihood.

Thwarted in their state and territorial efforts, unwilling to associate with the Populists, yet unable to influence the established parties, and all the time feeling the growing impact of technological change, railroaders in the last half of the 1890s increasingly voiced their opinion of the sources of their political impotence and gave suggestions to reverse this state of affairs. All recognized that the inability to unite behind a single candidate and program was a basic problem. A Chanute brakeman found that too many railroaders voted against fellow railroaders because of traditional party loyalties. A member of the Newton Brotherhood of Locomotive Firemen complained that railroaders failed to trust their own judgments and instead were "Democrats, Republicans or Greenbackers because their parental ancestor was."[35]

There was no shortage of prescriptions to boost railroader political power. The same Chanute brakeman suggested that railroaders start building up mutual confidence, cooperation, and strength on the local level. He wanted the town's railroaders to unite to swing local elections and gradually expand and raise their sights to include more powerful offices. A new party was a commonly suggested solution. The Newton BLF man mentioned earlier advocated that all labor unions in the country meet in a congress to establish a workingmen's party. In September 1900 representatives of six railroad unions met at Pueblo, Colorado, to mobilize all the state's railroaders behind a new labor-oriented political organization. Other union men suggested a compulsory legislative board in each state that would reflect railroad worker interests and which could expel any railroader from the union who openly opposed the organization's position.[36]

By the end of the century, railroaders turned their attention to Washington. The Supreme Court was making it clear that interstate commerce and laborers' connection with it came under the national government's regulatory power. Moreover, federal regulation skirted the problem of parochial state interests in appeasing railroad companies. Santa Fe railroaders wrote to their union journals, urging such steps as placing a railroad workers' lobbyist in Washington and moving the brotherhoods' headquarters to the nation's capital. The unions chose to lobby. In December 1896, the Order of Railway Telegraphers and the enginemen and trainmen unions initiated federal railroader lobbying by supporting the Brotherhood of Locomotive Firemen's W. F. Hynes in efforts for an arbitration bill. Hynes and H. R. Fuller, his successor from 1899 through the first decade of the twentieth century, gave railroaders a voice before the highest government officials. And since Populist and Progressive politicians were eager to prove themselves the friends of the common man and at the same time attack the railroads, labor union initiatives for an arbitration law, antiblacklisting legislation, and a change in the common-law doctrines regarding employer liability bore fruit in the decade following Hynes's installation.[37] Despite disappointments on the state and territorial levels, at least along the Santa Fe, railroaders began to gain victories in Washington and took a leading role in labor's move to the interest group politics that came to play an important part in twentieth-century government.

CHAPTER 6

Brotherhoods:
The Protective
Function

Like other nineteenth-century American wage earners, Santa Fe men strove, through a multitude of organizations and with varying degrees of success, to secure higher wages and a voice in the rules determining how they spent their workdays. Occasionally, Santa Fe officials conceded them their wishes informally. At other times workers won contracts. Company officers frequently acted cordially toward unions, even weak ones, as they pursued policies designed at minimizing strife. But employees also learned that contracts were mere paper documents that Topeka managers could scrap when unsupported by a vigilant and strong union.

As was the case nationally, the enginemen and trainmen were the first to organize on the Santa Fe. The Brotherhood of Locomotive Engineers and the Brotherhood of Locomotive Firemen established lodges in Topeka in 1876, thirteen and three years, respectively, after the writing of their national charters. Four years later the Order of Railway Conductors set up its first Santa Fe local, followed in 1885 by the Brotherhood of Railroad Brakemen (later renamed Brotherhood of Railroad Trainmen). These organizations, known as the Big Four, achieved almost thorough unionization along the Santa Fe. In the late 1880s newly formed unions of switchmen, telegraphers, machinists, boilermakers, and blacksmiths nearly matched the Big Four in strength. The late 1880s and early 1890s witnessed the emergence of a host of other railroad unions on the Santa Fe. Some, such as the Brotherhood of Railway Carmen and the Brotherhood of Bridge and Building Men, were beginning to approach the power of the bigger brotherhoods in the years just before the depression of the nineties. Many others, covering virtually all railroad positions from stationmen to boilermakers' helpers, offered some social benefits but did not pretend to have any influence with company officials. The hard times of the mid-1890s killed off these weak organizations and severely cut into membership in all but the telegrapher and Big Four unions.[1]

The ability of unions to coax or demand concessions from the Santa Fe fluctuated over time. Notwithstanding the Santa Fe was over thirty years old at the beginning of the twentieth century, the company signed a majority of its contracts in a four-year period of peak union activity beginning in 1888. Through the late 1870s and all the 1880s, only the enginemen worked under a contract, though the strength of the trainmen also won some noncontractual concessions. In a flurry of agreements in the early 1890s most of the skilled workers obtained recognition and their own schedule of wages, work rules, and prerogatives. Yet in 1893, depression undercut the workers' power—a weakening confirmed and exacerbated by the crushing of the Pullman strike the following year. For the remainder of the century unions took few aggressive steps. They made virtually no new demands on Santa Fe officials, the company violated some old contract provisions with impunity, and management introduced a host of changes in working conditions detrimental to employees without effective union opposition.

Management unilaterally imposed work regulations and pay schedules on the great majority of Santa Fe employees. With the exception of the pressure of spontaneous work stoppages unsponsored by any organized labor union, Santa Fe officials could hire, fire, promote, punish, rule, and pay all trackmen, bridge and building men, unskilled shopmen and station men, and a small army of other unskilled and semiskilled employees pretty much as they pleased. The company usually allowed these workers to appeal grievances to higher corporate authorities, and in many instances seniority did gain men promotions. However, there was no guarantee that officials would always follow these normal practices. In rare cases unorganized workers successfully petitioned for an increase in pay or shorter hours.[2] Despite the multiplicity of unions, only the enginemen, trainmen, switchmen, telegraphers, and skilled shopmen had any effective bargaining power prior to 1900.

Some unions influenced Santa Fe policy before they gained full bargaining agent status in a written contract. When they felt they had been wronged, brotherhood men created grievance committees that met with company officers. This was the case with the Brotherhood of Railroad Brakemen on the Atlantic & Pacific in 1886. Charging that their pay was too low, the union grievance committee met with the general manager and succeeded in gaining raises of up to ten dollars a month. This occurred four years before the brotherhood won a contract on the Santa Fe and a year ahead of the organization's first written agreement on any road in the country.[3]

Unions also attained some concessions without direct confrontation with the company. The Order of Railway Conductors probably presented its desires to the Santa Fe before the company's 1883 edict establishing a new set of wages. As a result the general superintendent tacked on a seniority clause guaranteeing that should traffic decline, the trainmaster would not lay off the conductor with the least seniority, but instead put him back to brakeman at the highest pay allowed for that position. Also, the National Brotherhood of Boilermakers had a verbal understanding on overtime with the foreman of the Topeka boilermakers and the superintendent of machinery at least a year before that organization received a written contract.[4]

Varying levels of skill helped determine the brotherhoods' success in organizing and bargaining. Skilled men received wages high enough to furnish them with the twenty to thirty dollars a year necessary to maintain membership in their brotherhoods. For some employees such expenditures were prohibitive. An 1897 Kansas survey revealed that costs played a significant role in dissuading trackmen and, to a lesser extent, track foremen and telegraphers from joining a union.[5]

More important, greater skill gave men increased job security and bargaining power, which made for a more successful organization. Success in turn encouraged thorough unionization. Engineers, conductors, switchmen, operators, and journeymen shop employees all possessed these special talents. Brakemen and firemen, who were only semiskilled, would have had little bargaining power, except that they associated themselves with their immediate superiors. The conductors and engineers were willing to lend their prestige and power to their coworkers out of sheer self-interest. While the company would find it impossible to recruit competent conductors and engineers off the streets, it could find well-qualified men among the brakemen and firemen. Thus in collective bargaining these two groups of the minimally skilled achieved a cooperative power that they lacked by themselves. To a certain extent this also helped account for the strength of switchmen, another entry position, for engine and train crews were reluctant to work with large groups of inexperienced scab yardmen.

Besides getting higher wages, unions strove to limit the authority of lower-level bosses, define the limits of the workers' responsibilities, and restrict the number of men with their skills. Unions gained relief from the arbitrary authority of local officers through a guarantee of the right to appeal all grievances and disciplinary matters to Topeka officers. Seniority provisos served to curb favoritism. The company also promised trainmen and enginemen that unassigned crews would be given runs in the order in which they returned from their last trip, thus assuring that the best runs would not all go to a local boss' friends. The outer bounds of employee responsibilities were defined by establishing a standard number of hours for work, by promising enginemen the right to eight hours rest whenever the men felt they required it, by stating that telegraphers and shopmen would have to work Sundays and holidays only when absolutely necessary, and by making it clear that men would not be asked to perform types of work for which others had been hired. Finally, to tighten the supply of men with their skills, the shopmen's 1892 contract established a ratio of skilled men to apprentices and the 1899 telegrapher accord pledged that no operator would be ordered to teach the mysteries of the key to others.[6]

The history of unionization on the Santa Fe offers a study of management policy that displayed far more leniency toward worker organization than has commonly been recognized. In a period of some twenty years, there were nearly two dozen labor organizations represented among Santa Fe employees. Most of these, such as the Brotherhood of Bridge and Building Men and the Brotherhood of Locomotive Wipers, were too weak to put up a fight should management have moved to stamp them out. But with only one exception, when the Brotherhood of Stationmen began to organize clerks and agents whom the company considered officers in sensitive positions, Santa Fe leaders maintained cooperative relations with these weak associations. The Santa Fe showed tolerance, if not encouragement, for many union activities. It allowed James DeWitt to travel free from Atchison to Topeka in 1876 for the expressed purpose of organizing the first Brotherhood of Locomotive Engineers lodge. Management provided transportation to national union functions throughout the nineteenth century. Company officers made it a practice to attend the brotherhood lodges' annual balls and say kind words to those present. They often tried to arrange work schedules so that as many workers could attend as possible. Grievance committees that met with company officials usually reported themselves satisfied with the results of their meetings and felt they had been treated with respect and sympathy. Some union members rose to high office in the company. In 1884 the Santa Fe promoted Order of Railway Conductors member Charles Dyer from trainmaster to division superintendent. In 1891 two other men from the order and two members of the Brotherhood of Locomotive Engineers attained the positions of trainmaster and master mechanic, respectively. Even Israel Conroe, who led a wildcat strike of engineers in 1888, gained a promotion; within five years of the strike, he had risen from engineer to master mechanic. In 1893 the *Switchmen's Journal* attested to the freedom the Santa Fe gave unionizing efforts, saying, "The company did not in any way interfere with the organizations of men employing spies or resorting to other disreputable methods such as are in use by a great many other corporations."[7]

The Santa Fe established a record of reaching accords with its unionized men before most other large roads recognized their brotherhoods. The corporation first signed an agreement with its enginemen in early 1877, only a matter of months after the brotherhoods of locomotive engineers and firemen formed lodges on the road and within two years of the engineers' first compact with the New York Central. The Santa Fe's written settlement with its trainmen came in 1890, three years after the Brotherhood of Railroad Trainmen's first agreement with any road. In 1891 the telegraphers won their first contract in the country with the A & P and followed this up the next year with a similar pact with the mainline of the Santa Fe. Also, in 1892 the Santa Fe was the first to sign contracts with the International Association of Machinists, the International Brotherhood of Blacksmiths, the National Brotherhood of Boilermakers, and the Brotherhood of Railway Carmen.[8]

Without any internal records of the Santa Fe's management, it is impossible to be certain of the reason for company courtesies toward brotherhood functions or union success in gaining early contracts. Certainly, solicitude for the unions could instill in workers a sense of moderation, compromise, and company loyalty. But corporate weakness was the primary motivation. Many railroaders found the territory through which the Santa Fe passed, especially that in New Mexico and Arizona, so inhospitable that they preferred to work for virtually any other road. Not only was the summer weather uncomfortable and entertainments scarce, but Arizona railroader Doc Seagondollar claimed that women were so rare that he had seen three men simultaneously hugging the same girl. To get enough workers the road sometimes had to hire the dregs of the profession, so the company was in no position to either dispense with or ignore union employees.[9]

The road's precarious finances during the late 1880s and early 1890s, when the national economy prospered, proved a more important reason to treat the unions respectfully. In prosperous periods workers could more easily afford the 4 to 5 percent of their annual earnings that union dues often required, and they were emboldened by the ready demand for their labor on other lines. Conversely, Santa Fe managers, struggling to keep the road out of receivership, needed an uninterrupted share in traffic to meet enormous fixed debt obligations. Unlike those firms in a healthier fiscal condition the Santa Fe could not absorb strike-induced short-term losses in the interest of long-term saving. Not surprisingly, then, eight of the Santa Fe's nineteenth-century contracts were drawn up between 1888 and early 1893.

The *Emporia Gazette* in 1892 held the Santa Fe's pioneering role in recognizing labor unions as "a refutation of the calamity theory that capital [had] labor by the throat." The paper commented, "On the Santa Fe railroad labor has a tail hold and a down hill pull and the company can only make the best of it." By recognizing the brotherhoods, the Santa Fe in these years of weakness did grant more to its unions more rapidly than most companies. On substantive matters related to work rules, though, the company's concessions were often more apparent than real. Managers did not feel a strong commitment to abide wholeheartedly either to the spirit or the letter of the agreements they made. The Santa Fe frequently conceded that which it already generally practiced and ignored those portions of agreements that called for changes in established procedures. That was the case with the first two accords with the enginemen in 1877 and 1886. No statement of the text of either has survived. However, in explaining their strike of April 1878, enginemen pointed out that the Santa Fe unilaterally lowered wages from those of the previous year's agreement, that a division superintendent acted more arbitrarily in dismissing men than the contract allowed, and that, contrary to one clause, the general superintendent refused to hear the grievances of the men. Some of the company's officers, probably at the divisional level, showed a similar disregard for the 1886 pact's seniority proviso. This was evident in the 1888 contract's flat admittance that some engineers still held down positions that they were not entitled to under the two-year-old accord.[10]

The company did not follow a more enlightened policy in the last decade of the century. In August 1892 management reached an agreement with three skilled shopmen's unions, covering the issues of foremen's pay, overtime, promotion, and apprentices. Within months, workers complained that the contract was a "virtual dead letter." Some head blacksmiths and boilermakers received the same wage as those immediately under them—a violation of contract provisions—and the number of apprentices exceeded the agreed to ratio of skilled men to apprentices. The workers' accumulating discontent led to a futile two-week strike in 1893. Failure to force company compliance with the year-old document meant that the Santa Fe continued to ignore portions of it and may well have abrogated it entirely by the dawn of the twentieth century. Nor did the Santa Fe annul the contract only with the relatively new and weak shop unions. In 1900 the press announced that enginemen would henceforth be allowed to demand eight hours rest whenever they had seen continuous service of sixteen hours. Since the brotherhoods of locomotive engineers and firemen's contract of 1888 had guaranteed this right to enginemen even without the sixteen-hour minimum, the 1888 rule must have fallen into disuse, if it had not been impotent from the outset.[11]

Such failures did not mean that negotiating contracts was futile. The records necessary for a year-to-year examination of wage fluctuations no longer exist. Still, a comparison of the payrolls of 1874 and 1895 clearly demonstrates the importance of unionization (see Table 4). During the twenty-one-year interval between these dates there were three periods in which economic crises exercised downward pressures on wages— 1877–78, when the costs of the recession that began in 1873 finally caused railroads around the country to lower wages; 1888–89, when the Santa Fe's own financial problems called for belt-tightening; and 1893, when the great depression of the 1890s began. The steady national deflationary trend that decreased prices 25 percent in the eastern United States between 1874 and 1895 and the even more rapid drop in the cost of living, which probably took place as the Santa Fe region became settled, also tended to encourage a lower dollar wage. These downward pressures bore heavily on many railroaders, yet the wages of some Santa Fe employees resisted decline and advanced to a startling degree. Few if any railroaders suffered a loss of buying power, but most lost in terms of money wages. The line between wage losers and winners ran squarely between the weakly unionized and those employees who had negotiated written wage accords. Every group whose pay increased—enginemen, trainmen, yardmen, and operators and dispatchers—had contracts with the company that included wage schedules. Among those whose earnings dropped, only the newly unionized carmen had a contract with pay provisos. Track crews retained about the same pay scale, despite extremely weak unionization, probably because the Santa Fe found it impossible to recruit men for less than their survival wage.[12]

Table 4: *Average Daily Pay by Occupation*

	1874	1895	Percent Change
Engineer	$3.35	$4.70	+40
Fireman	2.01	2.75	+37
Conductor	3.15	3.36	+7
Brakeman	1.96	2.15	+10
Switchman	1.85	2.60	+41
Dispatcher	3.33	4.00	+20
Operator	1.88	1.98	+5
Machinist	3.02	2.72	−10
Blacksmith	3.25	2.62	−19
Boilermaker	2.94	2.61	−11
Car repairer	2.75	1.85	−33
Blacksmith helper	2.25	1.71	−24
Shop laborer	1.66	1.35	−19
Station agent	2.06	1.73	−16
Station clerk	1.91	1.60	−16
B & B carpenter	2.88	2.16	−25
Track foreman	1.69	1.60	−5
Track laborer	1.28	1.25	−2
Total payroll (nontrack)	2.25	2.21	−2

Source: Payrolls, June 1874 (entire line), June 1895 (middle division only), AT & SF. The middle division data is the best for comparison purposes since it covered most of the 1874 trackage.

Once unions attained higher pay, the Santa Fe showed a marked timidity about rolling wages back, even in times of economic crisis. While the company made one or more cuts in the wages of many of its nonunionized workers in 1877, it made no move against the wages of the unionized enginemen until the following year. And in 1888 the *Railway Gazette* credited union power when the Santa Fe excluded the enginemen, and possibly the brakemen and switchmen as well, from a general 10 percent wage cut.[13]

The company abided by contract clauses insuring railroaders a fair hearing in cases of dismissals and suspensions and also upheld union-contract seniority clauses. Even before brotherhoods established it as a contractual right, both management and men accepted the seniority principle and workers complained bitterly and sometimes struck if local officials did not abide by it. Peer pressure also proved effective. In the early 1880s, at the master mechanic's request, Dan Sulier stayed in New Mexico instead of taking a transfer to Topeka. The appreciative master mechanic promoted Sulier to passenger fireman ahead of men who had seen more lengthy freight service. Sulier, however, felt this would cause hard feelings with his fellow employees, so he asked his superior to put him back to a freight engine.[14]

Through seniority rules the enginemen and trainmen eventually took virtual control over job assignments. The unions even proved powerful enough to thwart seemingly justifiable exceptions. After J. K. Pare, a long time Santa Fe engineer, had been incapacitated for further engine service in 1889 a New Mexico Division official gave Pare a good passenger-conductor run. But the conductors' brotherhood complained vehemently to local and Topeka officers. Even though the Santa Fe had not yet recognized the Order of Railway Conductors in a contract, the company quickly found another job in which to place Pare. In 1896, the Santa Fe's Texas line demoted trainmaster Smetten to passenger conductor when the company eliminated his trainmaster post. To do this involved the discharge of a veteran conductor. Despite union weakness during the depression, the Order of Railway Conductors successfully protested the move and the conductor retained his post.[15]

By the late 1890s, the Santa Fe relinquished all questions of seniority of trainmen and enginemen to their brotherhoods. In cases in which the road established new divisions or runs the brotherhoods were practically on their own in deciding how to apportion the available work. The greatest furor arose not between the company and its employees but among the railroaders themselves. This was particularly the case between conductors and brakemen. Brakemen generally favored seniority, which they saw as the fairest and surest avenue to advancement to conductor. Those already holding conductor jobs were less certain of the benefits of seniority, for they all feared and, in the depressed nineties, many knew the hardships of being thrown out of employment and having to start their advancement all over. Presumably at the Order of Railway Conductors' insistence, the Santa Fe in 1892 modified its contract-affirmed strict seniority practice to a system in which for every two brakemen promoted on the basis of seniority, the company could lift one man from the ranks of brakemen regardless of length of service, so long as the man had one year's experience as a conductor. In 1893 depression conditions set in motion a movement to end seniority on the Santa Fe. Within a year conductors succeeded in ending strict seniority on the A&P and the Gulf, Colorado & Santa Fe subsidiary lines, and narrowly missed a similar triumph on the mainline.[16]

A look at the contracts that the Santa Fe signed and the provisions the company most frequently violated reveal the designs of those Topeka officials who guided labor policy. As their recruitment, discipline, and paternalistic practices indicated, Santa Fe management's basic desire was to maintain a steady, productive work force. In times of union strength this required concessions to avert or end strikes. At all times it dictated a wage level at least comparable to that of neighboring lines. Because violations of wage levels were by their nature general and affected all workers while violations of other contract provisions had a more scattered and less simultaneous impact, union insistence and, consequently, corporate acquiescence in maintaining wage levels was more marked than other contract clauses. The need for dependable employees also made top management cognizant of the need to restrain the arbitrary power of local officials. Divisional officers may have had a personal stake in promoting certain favored employees over others or exercising greater leniency in punishing some men. But top company officers who answered first to stockholders cared little who did the work so long as it got done and the workers were content and consistent at their tasks. Therefore, Santa Fe general officers most regularly conceded and uncomplainingly maintained and enforced seniority and discipline provisions of contracts. Even nonunionized workers could count on some degree of seniority privileges and could appeal grievances to higher officers. Significantly, in conceding these issues and allowing workers to appeal violations to the company's head officials, the top management relinquished none of its own prerogatives. Indeed, the general officers could use the unions' vigilance to help centralize oversight of seniority and discipline matters in their own hands.[17]

Pressure for an efficient and inexpensive labor force was also the motivation behind a number of escape clauses that the Santa Fe wrote into its contracts and the cause of many general and obvious company violations of the provisions. The shopmen's and telegraphers' agreements normally excused these employees from work on the Sabbath and on holidays. Nevertheless, Sunday and holiday labor could be required of both groups "where it [was] absolutely necessary to protect the company's business." Similarly, the conductors' 1892 contract made an exception to the right of trainmen to have eight hours rest after sixteen hours of continuous work: when there were snow blockades, washouts, or wrecks, the trainmen's right was to be disregarded. The company in 1895 rescheduled its trains to gain more efficiency, despite thereby violating a supplement to an Order of Railway Conductors accord limiting the miles crews could be made to run. The order protested, but the best it could do was a new supplement tailored to allow the company its money-saving schedule. Gross violations of the shopmen's contract limiting apprentices not only swelled the skilled shopworker market, they also provided a larger number of poorly paid semiskilled men for the Santa Fe shops. By the early 1900s the shop machinists complained of a similar circumvention of the contract as the company assigned machinist's work to lower-paid semiskilled machinists' helpers.[18]

General grievance committees, in conjunction with the national brotherhoods' leadership, had the responsibility of drawing up, negotiating, and overseeing the company's compliance with contracts. The Brotherhood of Locomotive Engineers' committee was the first to convene on the Santa Fe, meeting in Topeka in May 1886. A general grievance committee consisted of a representative from each lodge on the road and usually met at least once a year. Members discussed and conveyed to Topeka management instances in which local grievance committees had been unable to resolve disputes with lower officials. The committees of the brotherhoods of locomotive engineers and firemen commonly met together and jointly presented their complaints. The Order of Railway Conductors and the Brotherhood of Railroad Trainmen acted similarly.[19]

In enforcing contracts, however, grievance committees only reflected the strength of their organizations. In the late 1880s and early 1890s union power expanded rapidly. The committees took this opportunity to gain contracts and enforce them staunchly. Eugene Debs, as editor of the *Locomotive Firemen's Magazine*, called a temporary halt for his union in 1889 to the "blusters" and "arrogant airs." He pointed out that the previous year's long Burlington strike had so depleted the treasury that the time had come for a less assertive stance. Still, only the depression of the nineties quelled most brotherhoods' zeal. With the economic downturn, the International Association of Machinists' leadership warned its members not to strike. The *Railroad Trainmen's Journal* in September 1893 said that with at least one half of the work force unemployed, the brotherhood's bargaining position was undercut. The *Journal* told the grievance committees not to search out disputes and to accept the best possible settlements on the ones members did bring to their attention. The overwhelming weight of the economic collapse combined with the demoralizing results of the Pullman strike in 1894 made the grievance committees largely impotent through the rest of the decade.[20]

There were many grounds for union discouragement by the last years of the century. The shopmen's contract was virtually forgotten. The other unions were so weakened that their officers may have stifled complaints of isolated violations. In contrast to the almost boisterous pride of union men in the accomplishments of their grievance committees in the first years of the decade, workers mention few victories in the late 1890s. The defeat of the Order of Railway Telegraphers' strike of 1900 and the company's subsequent abrogation of previous contracts with the union and refusal to sign another accord punctuated the frustration of union activity at the end of the century.[21]

Nor were the Santa Fe's brotherhood men able to rejoice wholeheartedly in the prosperous years at the end of the century, because the company invested much of its new income in the most advanced technology and coupled this with revolutionary methods of operation. E.P.Ripley, who has a reputation as a kind paternalistic boss, became president of the reorganized Santa Fe in December 1895. He was the prime moving force behind the institution of the Brown discipline system and the revitalization of the Santa Fe's YMCA and reading rooms. But YMCAs and reading rooms would not revive the road just redeemed from receivership. When the company's top officials failed to increase efficiency as much as Ripley desired, he brought in J. M. Barr as third vice-president in charge of operations in mid-1899, with the express purpose of reducing operating expenses by 25 percent. Barr and the set of assistants he recruited then undertook the most drastic cutbacks in jobs and the most aggressive alterations in old work patterns ever imposed on Santa Fe workers. By doing so they achieved remarkable savings . . . and alienated thousands of Santa Fe employees.[22]

While nineteenth-century workers in a multitude of industries felt the pressures of advancing technology and methods of work, the requirements of the workday on American railroads changed little until the last years of the century, when greater emphasis on cost cutting prompted pooling and double heading of engines, the introduction of behemoth locomotives, substituting black porters for passenger brakemen, and experimentation with piecework in the shops. Before pooling, each regular engine crew had its own engine. When the men were off work their engines usually lay idle. By throwing all locomotives into a pool to be assigned at the start of each run to any available engineer and fireman the company could keep its engines in service virtually around the clock.

Other roads had practiced pooling at least as early as the 1870s, but the Santa Fe did not try it until the summer of 1898. For the company it may have had some satisfactory results. The *La Junta Tribune* estimated that under the new system, engines would run as many miles in six months as they formerly had in a year. For engineers and firemen it proved an unmitigated disaster. A Las Vegas fireman in 1899 said that only three of the many engineers and firemen he polled in his division liked the new system. When engine crews received a call to make a run they never knew whether the machine they drew would be a "good steamer or a scrap pile." Firemen complained that it took them fifteen to twenty minutes with a strange engine to calculate the best method of firing it. Fastidious engineers could never be satisfied with the way the previous engine driver left the machine. Most important of all, when the company took away their locomotive, enginemen experienced a shattering loss of prestige. Each engineer had a love affair with his locomotive and relished a sense of ownership over it. Under pooling, however, when company officers assigned the men to the first engine to become available, their relationship to the machine was prostituted and their illusion of any proprietary claim quashed.[23]

Within a year, though, pooling was abandoned throughout most of the line, not because of the brotherhoods' pressure, but because the old ways proved more efficient. With pooling the company had to hire new men to do the maintenance that engine crews formerly did on their own. The company tried to counter partially for this liability by requiring firemen to clean three engines a month and engineers to polish three headlights in the same time. Yet the men often put off these duties until the end of the month; the quality and steadiness of care mandated by rules could not match that inspired by pride.[24]

Enginemen achieved less success in reversing the Santa Fe's adoption of giant locomotives. The Santa Fe inaugurated its modern era of steam in 1898, when Baldwin built it forty-five

large 2-8-0s for freight service. The company purchased comparable 4-6-0s to carry its passenger trains into the new century.
Commenting on one of the recently arrived locomotives, an
Albuquerque conductor exclaimed, "The new engines make the
old ones look like watchcharms."[25]

Firemen found nothing charming about the new engines.
Some of the mammoth locomotives had almost twice the pulling
capacity of the older machines and their consumption went up
correspondingly. Most of the older engines required no more
than five or six tons of coal on a daily run. Yet the press reported
that a freight fireman between Dodge City and La Junta often
shoveled over twice that amount on one of the new engines.
Leaders of the Brotherhood of Locomotive Firemen complained
that the engines were "literally killing" their firemen and requested that the nation's railroads either shorten the runs of
firemen or put two firemen on each machine. One disheartened
Santa Fe fireman at Needles murmured, "If . . . the company
puts on any heavier engines, I do not see what some of us are
going to do."[26]

Of all the new practices adopted by the Santa Fe, double
heading was the one enginemen and trainmen most despised.
Double heading involved coupling two locomotives together to
act as one. The Santa Fe had used double-headers on mountain
runs at least as early as 1885. In the last years of the century,
however, Vice President Barr made double heading the rule in
every branch of the road.

In 1899 a Chanute brakeman summarized the workers' view
of the innovation: "Every double-header run simply throws 1
train crew out of a day's work. It increases the danger to life and
limb 40 per cent., increases our burden 50 per cent., increases
our hours of toil 20 per cent., and will, in a short time, increase
our insurance 25 per cent., but there is no advance in pay for
extra hazards and burdens." In 1898 railroaders already complained that the displacement of crews was brought about by the
larger engines, which could pull forty to fifty loaded cars across
the Kansas plains, as compared to the older locomotives' norm of
twenty to thirty cars. The *San Marcial Bee* noted in the summer
of 1898 that there were only half as many engine crews in town
as there were a year earlier, largely because of the new be-

hemoths. When management added double heading to this, employment for train crews became even more scarce. A force built up to handle trains of only two to three dozen cars could not find adequate employment when the Santa Fe's double-header "Barr Specials" of over seventy-five cars became commonplace.[27]

Railroaders also claimed that double-headers increased their hours and the work's dangers. The excessively long and heavy trains could pull out a drawbar or break a coupler, which might result in derailment. Enginemen normally felt they exercised some control over their fate by watching the track ahead, but, as a Wellington fireman noted, those in the second engine of a double-header "[could] see nothing in front of them—they just [had] to trust to Providence to get through safely." Moreover, Barr's emphasis on having each engine pull its maximum capacity meant the machines had to struggle to get over the line at all. There were many occasions for delays, including broken couplers or the complicated switching involved when side tracks were shorter than the trains. As a result, in 1900 an Emporia train took sixteen hours to travel the 73 miles to Newton, and an Argentine crew labored nineteen hours to go the 108 miles to Emporia. Both of these trips could have been done in half the time three years earlier. Instead, the crews incurred the expense and inconvenience of staying overnight away from home and, since overtime pay could not compensate them for their inability to make a second home-bound run, they suffered a substantial loss in wages.[28]

Automatic brakes and couplers further devalued work and increased unemployment for brakemen. The Santa Fe had adopted air brakes in some areas and on all passenger trains long before the late 1890s. Nevertheless, it was only under the compulsion of the Federal Safety Appliance Act of 1893 that the Santa Fe equipped all its rolling stock with both air brakes and automatic couplers. Trainmen had long sought the adoption of these devices since they made their jobs less hazardous. Unfortunately, the new equipment also made their positions less necessary. Brakemen still could help conductors care for passengers, and they were essential in switching at small stations and for emergency flagging out on the line. However, increasingly trainmasters sent out conductors with one rather than the standard two helpers.

Passenger brakemen were the primary victims of the air brake and automatic coupler. Agile, skilled, and courageous brakemen no longer held the key to travelers' safety. Instead passengers placed a higher value on courteous and complete service from railroad personnel. Crews promoted from the ranks of the often rowdy freight brakemen, however, were not known for overwhelming their passengers with assistance. One train rider of the 1880s described a passenger brakeman as "a gentleman of considerable leisure, and by the nonchalant way in which he [came] through a car and [tramped] on the passengers' feet [was] often mistaken for the conductor." To meet the demand for more accommodating service, railroads in the last years of the century began hiring blacks as train porters. Northern white society and railroad managers had always been reluctant to hire blacks as brakemen. However, they considered them ideal to handle such duties as emptying cuspidors, making down berths, cleaning seats, and looking after soap, towels, and brushes. Not only were blacks more willing to handle these menial tasks; they were willing to do them for forty-five dollars a month, compared to a brakeman's pay of sixty dollars.[29]

The Gulf, Colorado & Santa Fe replaced both brakemen on their passenger trains with porters in late 1898. The road relented within a few months after a vigorous protest by the Brotherhood of Railroad Trainmen's grand master. Instead it adopted the formula of one brakeman and one porter, which had gone into force on the Santa Fe in southern Kansas and Oklahoma in August 1898. Under this plan the porter saw to the comfort of the passsengers while the remaining brakeman assisted the conductor in handling the train. After a successful experience with porters on this area of the road, blacks went to work in place of white brakemen all along the main line in March 1899. As a result, well over a hundred brakemen lost their jobs and those who remained saw their status sinking and worried over their ability to maintain their wage level.[30]

Increasingly thorough medical examinations further jeopardized railroaders' jobs. In 1899 the *Railroad Trainmen's Journal* deplored the recent practice of company physicians rejecting men for "a finger missing, a stiff joint, a lost toe, or any of the little evidences of service." Why brakemen or switchmen were considered unsuited for further rail service because of a couple of missing fingers remains unclear. Tens of thousands of men with this handicap had worked in these positions for decades. Some trainmasters, when looking for good veteran brakemen, preferred men with such signs of experience.[31] Moreover, at the turn of the century air brakes and automatic couplers made their jobs safer and easier. Part of the company's motivation probably was to increase efficiency by retaining only the more vigorous employees. There also may have been a fear that maimed men could be more susceptible to further injury. Railroads could have decided that this would add to their financial burdens through payment of compensation and medical expenses. Finally, a simple revulsion for the sight of maimed employees as railroads entered a safer era may have formed the basis for this prejudicial policy.

Other physical requirements were more justifiable. Probably prompted by the heavier work that the new breed of engines required, the company placed strict age and weight limits on applicants for fireman, and in 1900 extended these guidelines to the hiring of engine wipers, the position from which the road drew most firemen. The Santa Fe weeded out men who suffered from color blindness or hearing deficiencies because they were a danger on the road, where it was essential that they understood color-coded flags and lanterns and heard the engine's whistle. Unfortunately the tests that occasionally cost men their jobs did not always conform to high scientific standards. For example, Topeka doctor J.E. Minney's procedure to test color blindness by having the men name the colors of the dresses or hats worn by the women who passed his office was an accepted practice.[32]

Company officials also strove for greater efficiency in the shops. Through the 1890s the Santa Fe introduced new technology, especially pneumatically powered equipment, with little complaint from employees. However, the men accepted piecework with less equanimity. In November 1899 Barr instituted a piecework system, similar to that on the Norfolk & Western, in the Topeka blacksmith and car shops. With winter coming, workers had little alternative but to stay with their jobs, but one Santa Fe employee noted that had Barr introduced piecework in the spring, "the Santa Fe would have had an exodus of skilled mechanics, the like of which was never seen before." Shortly after piecework began, a committee of shopmen registered their strong complaints about the system to management. Whether this meeting achieved desired alterations or whether the men simply grew accustomed to the new regime, workers began to express approval of piecework. A car worker wrote his labor journal that on the Santa Fe piecework schedule "a good carman [could] make good wages." Payroll data indicates that those who worked under piecework prospered more than those in the same shop who remained on straight day pay. Still, workers and union leaders were wary of the system for all realized that the company could all too easily alter the schedule to the workers' detriment. Partly due to worker discontent, piecework was not introduced into any other departments and in the first years of the new century it was abandoned in the blacksmith shop. However, by 1906 all Santa Fe shops came under a modified piecework system that guaranteed a minimum daily wage.[33]

One day in 1891 A&P conductor Mickey Brennan discovered that the train the company ordered him to haul carried over eighteen fully loaded cars. He immediately kicked up a storm of protest with the trainmaster, saying that such a train was far too heavy and he would not run it. Within a matter of minutes local officials ordered the yard crews to detach a third of the load and a molefied conductor Brennan took charge of his train.[34]

That was 1891, the heyday of railroad union power. In the last years of the decade the brotherhoods failed to fight off company impositions of heavy engines, double-headers, black porters, strict physical requirements, and piecework. The deteriorating position of railroaders led a Winslow member of the Order of Railway Conductors in 1900 to comment, "It is a common occurrence to hear a Brother say he has his caddy packed to fly at any time." Flight, however, was not a realistic alternative. Although the Santa Fe may have undertaken a more accelerated series of innovations than other railroads, all American lines were adopting these new practices. With escape impossible and unions proving ineffective, more and more cries went up demanding legislation. A Santa Fe fireman at Wellington cited twenty-four-hour-long double-header runs as necessitating legislation limiting the hours of work. A Chanute brakeman suggested a law to forbid anyone to work on a passenger train without at least one year's experience on freight. Although the ostensible goal was the safety of passengers, the admitted object was to do away with black porters. Las Vegas brakeman W. W. Beebe spoke more forthrightly in advocating a simple ban on hiring blacks as railroaders. The greatest agitation focused on double-headers. In 1900 Texas railroaders called for a legal remedy, basing their case on the safety factor. The state legislature sidestepped the issue by referring it to the railroad commission, which after study decisively buried it, saying that double heading was probably even safer than single locomotive operations. Despite this setback, the series of innovations adopted by the Santa Fe and other roads in the waning years of the century continued to motivate railroad workers to search for political palliatives where union protection had failed.[35]

In the end, what did unions accomplish? What did they protect and how well did they protect it? To start with, there were a number of "nonaccomplishments." The company accepted the principle of seniority and the right to appeal arbitrary discharges and other mistreatment by local officials, not at the insistence of the brotherhoods, but as part of an effective labor policy. Including provisions dealing with these matters in contracts largely only confirmed what was standard corporate policy. At the same time, the Santa Fe accepted some union demands only to abrogate them after the grievance committees returned home and the intensity of the brotherhoods' militancy subsided. This proved most clearly the case with the shopmen's contract, but the violations of the enginemen's accords demonstrated that even that elite group could not always count on the company living up to the letter of their contracts. Finally, at the end of the century the brotherhoods proved too weak to combat the adoption of new machinery and methods or to exact compensatory concessions comparable to the losses incurred through the innovations.

Nevertheless, the protective unions did achieve real victories for their members. Most obviously they won higher wages and caused the company to hesitate in reducing them. The unions also secured some beneficial work rules and demonstrated special effectiveness in guaranteeing that general company seniority and discipline practices remained absolutely inviolable.

Another aspect of unionization may have been more important. In the railroad's hierarchy, employees in the shops, offices, trains, and engines could easily feel overlooked and unappreciated. Psychologically, unions afforded an indispensable vehicle to surmount such feelings of insignificance. To an extent, those weak brotherhoods that limited themselves to social functions were able to enhance workers' self-esteem by mimicking the more powerful unions and by winning such minor triumphs as having local company officers attend annual balls and say kind words about the brotherhood and its members.

Union men, however, derived far more status from reaching a written agreement with the corporation's leaders. The signing of a contract, even of a document that encompassed few alterations of independent company policy, placed workers for a moment on an equal footing with management. Those without contracts might be treated almost identically by their superiors, but for them such treatment was a privilege; for those with contracts it was a right. Influence over their working lives afforded railroaders a greater measure of self-respect. It was at the heart of "protective" unionism; and when the company denied workers this measure of dignity, the railroaders' struggle for recognition often impelled them to the last resort of a strike.

CHAPTER 7

Brotherhoods:
The Fraternal
Function

Many histories of labor organizations have focused on unions' ideological and economic goals and their success in achieving them, but have expended surprisingly little effort to ascertain why men became members.[1] Most have assumed that men joined for readily apparent economic motives, or possibly because they shared in a utopian or revolutionary vision espoused in union proclamations. Surely such conclusions have considerable merit. Yet, Kansas railroad brotherhood men questioned in the 1890s about what benefits they derived from membership pointed to a whole range of social benefits quite apart from economics and ideology. Brotherhoods were centers of good fellowship offering entertainment, education, moral uplift, assistance for traveling members, and insurance against sickness, injury, and death. "Organization . . . brings the men closer together, and there is less trouble and more friendship," the Newton Switchmen's Mutual Aid Association secretary contended. An Emporia brakeman noted that because of unions "the moral condition of train- and yard-service employés [had] been improved, as drunkenness [was] prohibited, as well as unseemly and immoral conduct." Many other respondents pointed to the more tangible results offered by the brotherhoods' insurance programs. Indeed, about half of those questioned claimed some social benefit derived from union membership.[2]

A new member's first experience at a union meeting was the solemn initiation rite. Although the ceremonies could not awe an initiate who worked and lived in daily contact with those performing the ritual, they could impress on him the responsibilities of being a brother. Moreover, gaining entrance to the lodge signified that his peers recognized and accepted him into full fellowship. Yearnings for approval and a sense of belonging made the last quarter of the nineteenth century the heyday of fraternal organizations. However, railroaders, particularly the mobile enginemen, trainmen, and switchmen, often found themselves at least partly alienated from the larger community. When the U.S. commissioner of labor in 1900 looked back over the history of railroad brotherhoods, he noted, "Railroad service, . . . is a life in itself, somewhat apart from that of an ordinary man . . . in an occupation that follows the conventional hours of work." This fact, along with

the peripatetic aspects of the occupation, and, . . . the element of risk and danger which has had an influence in binding railroad men to each other wherever they meet, are the causes which have led railroad men to form these organizations made up exclusively of their own members rather than participate in similar organizations outside the limits of their occupation.[3]

If railroaders, like those in Emporia, found community with many of their nonrailroading fellow townsmen, they also held special attachments for other railroaders, especially those with the same occupation.

Brotherhood membership provided an instantly recognizable badge of fellowship and respect. The Brotherhood of Railway Carmen's motto—"Friendship, Unity, True Brotherly Love"— emphasized the union's role in pulling men closer together. International Association of Machinists men who took jobs in the Topeka shops in the last years of the century credited union membership with helping them make friends at work. One Kansas machinist said that brothers sometimes harassed recently hired nonunion employees, but helped fellow members adjust to a new workplace. A brotherhood card also served as a solace to those who felt their self-esteem threatened by demotion. In 1898 a Dodge City Order of Railway Conductors member reflected, "To those who are so unfortunate as to be reduced [to brakeman] or out of a job altogether, the one oasis in the desert of their unhappiness is that they can still retain full fellowship with their Brother conductors."[4]

Brotherhood lodges were not utopian communities. Their history reveals both apathy and acrimony among members. In

1886 a correspondent from Kansas City's Switchmen's Mutual Aid Association lodge noted that over half of his fellows were behind in their dues. A leader of the same city's Order of Railway Conductors lodge admitted in 1893 that members lacked enthusiasm for the union's monthly journal, regularly throwing it away without even removing it from the wrapper. Local leaders most commonly complained of the failure of brothers to appear at semimonthly meetings. In 1893 an Emporia switchman declared that he knew of a fellow SMAA member who had not been to a union meeting in five years. The Order of Railway Conductor's grand chief conductor in 1888 speculated that in the preceding year at least a third of the total membership had not entered a lodge room. Moreover, petty wrangling and jealousy afflicted a few lodges. The situation became so bad among the brakemen at Winslow in 1888 that an outside union leader had to come and restore calm. And occasionally local treasurers violated their trust and skipped town with hundreds of dollars of brotherhood money.[5]

In the main, however, the record of brotherhood lodges was overwhelmingly positive. They were democratic in their organization and shared responsibility to the extent that rarely did any member serve as an office holder for more than a couple of years.[6] Poor attendance at lodge business meetings did not indicate that the organizations had failed in their fraternal mission. On the contrary, social activities were a key benefit of railroad brotherhoods. In the members' correspondence to their union journals, annual balls, socials, and parties drew mention far more often than the growth of the lodges, the accomplishments of the members, or the grievances of the workers. These events helped to support worthy union activities, but the primary reason for them was to provide an entertaining social round.

Railroaders organized some balls even before they set up union lodges. For example, in 1881 the engineers and conductors of Las Vegas sponsored what was reported as the largest gala in town history, with over six hundred Santa Fe employees and guests from as far away as Trinidad, Colorado, and San Marcial in attendance. Most such events, though, awaited the formation of local brotherhood lodges, some of which held balls within months of their founding. The Topeka Switchmen's Mutual Aid

Association lodge and the national organization itself were less than a year old when the Topeka switchmen held their first annual ball. The International Association of Machinists in Raton and the National Brotherhood of Boilermakers in Topeka and Albuquerque exhibited similar promptness. The organization of more lodges of more unions in the same town led to a continuous cycle of dances to entertain the railroaders, much of the railroading population showing up at each ball. The Brotherhood of Railroad Trainmen might hold a Thanksgiving gathering, which the Order of Railway Telegraphers would try to surpass at Christmas. The Brotherhood of Locomotive Firemen then sponsored the New Year's Eve celebration, which would be followed by the Brotherhood of Locomotive Engineers' Valentine's festivity and an Order of Railway Conductors' revelry in honor of St. Patrick.[7]

The formation of ladies auxiliaries to the brotherhoods further enhanced the social life of railroaders and their families. In 1887 the women relatives of members of the engineers', firemen's, and switchmen's unions initiated auxiliaries, and those related to union conductors, brakemen, and telegraphers soon followed. By the turn of the century the idea was also gaining adherents in the International Association of Machinists and the Brotherhood of Railway Carmen. The women along the Santa Fe, often encouraged by their husbands, continued to form these adjuncts until by 1900 half of the lodges of the enginemen and trainmen unions had auxiliaries.[8]

The unique trials the women relatives of railroaders faced accounted for the founding of these institutions long before auxiliaries for any other union developed. Wives, mothers, sisters, and daughters were just as much a part of the railroad population, which was cut off from full participation in town life, as were the railroad employees. Moreover, while other husbands came home every night and often at lunch time as well, trainmen and enginemen frequently spent their days and nights on the road. In 1892, "Flora," a Topeka brakeman's wife, wrote, "Like the other dear sisters of the B. of R. T., I am alone most of the time." Frequent moves exacerbated this loneliness. "Eve," the wife of a Las Vegas brakeman, felt auxiliaries would ameliorate this condition:

Those of us who have traveled around and lived in different railroad towns, know how lonely and desolate it seems to be a stranger in a strange place, not knowing whether there is anyone who would befriend us in sickness or sorrow. But now, as members of the Auxiliary, we know that if we need assistance we shall not have to look desparingly around us for doubtless sympathy.

Railroad wives, especially those in the more isolated areas of the line, also battled boredom. An Order of Railway Conductors member's wife noted that winters in Needles were abominably dull and that "the pleasure derived from [an auxiliary] would be very welcome where the amusements are so limited."[9]

Most auxiliaries succeeded in relieving the railroad women of loneliness and tedium. Some of the women's lodges, such as that of the Brotherhood of Locomotive Engineers in Albuquerque, met every other week and the engineer wives of Ft. Madison, Iowa, reported that their meetings ran so long that husbands came home to find their spouses were not there to prepare supper. The ladies had their own secret rituals and enjoyed themselves at their meetings with sewing, quilting, and card playing, although a few auxiliary units forbade the last as immoral. The women of an Argentine lodge bought a piano to entertain themselves. If an auxiliary member became ill, other members would attempt to cheer her with visits and sisterly assistance.[10]

The wider scope of sorority offered by their national women's organizations brought further comfort. A number of the union journals allotted a large section to articles of special feminine interest as well as correspondence from auxiliary members. Letters covered topics ranging from temperance, education, and women suffrage to "how to manage a husband," the best method to wash dishes, and recipes for bread and pork cake. The auxiliaries sometimes organized joint gatherings at which women from different towns could meet. Particularly active in this were women of four or five auxiliaries of the Kansas Brotherhood of Locomotive Firemen, who organized joint annual gatherings in the late 1890s. There were also special sessions for the women held in conjunction with the national meetings of the brotherhoods.[11]

The auxiliaries provided many services for the men in their

affiliated lodges. Near the end of the century a Raton wag satirized the function of the women's organizations. He had a Mrs. Grogan boost the idea of forming an auxiliary for the town's Brotherhood of Railroad Trainmen lodge. Convinced of the utility of auxiliaries by her husband, Mrs. Grogan explained to her neighbor, Mrs. Dooley, that organized into such an association, the women would be able to go up to one of the lodge's meetings and tell the men that

there's goin to be a supper in the nixt room so thay can surprise thim. Thay till thim that aint marriet to bring up their old clothes so thay kin be minded, and if enny of thim git drunk the wimen take thim in hand and give thim the Kaley cure wid a shtick and if enny of the byes git sick, we, the Ladies Artillery, go and set up wid them, so we can wate on thim.

Mrs. Grogan said her Jimmie liked the idea: "We will all be insured, thin whin I dies he will have $300 to burry me." It is doubtful if the auxiliary took on much mending of clothes and even less likely that the women, at least as a group, administered "the Kaley cure wid a shtick." Still, the brotherhood affiliates did have their own insurance plans and took part in a great deal of work in the interest of the brotherhoods.[12]

From the outset of Santa Fe unionization the brotherhood men called on their female friends and relatives for such services as providing a suitable altar cloth for the lodge room and ceremonial regalia for the members. Instituting the auxiliaries increased and regularized their assistance. Some auxiliaries had monthly meetings with the men. Others simply "surprised" the men, as Mrs. Grogan anticipated, by bursting in upon the lodge meetings, and bringing the men meals to justify the intrusion. The women aided the men in the brotherhoods' annual balls and added socials, dances, and parties of their own. The Brotherhood of Locomotive Engineers auxiliary in Winslow set some sort of record in this respect. In less than ten months of existence in the late 1890s, the seventeen members put on two balls, two socials, and a party.[13]

These activities brightened the railroad people's lives and, as one Topeka switchman's wife rejoiced, compelled the men to "spend an evening once in a while in a more profitable way than for them to go to town and get a little too much strong drink."

Money from admission tickets, contests, and games also assisted the charitable projects of the auxiliaries and the brotherhoods. Benevolent activities were most common among the wives of the elite engineers and conductors, who gave relief to the poor of their towns. The Chanute auxiliary was exemplary by annually collecting food and funds for poor families on Christmas. In 1895 they fed thirty families, including over one hundred children. However, they directed most aid toward the families of fellow railroaders. The ladies frequently turned over the proceeds of their social activities to bolster the brotherhoods' own charitable funds. Santa Fe women contributed directly by giving to national causes such as the Brotherhood of Locomotive Engineers auxiliary's home for orphaned children of engineers or the Highland Park, Illinois, home for disabled railroad men. They also gave aid to those members across the country who had experienced personal disaster. Some auxiliaries spent meetings making clothes and other household items for charity. Others undertook more substantial projects. In 1891 the Brotherhood of Locomotive Engineers' auxiliary in Dodge City, after great promotion and planning, held a calico ball, which attracted couples from as far away as Newton. The auxiliary used the proceeds of over two hundred dollars to purchase a three-room cottage for one of their sisters whose husband had died suddenly, leaving her homeless with four small children.[14]

Although the brotherhoods spent much effort entertaining their members, they also attempted to improve themselves morally and intellectually. The Brotherhood of Locomotive Engineers' motto was "Sobriety, Truth, Justice, Morality." Some Santa Fe union men contributed technical writings to the brotherhood journals while others wrote in asking questions. Numerous lodges sponsored classes to instruct members. Union men counseled each other on how to handle alcohol problems. Those who ignored warnings of their brothers and brought disrepute to the union were dealt with harshly. In 1884 the Las Vegas Order of Railway Conductors suspended conductor George Blue "for unbecoming conduct and deemed [him] as unworthy of their fellowship." The Emporia Brotherhood of Locomotive Engineers lodge in 1885 expelled Charles Lyman for deserting his family. The Switchmen's Mutual Aid Associa-

tion in Albuquerque expelled a member for defrauding his creditors and "taking on too many loads of tangle-foot whiskey." The
leadership of the lodge, furthermore, threatened to eject half the
members if that was necessary to form a good lodge and keep the
order's reputation unsoiled. And since these punishments were
published in the national union journals, the ill fame of these
men was not easily escaped.[15]

The ultimate goal of the emphasis on self-improvement was
to acquire the respect of employers and of the community at
large. Brotherhood of Locomotive Firemen editor Eugene Debs
wrote in 1884, "Ours is to be a Brotherhood of gentlemen—
honest, faithful, sober men." An Albuquerque Switchmen's
Mutual Aid Association leader stated in 1891, "what we want is
good, sober men, who are upright in their business dealings.
Then we can command the best treatment from both the railroad
officials and the business public."[16]

Union members did gain special consideration. Some
women shunned nonunion employees. More importantly,
Santa Fe officials came to value union members. The Kansas
Bureau of Labor and Industrial Statistics stated in 1890 that
railroad management noticed the brotherhoods' ability to develop more efficient employees. Union men commonly reported
that Santa Fe officers, some of whom were brotherhood members themselves, gave preference in hiring to brothers. In 1893,
after purging its line of members of a new radical industrial
union, the A & P management boasted that in place of the trou-
blemakers, it had acquired good replacements—all of them
belonging to established brotherhoods. Some considered union
men steadier. Furthermore, according to one railroader, in 1888
a prominent Santa Fe official had stated that drunkenness and
theft among the company's trainmen had dropped 95 percent
after the company began employing members of the Brotherhood of Railroad Trainmen.[17]

Brotherhood members also rendered economic help to
others holding a union card. The practice of trainmen allowing
union men seeking employment free rail passage was especially
common. They extended this privilege even to members of such
small unions as the Brotherhood of Railway Bridge and Building
Men. Brothers, though, went far beyond this in aiding unem-

ployed members. Some recommended a brother for a job, knowing little about his background except that he held a union card. Still more provided free meals and housing for those passing through town and, if they landed a job there, loaned them cash to help them to the first pay check.[18]

This generosity was dampened by the parasitic part of the membership who traveled about the country professing to be looking for work, but actually only "working" the brothers. The mainline of the Santa Fe, particularly the section running from La Junta to the west coast, became notorious as a transcontinental avenue for deadbeats. Some of these transients were union members with no determined plans or ambition. A Winslow Order of Railway Conductors member despaired of the abuse of union ties perpetrated by members not seeking steady employment, but "simply looking up old friends or a job for a month, then [getting] drunk and . . . discharged." There were many complaints of men skipping town, leaving charitable brothers poorer for having lent them money. Some lodges found their treasuries depleted because, to defend the brotherhood's honor, they felt compelled to pay the bills of shiftless brothers, who spent only enough time in town to run up debts to boardinghouse proprietors and local merchants. The Brotherhood of Railroad Trainmen at Temple, Texas, was exceptionally hard hit in early 1895, when William Irwin of a Colorado lodge wandered into town and signed on with the Gulf, Colorado & Santa Fe. The Temple brothers furnished him food and lodging from the day of his arrival. Before Irwin's job began, he came down with typhoid fever. The Temple lodge members saw that he received proper treatment. However, he no sooner recovered from his illness than he skipped town, leaving Temple railroaders $135 in debt for food, lodging, medical care, and drugs. Still, the spirit of brotherhood continued to compel many union men to assist compatriots down on their luck.[19]

Brotherhoods provided useful service to their bedridden members. Sickness or an all-too-common injury could cut drastically a railroader's income. A member of an Arkansas City Brotherhood of Railroad Trainmen lodge noted that if a union man was "overtaken by sickness or some other misfortune, . . . the brothers [would] come to his rescue and enable him to maintain himself and family until the clouds of adversity [had] passed away." Ad hoc committees sometimes raised contributions to help incapacitated nonunionized employees. The action of Raton shopmen in 1885 in sending funds that assisted a former fellow employee injured while working for a nearby Colorado road provided an extraordinary example. However, a worker seeking a measure of economic security could not count on such aid. The vicissitudes of recent economic trends, the persuasive powers of the man passing the hat, petty personal antagonisms, and whether the request for aid came just before or just after payday too easily affected worker generosity when the employee in need was unassisted by an ongoing organization whose membership pledged cooperation to each other.[20]

Brotherhoods provided the necessary structure to coordinate charitable activities. Policy on giving differed from lodge to lodge. Rarely, if ever, were there contractual arrangements ensuring that fellow lodge members would support incapacitated brothers with any fixed stipend. Even well-meaning lodges could not stretch their resources to meet all the needs of the ailing if lodge membership was small and several workers were disabled simultaneously. Economic adversity could also drain the reservoir of funds for charitable purposes. Far fewer lodges granted health benefits in depression times, and in the depths of depression in 1895 complaints from International Association of Machinists locals compelled the national organization to nullify its requirement that lodges provide members with sickness and injury benefits.[21]

At least in good times, though, most lodges assisted those whose incomes were cut off by sickness or injury. An inquiry into the practices of Kansas lodges in 1889 revealed that of seventeen Santa Fe trainmen, enginemen, and switchmen lodges, all but five had a sickness insurance program and only two had no policy for members injured on the job. Records on dispersements reflected the disparity in the risks of railroad work—the engineer and conductor lodges not being called on to compensate any of their members while one of the switchmen's lodges claimed to have spent over one thousand dollars for brothers injured on the job. More commonly, expenses fell between one hundred dollars and three hundred dollars a year.

Some larger lodges could disperse these from their general funds, but others were forced to make special assessments on members. The benefits granted to workers also varied greatly. In 1889 a member of Raton's Brotherhood of Locomotive Firemen's lodge received the modest sum of twenty-five dollars when he was bedridden for three months with smallpox. In the same year Emporia's Brotherhood of Railroad Trainmen voted four dollars a week to those out of work because of sickness. At the other extreme was the assistance given by Chanute's one-hundred-member Brotherhood of Railroad Trainmen lodge, which supported on a continuing basis a totally disabled member who had no chance for recovery.[22]

The brothers showed their greatest compassion when stirred by the plight of a dying member. As Christmas 1887 approached, Topeka switchmen gave three hundred dollars to Joe Reece, a fellow unionist long out of work because of consumption, and seven brothers spent Christmas Eve with Reece to brighten the season. The ties of brotherhood reached beyond the locality. When Reece had a relapse in La Junta in the spring as he was returning from a trip to Denver to improve his health, the brothers of the La Junta Switchmen's Mutual Aid Association lodge gave him assistance—"Every——one of them," as Reece himself appreciatively reported. The heartfelt thanks of more than one new widow appeared in brotherhood journals. Mrs. George Dice's letter expressing gratitude to the men of Newton's Switchmen's Mutual Aid Association was typical in saying that during her husband's sickness "he never expressed a wish but what they granted it; any and everything they thought he needed was bought at their own personal expense."[23]

When a Santa Fe employee died, his coworkers extended sympathy and charity to his dependents. Among the unorganized workers, this amounted to little more than donating flowers for the funeral and taking up a collection for the man's widow. The wives and children of union railroaders fared better. When a brother died, the lodge to which he belonged saw that he was buried properly, including the solemn ceremonial rites designed by each union. Lodge members also raised money among themselves to assist the heirs of men not covered by an insurance policy. Most commonly the contributions were one-time affairs, but Brotherhood of Locomotive Engineers Number 130 in 1882 made the ironclad pledge that the widow and children of Brother S. B. Fisher, who had no insurance coverage, "shall never be in want, pecuniarily, while Division 130 exists."[24]

In 1879 T. P. O'Rourke, a Brotherhood of Locomotive Firemen bard from South Pueblo, described in romantic terms the role of the local brothers upon the death of a member:

> To the widow and the orphan they gave
>   comfort and assurance,
> Supplied all her immediate wants from
>   the Brotherhood Insurance,
> Assuaged her grief, renewed her hopes
>   and round her pathway cast,
> Such brilliant rays, for future days—
>   She'd most forgot the past.

Given that the majority of the unions' insurance policies were for at least one thousand dollars, more than a widow's immediate monetary wants could be satisfied. Most larger brotherhoods, and some minor ones, such as the Brotherhood of Bridge and Building Men, developed death and disability insurance plans to provide security to dependents. The Brotherhood of Locomotive Engineers was a pioneer in this area in 1867. Two years later the newly formed Ancient Order of United Workmen became the first fraternal insurance order. Throughout the rest of the century, other brotherhoods and fraternal societies instituted similar programs offering cheaper coverage than commercial insurance firms. Until the last decade of the century, when the fraternal associations began to exclude those in the more dangerous railroad occupations, railroaders took advantage of both union and fraternal insurance to construct a measure of financial security for their families.[25]

The dangers of railroading required that brotherhood rates be higher than those of the associations. Not unreasonably, most railroaders preferred the fraternal plans. Throughout the first decade of Brotherhood of Locomotive Engineers Number 130's existence, no more than two of its members were simultaneously enrolled in the union's insurance. Even in the late 1880s and early 1890s, when insurance participation grew, few, if any,

Santa Fe engineer locals could claim a majority of the lodge as beneficiary fund members. In 1878 the Brotherhood of Locomotive Firemen made its insurance compulsory for its members. Other unions followed suit, so that by 1894 all of the big four brotherhoods and the Switchmen's Mutual Aid Association had mandatory programs. This did not make policies any cheaper, and complaints arose, especially from men in the lower-paid occupations, some of whom had to give up union membership because of the added expense.[26]

The importance of the fraternal functions of the railroad brotherhoods should not be exaggerated. Members did not always act brotherly. They did not exhibit universal interest in the mundane management of the local lodge. Many became reluctant to extend the hand of fraternal friendship to traveling brothers, when some who accepted it were unworthy and ungrateful. The workers' slowness to subscribe to the brotherhoods' insurance suggested that at least until the end of the century, when fraternal societies began to proscribe membership to those in the hazardous railroad jobs, union men placed limited value in the labor organizations' beneficiary role. Moreover, by the turn of the century, members seemed to begin to move away from the idea of unions as social and reformist organizations. The young Eugene Debs in 1884 stressed the importance of the Brotherhood of Locomotive Firemen as an association of good and industrious men. But in the last years of the century the International Association of Machinists eliminated its long-standing practice of allowing blackballing to exclude unsociable or undesirable men. In doing this, an association leader noted, "A trade union is not a social society, but is a purely business proposition . . . it is not so much a case of high morality that is necessary in a candidate, but . . . whether he is likely to be a competitor or not—whether he is likely to take your place in the event of trouble.[27]"

Still, historians have not given the nonprotective aspects due emphasis in explaining workers' motives for joining unions. Economic and ideological factors probably were more significant for those outside railroad employment. Yet, the lodge halls of many unions housed small reading rooms and members of such diverse labor groups as the Knights of Labor, the International Typographical Union, the Western Federation of Miners, and the Industrial Workers of the World took comfort in the social offerings of their organizations.[28]

Mobile railway men's peculiar social needs and the less mobile railroaders' tendency to model their unions after those of the big four accounted for the brotherhoods' heavier emphasis on the fraternal function. Not only did national railway labor organizations grant peer recognition, entertainment, education, moral uplift, and insurance, they also allowed workers to transcend the loss of community occasioned by geographic mobility. The scattered lodges assisted traveling job-seekers with favorable references, shelter, food, medical care, and friendship. And once the traveler settled in a new town, union membership created an instant bond that carried with it respect, fellowship, and mutual responsibilities.[29] The story of the unionization of the Santa Fe, therefore, cannot be told only in terms of economic and political pressure groups. It also reveals the workers' search for community.

CHAPTER 8
Santa Fe Strikes

Although the Santa Fe maintained relatively good relations with its workers, it suffered at least thirty strikes during the nineteenth century.[1] Causes included wage reductions, unfair and arbitrary management practices, a sense of class or union solidarity with workers striking other companies, and fights for contracts, higher pay, and better working conditions. Only a few walkouts succeeded, and most of them were in the early 1890s, when the Santa Fe was particularly vulnerable. Before then workers were so unorganized and the company's position so unassailable that labor initiated few strikes and generally lost those attempted. After the Pullman boycott of 1894 the subdued workers undertook no major action against the Santa Fe until the last year of the century.

Whatever cause could be assigned to a particular strike, the motivation behind the decisions of individual railroaders was more complex. An individual worker had to consider his family, his chances for reemployment, and whether striking could jeopardize his ownership of his home. Moreover, he was affected by his social relations: failure to strike when most of his peers were struggling against the company could cost a man the respect and friendship of his closest associates.

The character and success of Santa Fe strikes also was affected by the attitude of strikers' fellow townsmen. In many towns railroaders gained the sympathy of other workers, but their political and economic clout was insufficient to bring meaningful backing from the town as a whole. However, very small communities and those with a large proportion of railroaders often supported strikers. They could hinder company and outside government officials' efforts to resume normal operations and make life most uncomfortable for new employees brought in to replace local workers.

A view of the men during and after strikes adds to our appreciation of the experience of nineteenth century workers. An especially passionate minority committed crimes against persons and property. Most strikers, though, shunned such actions, confining their activities to participation at union rallies or to cursing scabs. Once a conflict was resolved, workers might acclaim victory with parades, bonfires, and generally unruly celebration. But more frequently, they had to look for new employment. Committed as many were to railroading as a way of life, they were compelled to uproot themselves and their families. Nor were other jobs always easy to find, especially when, as after the Pullman strike, the Santa Fe in cooperation with other roads blacklisted their rebellious employees.

Strikes primarily of trainmen in 1877 and of enginemen a year later inaugurated labor-management confrontations on the Santa Fe. Both were in part echoes of the walkouts that took place on the great eastern roads in July 1877, but they also had their local causes. The trainmen of Newton staged a two-day strike in July after general superintendent C. F. Morse remained unmoved by their protest that the 25 percent wage cut recently enacted and a threatened additional 5 percent cut allowed them an income "insufficient for the absolute necessaries of life." Although some employees in Emporia joined the job action, the men lacked organization and resolve and returned to work when Morse threatened the forfeiture of their jobs. Grievances against a division superintendent, including the firing of a union leader, triggered the more significant enginemen's strike of 1878. Most engineers and firemen east of Emporia quit and Emporia and Topeka witnessed numerous violent incidents. Passenger trains were interrupted and freight traffic ground to a halt from April 4 to April 8, when the Kansas militia overawed all opposition. The following ten years saw only two walkouts—both of these local, short, and unsuccessful. This lull reflected the general reluctance of labor to wield the strike weapon after the defeats of 1877 and the easing of the stresses on workers as the economy strengthened.[2]

In 1888 the wildcat sympathetic strike of Santa Fe members of the Brotherhood of Locomotive Engineers in the interest of unionized engineers on the Chicago, Burlington & Quincy initiated a return to a more militant stance. Nearly all the company's locomotive drivers quit and for three days the line shut down. However, the strike came to an abrupt halt when P. M. Arthur, the brotherhood's national head, overruled the Santa Fe union leadership's call to stop work. The first victory for workers on the Santa Fe came later in 1888, among the least skilled and thoroughly unorganized track workers. The next few years witnessed a sharp rise in local strikes by switchmen. These rarely if ever were connected with union activity and met with mixed results.

The same resurgence in workers' confidence that ushered in the new wave of strikes also spurred union organization. The older enginemen's and trainmen's brotherhoods had proved their strength on other roads and the Santa Fe, therefore, drafted contracts with them without a fight. In contrast, Santa Fe shop and telegraph workers in the early 1890s pioneered for their organizations by forcing their employer, through walkouts, to sign some of the first contracts their unions ever gained. The last of the shopmen's strikes and the most widespread was that of April 1893. The workers charged the company with not living up to a year-old agreement and clamored for more favorable work rules. The strike lasted two weeks and, although the shopmen could not stop traffic immediately, by the second week management experienced grave difficulty in keeping an adequate engine force in operation. The company utilized its connections with the General Managers' Association to recruit scabs and held to its commitment not to accede to worker demands. However, with the national economy still healthy, the railroad failed to recruit enough new men and was forced to reinstate the strikers in their jobs and reaffirm a contract with them.

Within two months of the end of the walkout the economy, and workers' power along with it, collapsed. This was evident in the Pullman strike. Eugene V. Debs' American Railway Union had organized western railroaders and in late June 1894 they refused to handle cars made by the Pullman Car Company in sympathy with union members then striking that firm. When the railways fired the boycotters the American Railway Union called a strike against the companies. As elsewhere, the strike on the Santa Fe began in late June and incited intimidation and violence. Although the Santa Fe men did not concede defeat until mid August, the company resumed normal operations in the second week of July. Corporate interests were assisted by the General Managers' Association, which recruited workers; the federal courts, which ordered employees to go back to their jobs or face contempt charges; and the U.S. army, which quelled disturbances in the violent strongholds of the walkout. Santa Fe railroaders again entered a quiet period, a calm finally punctured in the last year of the century, when the Order of Railway Telegraphers staged a series of strikes, the last one so irritating to management that the company quashed it and destroyed the order on the Santa Fe.

Employees usually timed their strikes to avoid seasonal and cyclical lulls. The Pullman strike was a model of bad timing, coming a couple of months before the peak traffic period and in the midst of a depression that left tens of thousands of the unemployed eager to take American Railway Union men's jobs. Other actions, though, showed sounder judgment by the workers' leaders. For example, the Brotherhood of Railway Employees' 1893 strike on the A & P succeeded temporarily because it was initiated when expensive shipments of perishable fruit were crossing the Arizona desert. Nor was union organization essential to a calculated and victorious strike. Nonunionized Kansas and Colorado trackmen and Albuquerque yardmen won strikes and were careful to limit their actions to the company's vulnerable years in the late 1880s and early 1890s.[3]

Although brotherhood-sponsored walkouts were little more effective than those of nonunionized men in gaining stated demands, four points can be made in favor of union strike policy. The strength, discipline, and acumen of the older brotherhoods achieved some gains without striking and restrained the men from vainly pushing for the unachievable. Union strikes generally aimed at more significant concessions than nonunion actions and, when victorious, the union attempted to compel adherence to the concessions. Moreover, shop and Order of Railway Telegraphers victories on some segments of the Santa Fe system in the early 1890s probably were more readily transferable to the entire line because of those organizations' presence throughout the road. Lastly, the failure of the American Railway Union was a failure of leadership rather than of followers. Once the leadership called for a boycott and strike throughout the country, the pledged word of union members brought a unanimity of action that would have been impossible without the organization.

A man's decision whether to strike was one of the most important he could make. On it hinged not only his livelihood but also a wide range of social relations. It could be a traumatic experience. A Newton paper during the Pullman strike gave some of the causes for railroaders' inner turmoil: If they

desert the company they are blackballed and will find it hard to get employment again and if they remain when a strike is ordered they will forever afterwards be considered as scabs. . . . The boys are sewed up between the devil and the deep sea, and many of them are heartily wishing that the strike will soon be over.

Worry over the shopmen's strike in 1893 drove the already troubled Charles Nelson, a Topeka brass worker, over the brink of insanity. Nelson's was an extreme case but for all workers who were not wholly committed to the laborers' cause the choice of whether to strike was surrounded with anxieties and misgivings.[4]

The realities of personal economics proved less important in determining individual stances during walkouts than did social pressures and responsibilities. The higher-paid employees and those with homes showed a slight tendency to stick with the company, though within any given occupation this relationship was not strong. In contrast, a clear tie existed between age and striking among workers in Emporia during the Pullman crisis (see Table 5). Those under thirty-five felt far freer to quit than did their elders. Nor does this tendency weaken much within various occupation groups. Of ten yard and shop laborers under the age of thirty-five, nine struck, compared to only three of seven-

Table 5: Percent of Each Age Group of Emporia
Railroaders Not to Strike, June–July 1894

Age Group	Number	Percent Nonstrikers
21–24	23	30.4
25–34	63	31.7
35–44	47	57.4
45 +	42	76.2

Source: Payrolls, June 1894, AT & SF; Kansas Census 1894 for Emporia,
Lyon County Courthouse, Emporia, Kansas.

teen of their elders. Similarly, thirteen of eighteen brakemen in
the lower age group followed Debs, compared to only one of four
who were thirty-five or older. Two factors explain this. Those in
their late thirties and forties were somewhat more likely to be
married and to have several children. Besides these heavier
responsibilities, older men faced a more difficult time finding
another job since employers preferred to hire those in the physical prime of life.[5]

Some social pressures on the workers' choice were exerted in
the home. The *Chanute Vidette* reported that one wife left her
husband for refusing to strike. The *Las Vegas Daily Optic* observed in the last days of the strike that only at the insistence of
their wives did some machinists return to work. And Mrs. Rumble told trainmaster Bailey of Nickerson that she supported her
husband's decision not to take a train out during the strike,
remarking that Mr. Rumble would go without supper if he
worked and forfeited his honor as a railroader. She said she
would rather go to the poor house than have her husband lose
his respect among his peers.[6]

The stances taken by the more decisive and committed men
constituted another important social influence. Peer pressure
can not account for the creation of the dominant attitude toward

a strike. Nevertheless, once a concensus was formed, it could have a powerful impact on those uncertain workers who found themselves "between the devil and the deep sea." Working side by side in often dangerous occupations and usually living near one another, railroad men formed close associations. If one's coworkers remained on their jobs it was easier to resist the calls to strike. If most of one's friends struck, it was very difficult to remain at work. The inclination to follow the crowd was increased by the turbulent atmosphere common at the outset of a strike. In 1894 a number of Ratonites probably related the experience of many when they admitted that they had been caught up in the excitement of the moment and had joined the Pullman strike without careful consideration of the risks.[7]

Workmen's efforts to convert their coemployees sometimes took the form of violence. In 1878 Emporia and Topeka strikers stoned every locomotive that moved and taunted and threatened those who ran the engines. In the Kansas capital, there were several beatings of working enginemen. Topeka engineer C. F. Tenney, who defied the strikers in taking a train out, later reversed his decision, saying that he had no relish of being shot at. Violence was the essence of the New Mexico White Cap strikes. The White Caps were a terrorist organization that waged war on white economic institutions, including the Santa Fe. In 1891 and 1893 it called for higher wages for those in the low-paying jobs held primarily by Chicanos and threatened violence to anyone who did not join the strikes. Almost all employees were scared away from their jobs. Considering the number of men involved in strikes against the Santa Fe, there was not a great deal of physical violence, but the possibility of it could be unsettling enough. Santa Fe Kansas City superintendent J. Z. Roraback estimated that half of the area's Pullman strikers quit reluctantly, fearing retaliation if they continued to work. Certainly loyal Topeka employees who faced crowds attracted to any sign of business as usual in 1878 could never be sure that angry taunts, such as "You better order your coffin," would not escalate into attacks which would put them in a sling, if not a wooden box.[8]

While potential violence must have been in the back of workers' minds, the most important impact of peer pressure was more subtle and peaceful. In the 1878 engineer's walkout, strike leaders pointed to the arbitrary rule of William H. Pettibone, division superintendent at Newton, as the primary cause for the strike. Yet the vast majority of the engineers on the western half of the line that Pettibone headed remained loyal, while virtually all the workers on the eastern half struck. The key to understanding this paradox appears to have been the personal influence the three very talented and self-willed strike leaders based at Emporia were able to exercise over the eastern engineers, many of whom quit without any inkling of what grievances justified their action. And most westerners refused to strike largely because their informal group leader, James M. Anderson, an engineer who sat on the Newton city council, opposed the Emporia clique.[9]

More indications of the influence of fellow local workers are found in an analysis of Pullman strike payroll statistics for fifteen Santa Fe towns in Kansas, Colorado, and New Mexico. If the impetus to strike came only from the issues of class solidarity, one would expect a measure of consistency in the amount of striking from one town to another. This was not the case. (see Table 6). Few struck where the American Railway Union had not formed a lodge prior to the strike; Santa Fe examples were San Marcial and Wichita, where almost no one struck. A lodge would have given the union an inroad to battle for the loyalty of local railroaders. Without one, Debs' calls from Chicago fell on deaf ears.[10]

But the basic cause for differences in strike activity was the local nature of the workers' sense of fraternal loyalty. The vast majority of shopmen, enginemen, and trainmen struck in Trinidad, Raton, and Las Vegas, in contrast to the relatively few workers who quit in Chanute, Newton, and Arkansas City. Besides reflecting the generally younger work force on the western end of the Santa Fe, the large difference in participation in the strike in these towns suggests that seeing many coworkers lay down their tools or, alternatively, stand by their jobs created a bandwagon effect to either strike or remain loyal to the company.[11]

The bandwagon effect applied to most employees within a town. Yet some men followed the lead of a smaller group of

Table 6: Percentage of Workers to Strike in the Pullman Strike
(total number of workers shown in parentheses)

	Engineers	Firemen	Conductors	Brakemen
Argentine	23.3	92.5	0.0	48.2
	(60)	(67)	(25)	(56)
Chanute	1.8	25.9	11.9	33.0
	(55)	(58)	(42)	(97)
Emporia	22.9	94.9	12.5	70.6
	(35)	(39)	(32)	(51)
Newton	3.4	45.1	0.0	13.4
	(29)	(31)	(30)	(67)
Nickerson	43.5	92.6	33.3	85.0
	(23)	(27)	(18)	(40)
Raton	64.6	92.5	67.6	75.4
	(48)	(53)	(37)	(61)
Las Vegas	59.5	91.7	3.0	29.8
	(37)	(36)	(33)	(57)

Table 6 *continued*

	Switchmen	*Trackmen*	*Shopmen*
Argentine	97.7	82.1	54.8
	(43)	(28)	(272)
Chanute	100.0	33.3	31.0
	(13)	(18)	(58)
Emporia	100.0	64.0	57.3
	(25)	(25)	(75)
Newton	87.5	0.0	41.9
	(16)	(17)	(43)
Nickerson	100.0	100.0	62.3
	(7)	(8)	(93)
Raton	100.0	11.1	100.0
	(5)	(9)	(205)
Las Vegas	16.7	0.0	100.0
	(6)	(9)	(61)

Source: Payrolls, July 1894, AT & SF.

coworkers. In Trinidad, Raton, and Las Vegas, where so many men struck, only one of the three towns' twenty-nine trackmen quit. The one striker was an Anglo, while all the other laborers were Chicanos. The sense of belonging to the same working class community did not extend across this ethnic line. Also, workers of one gang sometimes behaved different from most Santa Fe men of a town. For example, in Chanute, where most remained loyal to the company, twelve of fourteen machinists followed Debs. These men went against the grain, knowing that they maintained the respect and friendship of those with whom they worked most closely.[12]

Foremen played an especially important part in determining the number of workers in their groups who remained loyal to the company. Like all other employees, foremen responded to the action taken by many of those around them. Except for a head blacksmith in San Marcial, no shop foreman, in the fifteen towns studied, struck without being accompanied by at least half of those who worked under him. Of course, at this date it is impossible to know whether it was the foreman who led most of those under him to strike or pressure from the subordinates that caused the foreman to quit. Some foremen, such as the head machinist, blacksmith, and carman in Ottawa and the boss machinist and carman in La Junta, remained loyal to the company despite the defection of most of those under them. However, other cases point to the effect that a strong foreman might have on his employees. A greater percent of the shop workers in Ottawa and Nickerson struck than in Arkansas City and Argentine. Yet in Ottawa only five of twelve boilermakers struck, compared to twelve of thirteen in Arkansas City, and two of seven blacksmiths struck in Nickerson, while six of seven did so in Argentine. In each a majority of the gang followed the foreman's lead.[13]

A comparison of the striking figures for switchmen with those of trackmen, bridge and building men, and workers at small stations further supports the importance of peer pressure. A higher percent of switchmen struck than any other class of employees. The track and bridge and building men were at the opposite end of the spectrum. And of the 138 employees in the fifty-two small stations on the eastern division, only 3 struck, in comparison to all but 1 of the 43 yardmen in Argentine, the town with the largest station force on the division. One explanation for these contrasts was that switchmen had a longer experience with union activity. The switchmen were also more crucial in any walkout and more accessible in division centers, so it would be surprising if the American Railway Union leaders did not aim at and meet with greater success in organizing them. Nevertheless, the exceedingly high percent of switchmen striking in comparison to most other groups of employees and the propensity for those trackmen who did strike to work in the yards or on sections immediately adjacent to striking towns, suggests that another factor was at work. Bridge and building men, trackmen, and station men away from larger towns operated far from other workers. They were self-contained groups with minimum contact with other railroaders. Switchmen, however, came into close daily contact with stationmen, trainmen, enginemen, and shopmen. Moreover, their place of work was outdoors in the center of railroad communities, within range of strikers hurling insults and more substantial instruments at anyone who remained on the job. Trackmen, bridge and building men, and the personnel at small flag stations could ignore the actions of the wider railroader community with relative impunity; the switchmen could not.[14]

Among nineteenth-century Santa Fe strikes, Pullman was unique in involving conflicting union loyalties as one more cause for tension within many workers. Men could join the American Railway Union and still maintain membership in the older craft organizations. When the Pullman boycott erupted, most of the shop unions either openly sympathized with the union or remained quietly neutral. However, the national leadership of the switchmen's union and the big four unions of enginemen and trainmen were unanimous and outspoken in their opposition to Debs' strike.[15]

Men committed to the American Railway Union castigated the brotherhoods. Union men in Dodge City made blistering attacks on the Order of Railway Conductors and the Brotherhood of Locomotive Engineers. Strikers at a mass meeting in Topeka denounced all the nonstriking brotherhoods. As frustration set in near the end of the strike, the American Railway Union lodge secretary at Argentine declared that the strike was less a fight between capital and labor than between sets of labor organizations with the well-placed and selfish refusing to take part in the struggle.[16]

This conflict in union loyalties may have involved policies and principles dealing with class unity, union discipline, and faithfulness to contracts, but on the local level it also took on the nature of a tug-of-war between group loyalties. The Brotherhood of Locomotive Firemen's Santa Fe leader, Thomas Burke, urged in a letter to members that they stick together and encourage each other to resist pressures to strike. As the walkout spread, the usual reaction of old-line union men was to call a meeting of their local and attempt to decide on a united stand. Usually the union sustained national policy. The Brotherhood of Locomotive Engineers' lodge at Argentine tried a common compromise of conflicting loyalties by expressing themselves unwilling to work with nonunion crews. But when Santa Fe Superintendent Roraback told the men to work or quit, the engineers held another meeting and decided to go back to their jobs, except for switch engineers, who refused to work with scabs.[17]

The varying outcomes of the struggle between union loyalties in Santa Fe towns testified to the inner turmoil that many railroaders felt. That smaller percentages of trainmen and enginemen struck than shopmen is attributable to the persuasive powers of the big four unions' directives, reinforced by local lodges. However, in some towns traditional union loyalties were insufficient to prevent massive desertions to the American Railway Union. The Order of Railway Conductors' lodges at Raton, New Mexico, and San Bernardino on the Santa Fe's California line suffered huge defections to Deb's union and had their charters revoked by the national organization. The large memberships of brakemen at Dodge City and firemen at Emporia, Nickerson, and Las Vegas went over en masse and forsook their brotherhood charters, while other lodges barely retained an infrastructure. And the outcome of the struggle for switchmen's loyalty was overwhelmingly favorable to the American Railway Union. The head of the Switchmen's Mutual Aid Association, Miles Barnett of Kansas City, stood by helplessly as lodge after lodge, including those in Kansas City and neighboring Argentine, voted to back the strike and surrender their old charters.[18]

The effectiveness of strikes on the Santa Fe also was influenced by the degree of local nonrailroader sympathy. Town opinion and policymakers tended to either support, ignore, or scorn railroaders' strike actions, and the workers prosecuted their strike either with caution or vigor, depending on the role the workers played in the community. Essentially, there were three types of towns, each with a different reaction to local strikers. Towns of no more than several thousand, in which less than a third of the working population engaged in railroading, were small enough that close personal contact and a sense of community extended to all within the town borders. Class divisions, though not obliterated, were at a minimum. In many such towns there were only a few dozen to a few score of railroaders, so Santa Fe employees were not perceived as a separate community, nor could they have anything approaching an adequate social life without liberal mixing with their nonrailroading neighbors. This enhanced the probability that they would be fully incorporated into the wider community and that railroaders' interests would find sympathy from a large spectrum of townsmen.[19]

In the 1870s Newton and Emporia both fit this pattern. During a locally initiated trainmen's strike in 1877, Newton's population of under two thousand supported the strikers. Although not directly commenting on the confrontation, Reverend Beatty in his Sunday sermon lavished high praise on the Santa Fe trainmen, and the *Harvey County News* noted, "The sympathy of the citizens is with the strikers." The *Newton Kansan* concurred: "[A majority of the strikers] are old citizens here, . . . are worthy men, and our people take no small amount of interest in their welfare."[20] In the next year's engineers' walkout, Newton workers remained loyal to the company, so the town's papers attacked the strikers and defended W. H. Pettibone, the local Santa Fe official whom the strikers berated. Meanwhile the Topeka *Commonwealth* characterized Emporia, numbering about three thousand and being the focal point of the strike, as openly supportive of the rebellious workers. A local paper stated that at a public information meeting a "good many" citizens endorsed the workers' actions. Moreover, municipal officials displayed reluctance to take strong police action to pave the way for a resumption of regular traffic.[21]

Similarly, during the Pullman boycott, Strong City, a town of seven hundred, which lay twenty miles west of Emporia, backed its local railroaders, a sizable minority of whom struck. Out-of-town papers noted considerable sympathy for the strikers in Strong City. The *Emporia Gazette* called it one of the "hottest" towns in the state and charged that local residents scorned the scabs and the deputy marshals sent to protect them and refused to provide either with boarding places. The *Strong City Derrick* failed to confirm or deny this characterization of town sentiment. But it did praise the local strikers as "perfect gentlemen" and called the dispatch of deputies to the town unnecessary."[22]

Strikers also gained sympathy in towns in which railroaders were a sizable part of the population. The critical mass seems to have been about a third of the total working residents. In these places politicians tried to cater to railroaders' wishes, editors generally championed their causes, and local businessmen shrunk from criticisms of their actions. This problem for management was largely one of the Santa Fe's own creation, since most such towns would not have existed except for the railroad's decision to create division centers in them. On the Santa Fe, Argentine and Nickerson, Kansas, and Raton and San Marcial, New Mexico, matched this description. Trinidad, Colorado, housed a large proportion of railroaders, but Union Pacific employees far outnumbered those of the Santa Fe. Las Vegas, New Mexico, also may have qualified because, although the Santa Fe's employees constituted less than 20 percent of its urban population, the local Santa Fe workers made up a larger percentage of the Anglo community. Moreover, the vast majority of the railroaders lived in the city of East Las Vegas, where they constituted nearly a third of all workers and therefore exercised considerable influence over local politics and business.[23]

These division towns did not get Santa Fe facilities until 1879 or after, so a major test of their allegiance did not come until the Pullman boycott began. San Marcial men failed to strike. Nevertheless, Trinidad, Raton, and Las Vegas formed the stronghold of resistance on the Santa Fe and Nickerson and Argentine were two of the most solid striking centers in Kansas.

In all of these towns there was substantial backing for the strikers, though there is inadequate evidence to tell much of the story of the strike in Nickerson.

Argentine's reaction was clear. Its people were "as a unit in sympathy with the strikers and against the railway, for the population of the place [was] made up largely of Santa Fe employees and their families." Argentine's chief of police swore in five American Railway Union men as special officers during the strike and put a U.S. deputy marshal in jail for carrying a concealed weapon. At least one mass meeting addressed by a public official passed resolutions supporting the strikers. When the first group of U.S. marshals arrived they could find no boarding or lodging place. All the town's proprietors feared that their businesses would be boycotted or otherwise injured by the strikers if they accepted the deputies' patronage. Men taking the strikers' jobs got an even more hostile reception. None could eat at W. C. Jones' restaurant, over whose entrance hung an old musket with a placard reading, "This gun is loaded for scabs." The hostility of the town's businessmen to the new men lasted long enough that some did not find suitable lodging for several weeks.[24]

The deputies in the first days of the strike had to conceal their occupation to get meals, and they spent their nights in passenger cars rather than hotels. When the Santa Fe imported new men it began housing and feeding them and the deputies in the yards. As the strike approached its second week, the Santa Fe sent a bridge and building crew from Topeka to assist in constructing two barrackslike buildings to serve the deputies and new employees. Within a couple of weeks there were sufficient bunks and large enough kitchens to care for four hundred to five hundred men. There was also a general store and barber shop. The Santa Fe's Superintendent Roraback, who had taken similar measures the previous year during the shopmen's strike, said that these improvements, instead of Argentine businesses, would continue to serve the new employees "until the citizens . . . stop fighting us."[25]

By the third week of the walkout some businessmen realized that the strike was lost and cautiously moved toward reconciliation with the railroad. In a meeting they did not explicitly condemn the boycott of scabs and deputies, but they did not endorse it either. When forced to choose between railroaders and the company, merchants chose the local residents, at least in the short run. But when the strike was lost, good relations with the road and its new employees became increasingly important. Still, the local business leaders hoped to retain as many as possible of the old workers, a reaction shared among Nickerson business leaders who feared property owned by strikers would go to ruin while they searched for new jobs. As a result both cities sent delegations to Santa Fe headquarters in Topeka to plead for the reinstatement of local strikers.[26]

Strikers received even more support in Raton and Las Vegas. Ratonites were furious with federal troops in town. One out-of-town paper commented, "The whole town is in close sympathy with the strikers," and the sentiment against moving Pullman cars was "well nigh universal among the people." The U.S. marshals sent to the town had difficulty finding anyone who would feed them. The actions of Sheriff McCuistion of Colfax County and Raton marshal J. T. Thatcher gave the best indications of local opinion. On hearing that U.S. marshals were coming, Raton strikers and their sympathizers wrecked several cars south of town to force the deputies to walk in. When the marshals reached the city boundary, Sheriff McCuistion and a large number of strikers met them. The strikers ordered the marshals to remain on railroad property, an order supported by the county sheriff. This confrontation brought a direct admonition to McCuistion from a U.S. district court judge to desist in obstructing the marshals and ordering the marshals to arrest the sheriff if he persisted. At this McCuistion stepped back, but Raton marshal Thatcher was arrested when he drew his gun on a U.S. marshal, whose right to carry a weapon Thatcher questioned.[27]

Las Vegas did not confront outside forces as roughly, but at the insistence of strikers, city marshal Clay prevented armed U.S. marshals from protecting scabs off of company property. The Las Vegas Daily Optic blamed the railroads for the halt of the nation's traffic, since they should have continued to run their lines for the four-fifths of all passengers who did not use Pullmans. Even if the strikers were partly at fault for the inter-

ruption in transportation, the *Optic* declared on the second day
of the strike, "Public convenience has often to be made secondary to the settlement of great principles." Moreover, in a five-day
period at the outset of the strike Las Vegans held three meetings,
at which a judge and more than half of the church leaders in
town spoke. At these assemblies the local speakers unanimously
expressed sympathy for the strikers and usually culminated the
rallies with resolutions championing the workers' struggles
against the corporations.[28]

Nevertheless, as the Santa Fe gained the upper hand, support
for the strikers waned. At the beginning of the third week trains
were arriving and departing from Las Vegas and Raton on a
regular basis. The U.S. marshals had left, replaced by soldiers
who moved around town unarmed. With the tumult over and
the issue decided, the *Optic* did an about-face and opposed the
secondary boycott as unfair to the railroads. Meanwhile, Raton's
editor fended off charges from outside that his town had been the
most anti-Santa Fe on the road, and the municipal council
rejected Marshal Thatcher's request that the city reimburse him
for the expenses of his brief imprisonment, partly because to pay
Thatcher would lend support to the charge that Raton aided the
lawless element.[29]

The third type of town included those with populations over
three thousand whose railroad population constituted less than
a third of their workers. In such towns class divisions emerged.
Emporia's development after 1879 exemplified this. Commonly,
railroaders concentrated in one corner of these towns and they
and their working class cohorts were separated socially and
residentially from the local elites. Santa Fe strikers may have
received the sympathy of their nonrailroading working class
neighbors, but the leadership of the town opposed the strikers
and, partially as a result of this, the railroaders' activities were
more restrained than in Las Vegas, Raton, or Argentine.

In Topeka it was clear that town leaders were not as sympathetic toward the 1878 engineers' strike as were those in
Emporia. After a strike leader had properly arranged to rent the
Topeka Opera House for a speech, Mayor M. H. Case blocked the
meeting. A more emphatic expression of sentiment of some of
the state capital's leading citizens was the formation, in the

midst of the strike, of a militia company under the leadership of
Santa Fe general superintendent C. F. Morse. Among the nearly
fifty members of Morse's company were some of the city's most
prominent citizens, including the county attorney, a former state
senator, and five bankers.[30]

During the Pullman boycott, newspapers in towns of the
third type reflected the sentiments of the local upper class. Some
newspapers virtually ignored the arrival of deputy marshals and
the risk that scores or hundreds of town residents were taking by
striking. The *Newton Daily Republican*'s greatest concern was
for the impact of the strike on local business. The boycott had
closed off town manufacturers' supplies of coal, a situation that
threatened to cause shutdowns. Fresh fruit was fast becoming a
luxury and farmers who raised perishable crops would soon
experience difficulty selling their produce to wholesale merchants who now lacked the transportation facilities necessary to
market the goods.[31]

The three Emporia papers offered far more elaborate coverage of public sentiment. C. V. Eskridge, the crusty old editor of
the *Emporia Republican*, declared bluntly, "Strikes are un-
American." One of his more moderate editorials came closer to
expressing the opinion of the "society" class of Emporia's north
end when it stated that the public sympathized with the American Railway Union against Pullman but felt that the secondary
strike was unfair to the railroad companies.[32]

The town leadership's view of outside law officers was now
far different from what it had been in 1878. During the engineers'
strike such external interference was viewed as an invasion of
the community and an implied criticism of its ability to control
itself. All major town and county officials protested, in the most
vehement terms, the sending of state militia into their midst. In
contrast, in 1894 the city council scoffed at and killed a resolution introduced by two Third Ward politicians representing
local railroaders' desires to have the U.S. marshals removed. The
difference between 1878 and 1894 was that by the latter year
Emporia's one community had become two, divided by class. If
the sending of marshals implied that some town citizens might
be potential lawbreakers, this was less a concern than the 1878
implication that some community members might be lawbreak-

ers. By 1894 northenders had grown accustomed to thinking of railroaders as a separate, and sometimes undesirable, class. If they threatened the peace they had to be controlled, and northenders would not scorn federal assistance in this effort.[33]

Railroaders did find support among many Emporians of their own class. The antimarshal resolution was evidence of support, as was the barbers' union boycott of the U.S. marshals sent to town. So also was a resolution passed by the town's Neosho Tribe of Redmen, a working-class fraternal organization. At a special meeting called at the end of the first week of the strike, the Redmen backed a resolution sympathizing with "the honest laborers ... out of employment and subjected to unceasing abuse and persecution by heartless and wealthy corporations." The Redmen went on to pledge "the wampum of the Neoshos" to support the strikers in their "struggle for future protection to their princesses and children."[34]

Farmers, Alliance men, and Populists also rendered class-based sympathy to Pullman strikers. Farmers were the primary contributors to the material support of Debs' followers during the strike and in the days immediately thereafter when so many were destitute. In a number of Kansas division towns the American Railway Union men established centers where farmers could bring food to help the strikers. Fifty farmers of Shawnee County made regular contributions to the center in Topeka. In Argentine, wagons sent into the countryside soliciting vegetables met a generous response, one farmer offering a wagonload of potatoes for the digging. Kansas Populist politicians, from Governor Lewelling down, claimed the strikers' cause as their own. In Arkansas City, the Populists allowed the strikers the use of their headquarters. The People's Party of Shawnee County asked that farmers donate food and other goods to the struggling followers of Debs. The People's Party owed this to the American Railway Union since the union, just before the Pullman boycott, endorsed free silver and, indirectly, the Populist Party.[35]

For all the support railroaders could garner from their working-class neighbors and the surrounding farming community, towns of Emporia's type were less sympathetic to the workers than were the particularly small towns or those larger ones dominated by railroad men. Farmers were peripheral and could exert slight control over town policies. Urban workers had little more influence because the upper class dominated local politics, society, and economics. In small towns, communal affection bound those in power to the railroaders, while in towns in which railroaders composed the paramount economic and political bloc, the men in power felt compelled by self-interest to back their local workers. No such bonds existed in most cities, however, and railroaders were isolated from positions of power. As a result, Santa Fe strikers were more restrained in these towns than they were in worker-dominated towns such as Raton and Argentine, or in small united communities such as Emporia in 1878. They also were less successful in accomplishing their goal of bringing railroad traffic to a halt. That most late nineteenth-century strikes took place in unfriendly surroundings, both on the national and local levels, goes far to explain their general failure to achieve victory.

Although some strikers were violent and, in especially sympathetic communities, a majority may have engaged in verbal abuse of scabs, all was not turmoil and conflict. The majority spent most of their time on strike as they would on a vacation. Married men enjoyed the company of their families. In the brief Brotherhood of Locomotive Engineers strike of 1888 several dozen Arkansas City enginemen took advantage of an idle day to fish on Chilocco Creek. During various walkouts men wandered about town, met to play cards, lounged in the shade or whittled, while the story that beer was the only commodity exhausted before the Pullman boycott ended in the Santa Fe town of Williams, Arizona, suggested that others relieved tension and lifted spirits by a well-tested method.[36]

Strike leaders strove to keep their members united, resolved, and peaceful. They occasionally requested liquor dealers, saloons, and gambling houses to suspend business during strikes. There was also a seemingly endless succession of meetings at which leaders exhorted members and read the latest communications of solidarity along the line. Meetings in some towns numbered two, three, and even four a day. They tried to entertain as well as encourage and inform. Entertainment fended off boredom, from which men might otherwise have sought relief either in violence or a return to work. Frequently the meetings, which wives sometimes attended, included singing, dancing, comic songs, and patriotic music along with the stump speeches. Commenting on the shopmen's meetings in Topeka in 1893, the *Railroad Register* said they "presented more the appearance of men gathered together for recreation than to discuss the weighty matter which affected the future welfare of many of them." Nor did striking organizations limit their diversions to assembly halls. There were rallies in many towns to garner public support. These often reflected a festive mood, and during the Pullman strike American Railway Union lodges organized baseball teams, the one at Las Vegas playing a game against stranded passengers equally at a loss for something to do.[37]

The sense of expectancy that accumulated during a long strike could be expelled in wild celebration when anything like a victory was achieved. At the end of the two-week shop strike of 1893 jubilant workers in Nickerson built a bonfire, lit skyrockets, and boarded the company's engines to blow the whistles and create a general din. In Argentine the scene was a riot, with triumphant strikers running a dozen scabs out of town. This done, the town band paraded through the streets and the saloons threw open their doors to the celebrants.[38]

Defeat and loss of their jobs was the more common experience for strikers. No strike of the nineteenth century lost more men their positions than did the Pullman boycott. Five thousand or more became jobless on the Santa Fe system alone. Charity, family gardens, and the accumulated back pay collected on their discharge aided survival in the short run, but these resources were exhausted quickly and merchants soon closed their books to a man who no longer had a steady income. Therefore, another job was the top priority. Within two months of the boycott, Santa Fe management announced that men who had not taken an active role in the strike could reapply for work. By this time nearly all jobs were filled, but this ruling did provide relief for some former employees.[39]

Failing to return quickly to their old posts, many found local jobs outside of railroading. Las Vegas' Walter and George Boardman opened a restaurant. An Argentine switchman ran a popcorn stand in Kansas City. And some might have considered it ironic that R. J. Sloat, who led many Topekans in the Pullman debacle, entered the coffin trade. Others were fortunate to get factory work. A dozen Williams strikers found employment in the nearby mills and a handful of Argentine men took jobs at the local smelter. Strikers got positions on the police forces of Las Vegas and Newton. Others entered the ranks of common laborers, working in street gangs, joining in the seasonal harvesting that was going on as the strike collapsed, or doing odd jobs wherever available. The *Las Vegas Daily Optic* noted bitterly in October 1894 that some of the most skilled railroad men were reduced to pick and shovel labor in the excavation of the new Masonic Temple. For some, the loss of a steady paycheck was a long-term tragedy. Ed Winans was a twenty-three-year-old Newton roundhouse worker when he struck. Had he stayed with the Santa Fe he might have climbed the promotion ladder to engineer in five years. Instead, he struggled during that time period with odd jobs around Newton.[40]

Reflecting their attachment to railroading and demonstrating the tragedy of their ill-conceived walkout, the vast majority of Santa Fe strikers took to the road to find new employment. One Williams man found his three married daughters moving back in with him while their husbands scoured the country for work. An Argentine American Railway Union man bemoaned his forced exodus, saying, "I don't care for myself, I can stand it. . . . but, oh, it hurts to have to leave the wife and babies and not know when I shall see them again." Freight trains out of railway centers soon crawled with discharged railroaders looking for a free ride anywhere there might be work. But with a national recession and few available jobs, the unemployed had to travel great distances, some searching for work as far as South America and Africa. Moreover, blacklisting haunted the rebellious workers. The experience of telegrapher John O'Brien, whom the Santa Fe fired for refusing to take a transfer to Strong City during the walkout, was common. He had three jobs in the three months following the strike, but each time he was discharged after only a few days when the evidence of his disloyalty caught up with him.[41]

The only solution to blacklisting and the ultimate corporate humiliation of railroaders was the practice of adopting a new name. By denying their identity, railroaders could escape their past. In early 1895 the *Las Vegas Daily Optic* commented, "many of the employees . . . in Las Vegas do not readily recognize their present names, upon pronunciation . . . because they have changed from those the men went under, when they were stronger A.R.U. men than they are to-day." The practice was so prevalent among Nickerson's post-Pullman employees that the town's census taker in 1895 conceded that his work contained inaccuracies, for many of the railroaders were Pullman strikers "working under assumed names wherever they [could] get work." As such remarks indicate, the use of assumed names was not only common practice, but also common knowledge. Some foremen knew that the names of individuals in their gangs were only recently adopted, but, out of disdain for the blacklist, they went along with the fiction.[42]

The crushing of the Pullman strike and the hardship that ensued for the defeated men was extraordinary in scope and atypical of the nineteenth-century strike experience of Santa Fe railroaders. The men did win some walkouts. But all workers realized that their jobs and all they entailed were imperiled any time they joined a strike. Why did workers risk such losses? Ideology and economic interest ultimately provided the basis for strikes by impelling labor leaders to action and rallying many followers. However, in any large group of men there were the unconvinced and the faint-hearted. The unevenness of strike activity of different groups of men in various towns during the 1878 and 1894 walkouts suggests that the uncommitted composed a significant body of the American work force; sizable enough that their decisions could account for whether some strikes succeeded or failed. These men eventually committed themselves only after consulting more personal and noneconomic factors. Of these, the opinions and actions of others whose respect and affection an uncertain railroader valued proved critical. Striking was not solely an economic or political action. It was also a social act. Union principles and policies came to life only when small groups of men in dozens or even hundreds of communities decided to follow national orders and urged their coworkers to join them. To be effective, class consciousness and union loyalties had to be reinforced by local personal contacts.

As long as men could be inspired to join in organizations of their fellow employees, the potential for united action persisted. Once identified with their fellow employees in a union, individual calculations of risks and advantages could be transcended by loyalty to one's peers. If the dynamics of peer pressure spelled disaster for tens of thousands of jobholders, it also held the only promise for advance and victory. Class solidarity and union loyalty were fragile abstractions. Only when linked with fraternal feelings for those who labored daily at one's side could notions of the risks of losing one's job be muted and effective worker unanimity achieved.

Conclusion

On a March day in 1900, a few hours after the sun rose over the mountains, a party headed by A. R. Peacock gathered in Los Angeles to board a Santa Fe passenger car. Peacock, an officer of the Carnegie Steel Company, had arranged with the Santa Fe for a special train to run at top speed from the west coast to Chicago. About ten o'clock that morning the train pulled out from the station and began rushing eastward. All along the route other trains were shunted off to sidings to let the special pass. The Arizona desert rolled under the wheels of Peacock's train. Desert was exchanged for mountains as the train rushed up toward New Mexico's Raton Pass. Onward into the Colorado and Kansas flatlands the cars rumbled at increasing speed. After the train crossed the Missouri it whistled its way through substantial towns and cities, preludes to its arrival at the metropolis of the Midwest. Finally, just under fifty-eight hours after Peacock's train began its journey, the special came to a halt in Chicago's Dearborn Station. The average speed had been forty miles per hour, though it had reached nearly twice that rate as it coursed its way across the Plains. The entire excursion set a record as the fastest trip from the Pacific Coast to Chicago, comfortably eclipsing Nelly Bly's record over the same line eleven years earlier.[1]

During the three decades between the road's first seven-mile run to Cottonwood Falls in 1869 and Peacock's joy-ride, Santa Fe employees' work and ways of life reflected much that was common to men in railroading and other industries. Still, as sizable a class of laborers as these southwestern railroaders were, they constituted but a minuscule fraction of the late nineteenth-century working class. Moreover, the way Santa Fe men lived need not have represented in any exact way the lifestyles of those in nonrailroading occupations, or indeed of those railroaders in other sections of the country. Consequently, the following ruminations on labor historiography, even when buttressed by numerous perceptive recent studies, propose; they do not pronounce.

In the past decade it has become popular to differentiate between the old and the new labor history. Until the 1960s most investigations of wage earners focused on their developing class consciousness. This was accomplished by probing the nature of institutions such as unions and political parties. Not only was this methodology a convenient approach to summarizing the sentiments of millions of men and women, but it offered the most direct evidence on union leaders' ideology and the workers' effectiveness in translating their wishes into corporate concessions and political power.[2]

Since the 1960s another type of labor history has come into prominence that, while retaining a strong interest in class, highlights communities of workers grouped by skill level, social status, or occupation. This approach is more fitting to the questions concerning workers' off-the-job lives and their relations with the wider community that so intrigue current investigators. Because of many overlapping interests, the dichotomy between the old and the new labor history may easily be exaggerated. Yet in general the newer studies contrast with the old in concentrating on individual workers instead of institutions, culture rather than class, and worker relations with the community as well as with the company.

While accepting some of the basic assumptions of the old labor history, this work, along with other contributions of the newer school, modifies the traditional portrait of labor-management relations. The dominant theme voiced by John R. Commons and his students has been the development of "business" unionism to gain for workers a fair proportion of the rewards of their labor. In this view unions were primarily economic institutions. They were opposed by an equally economically conscious management. In the grips of bitter competition, managers strove to minimize costs and maximize profits. They spent as little as they could on workers, raising wages only when forced to by unions. Unions, consequently, suffered corporate America's nearly universal enmity.[3]

The dedication of railroad brotherhoods to bread-and-butter unionism is beyond question. Santa Fe unions struck and were quite successful in drawing up contracts to gain better pay and working conditions. They were conservative craft organizations interested in their own economic well-being, not that of the entire working class. The shopmen, operators, trackmen, enginemen, and trainmen each struck separately, but those outside their unions continued to work. Even within craft lines there was occasional discord, as in the fight over seniority between brakemen and conductors.

However, the old labor history's view of unions from the top down distorted the sentiments of many workers. Its preoccupation with institutional studies largely begged the question of how representative the statements of the leaders were of the membership.[4] How universal was the belief in bread-and-butter craft unionism? The history of the Santa Fe brotherhoods shows the national leadership to have been both too conservative and too militant for portions of their membership. On the one hand, although craft unionism predominated, Santa Fe men of all skills rallied to Eugene Debs' American Railway Union and joined other railroaders throughout the West in protest over the condition of a few thousand factory workers in Pullman, Illinois. And, on the other hand, workers sometimes displayed a more cautious attitude than their top union leadership. Leaders of the national railroad unions spoke out against piecework and would forcefully promote federal legislation on hours shortly after the turn of the century. However, some Santa Fe employees willingly accepted piecework, and a majority had no strong urge to reduce their hours of employment. Moreover, while national leaders expressed the hope that farmers and laborers might unite in common political cause, Kansas railroaders held to the narrower view that linked their interests, not to the laborers of the fields, but to their own capitalist employers. It is a simple point, yet one too often overlooked in institutional studies, that any union in order to be effective had to gather within its membership men of disparate opinions on even the basic issues of working-class life.[5]

Just as significantly, with the exception of Robert Hoxie and Frank Tannenbaum, old-school labor scholars understated the importance of the social aspects of unionism. Recent historians, such as E. P. Thompson, Eric Hobsbawm, and Herbert Gutman, in their emphasis on studying the culture of the working class, have pointed the way toward the recognition of a broader role for unions.[6] For most Santa Fe employees the brotherhoods provided important social functions. Indeed, the social role was probably more in evidence in the membership's everyday experience than were the unions' economic responsibilities. Railroad labor organizations were known for their exceptional interest in insurance and moral uplift programs. Nevertheless, they were far from unique. Workers as diverse as western miners and New York City printers also expressed grassroots support for similar projects.[7] From the perspective of labor organizers, such benefits were inducements to attract a large membership and maintain broad support during strikes. But for much of the rank and file, the fraternal functions were assumed as both integral to the union and highly desirable.

The union was a social institution, not solely because it provided insurance and entertainment, encouraged moral behavior, and assisted traveling members, but also because it was so easily associated with the community of workers. As Tannenbaum stated, unions reflected "the moral identity and psychological unity men always discover when working together."[8] Santa Fe men valued the acceptance by their peers signified by admittance to the local lodge. Because no large association could hope for ideological unity, the emotional ties implicit in the lodge proved of great importance when brotherhood leaders tried to affect a strong unified front. It was the associations and friendships initiated on the job that helped create workers' organizations, and it was these emotional bonds that formed an essential ingredient in uniting men in a single cause during strikes.

Historians of all schools have recognized the inherently antagonistic interests of employers and employees. Santa Fe management did resist pay increases, cut labor costs when corporate finances required, and attempt to maximize control of workers in the interest of greater efficiency. Yet for railroaders several factors mitigated what might have been an oppressive atmosphere of subjugation, exploitation, and resentment. Unlike the old labor historians' portrait of rampant mechanization devaluing skilled labor, there were few disruptive technological advances in railroading through most of the nineteenth century. Moreover, because the demands on their labor ebbed and flowed both with the season and, at least for many, with the arrival and departure of trains, nineteenth-century railroaders worked in something akin to the loosely structured and less intense manner labeled "traditional" by Peter Stearns.[9] Since men were accustomed to this rate of effort, they were generally contented with it, despite its demands for periods of arduous toil and long hours on the job.

Most significantly, and most unlike labor in any other industry, railroaders' distance from supervisors provided them with a degree of autonomy similar to that described by David Montgomery as an attribute of much work before scientific management.[10] Employees in track sections, flag stations, cabooses, and road engines escaped close supervision. It was not that management did not try. Officials used rule books, spotters, collectors, and Dutch clocks to control employee behavior. But they could only directly supervise their workers in the major shops, stations, and yards.

The impetus for strife was also lessened on the Santa Fe and numerous other roads because they instituted policies for peaceful coexistence with their workers. Contrary to the underlying theme of most labor histories, old and new, the Santa Fe showed itself willing to accept unionization, even if management would fight when it could to prevent "dictation" by the brotherhoods. In matters of seniority and discipline, unions and top managers could cooperate in narrowing the prerogatives of local company authorities. The corporation also took steps on its own to curb arbitrary rule by lower officers and initiated programs to help attract and retain worthy employees. Besides its own occasional fiscal weakness, the problem of turnover, and the paucity of housing, hospitals, and wholesome diversions—problems shared by other industries—railways had the special challenge of gaining loyal service where the scattering of laborers made strict discipline unrealistic. Because of this there can be no claim that the railroads' paternalism was in any way typical. Nevertheless, as Stuart Brandes has pointed out, the Santa Fe's activities were exemplary of an important, if modest, movement among American manufacturers that is too often overlooked by labor scholars.[11]

The fraternal aspects of the Santa Fe brotherhoods and the company's paternalism together pointed to the potential, at least within the railroad industry, for a less antagonistic industrial environment; one which recognized man as a multifaceted social being. However, such a development became impossible with the emergence of scientific management and twentieth-century inflation. The Santa Fe experience lends support to Daniel Nelson's contention that rationalization of labor management could benefit workers by freeing them from unfair treatment by lower-level bosses. But at the same time revolutionary industrial innovations disrupted the old ways railroaders had done their tasks. On the Santa Fe these innovations began in the late 1890s, with heavier engines, piecework, double heading, medical examinations, and black porters.[12] As a result, embittered railwaymen increased their agitation for laws to control relations with their employers, and there were signs of growing militancy in the brotherhoods. And just as scientific management became a perennially disruptive force for workers in and out of railroading, so too was the shift to an inflationary economy. The pressure of rising prices compelled employees to ask for higher wages; these requests naturally were resisted by all businesses, but maybe even more so by railroads, whose profits increasingly were jeopardized by progressive legislation and the introduction of the automobile.[13]

The new labor history, which frequently is hardly distinguishable from recent work in social history, has introduced some novel questions. Among the most important of these is the impact of ethnicity and class on relations in a community. Ethnic loyalties have been shown to have had an inconsistent impact on working-class unity and effectiveness. When the labor force was not ethnically divided, local cultural institutions and associations bolstered employee unity. However, if management employed diverse and antagonistic national groups, it proved difficult for union leaders to get workers to act in concert against the employer.[14] Compared with the work force in eastern cities, the Santa Fe offered less opportunity to examine these factors because of the latter's relative ethnic homogeneity. Still, the familiar promise and problem of ethnicity also appeared in the Southwest. Mexican-Americans composed the majority of New Mexico track laborers. When they twice quit work in the early 1890s, their White Cap actions were as much cultural protests against the Anglo disruption of their society as they were strikes. This Chicano rebellion, reinforced by vigilante terrorism, won a rare victory for unskilled men on the Santa Fe. However, the Chicano-Anglo division also undercut workers' strength. During the Pullman boycott Mexicans remained at their jobs, and in other conflicts the railroad hired Chicanos as special strike-breaking police.[15]

When communities were not divided by national origins, they could be cut by class. The case of Emporia reinforces the argument of those who have found class divisions, even in small cities.[16] Residential patterns and the rosters of social clubs reflected this division. The reactions of towns to strikes of Santa Fe employees adds greater dimension to an understanding of community, particularly as it affected working-class power. Herbert Gutman, in several articles that helped introduce the new labor history, contended that, unlike large cities, small towns possessed a democratic egalitarian ideology that rendered them sympathetic to strikes by local workers. Subsequent writers have multiplied the known instances in which small towns supported local workers. However, they found that this backing rested largely on the economic, political, and (at least potential) physical power the mass of strikers could exert on local businessmen and politicians.[17] This Santa Fe history postulates a more elaborate explanation. Most of those instances of local support revealed in other studies came in municipalities in which the striking laborers composed over a third of the population; in Gutman's example of the Braidwood, Illinois, coal strike more than two-thirds of the town's employed males worked in the mines.[18] Economic and political strength necessitated local sympathy for workers. In towns in which railroaders did not predominate, support was less assured. Inhabitants of small villages of three thousand or fewer stood behind fellow residents out of affection. However, larger towns, such as Emporia after 1880, were split by class and divided in their reaction. The working class backed the strikers as members of their working-class community, but the dominant economic and political leaders ensured that the town as a whole gave no substantive assistance to rebellious employees. Clearly this model requires elaboration. However, it is presented here as a basis for further testing and refinement.

Labor historians, old and new, have contributed much to our understanding of the common people who invested their lives in the construction of modern industrial society. The lives of workers can only be given their proper significance when they are related to the overarching issues of class and community. Still, there is also a place and a value to the narrative history of the innocuous happenings of the everyday lives of everyday people. Therefore, the very human working-class experience on the Santa Fe must include "Dad" McKanna passing out cigars when his repaired engine emerged from the shop, Jack Meierdick's daily six-mile trek between the Florence station and his rural farm, Tom Foley's drinking spree and "El Paso Special," and George Hill's sacrifice of a promotion to a passenger run in order to have more time with his family. These incidents were not earthshaking matters. Yet they were an important part of the whole fabric of the nineteenth-century railroading experience.

Appendix

The following is a roster of most of the census job descriptions included in each classification which are not self-evident.

Railroaders

Santa Fe officials: trainmasters, master mechanics, roadmasters, yardmasters

Foremen and skilled: all foremen except track foremen, machinists, boilermakers, railroad blacksmiths, railroad carpenters, car inspectors, engine inspectors, car repairers, railroad painters

Shop laborers: hostlers, wipers, cinder shovelers, fire pullers, shop workers, roundhouse workers

Yard and station men: switchmen, flagmen, yardmen, callers, baggagemen, car cleaners, railroad janitors

Railroad laborers: railroad men, railroad employees, works for Santa Fe

Nonrailroaders

Business elite: in 1880, 1885, and 1895, those people from small businessmen and small craft businessmen categories who were in the top 15 percent of this combined group in terms of their personal estate or real estate assessment. For 1900 the business elite is defined as businessmen who were in the top 20 percent of the same groups in personal estate assessment and who owned their homes.

Professionals: clergy, doctors, lawyers, dentists, civil engineers, architects

Small businessmen: merchants and store owners in businesses that did not require a craft skill; bankers; hotel keepers; restaurateurs; saloon keepers; keepers of livery stables; stock dealers; grain dealers; real estate agents; newspaper editors; contractors; manufacturers; traveling salesmen

Small craft businessmen: craftsmen whose skill was frequently associated with running one's own shop or store rather than working outdoors or for someone else; barbers; tobacconists; photographers; confectioners; bakers; butchers; druggists; watchmakers; gunsmiths; opticians; tailors; shoemakers; cabinetmakers

Craftsmen: carpenters, painters, masons, plasterers, printers, harness makers, bridge builders, music teachers, millers, broom makers, tinsmiths, undertakers, gardeners, telegraph operators, cigar makers, veterinary surgeons, plumbers, wagon makers, tanners, stationary engineers, paper hangers, book binders, electricians, compositors, decorators, foundry men, cider makers, handymen

Government employees: mayors, mail agents, teachers, sheriffs, policemen, county surveyors, mail carriers, judges, county treasurers, city assessors, registers of deeds, city clerks

Clerks and salesmen: bank tellers, clerks, bookkeepers, stenographers, grocery salesmen, clothing salesmen

Menial service jobs: cooks, janitors, dishwashers, hotel waiters, porters, laundrymen, bartenders, bellboys, servants, delivery boys, messengers, waiters, butlers

Physical unskilled: teamsters, draymen, drivers, laborers, coal men, well diggers, lumberyard workers, bus drivers, expressmen, miners, freighters, stock drovers, house movers, lumbermen, hod carriers

Notes

Abbreviations

AT & SF	Atchison, Topeka & Santa Fe
BLE	Brotherhood of Locomotive Engineers
BL & IS	Kansas Bureau of Labor and Industrial Statistics
IAM	International Association of Machinists
IBB	International Brotherhood of Blacksmiths
LEJ	*Locomotive Engineers' Journal*
LFM	*Locomotive Firemen's Magazine*
NBBM	National Brotherhood of Boilermakers
ORC	Order of Railway Conductors
RC	*Railway Conductor*
RT	*Railroad Telegrapher*
RTJ	*Railroad Trainmen's Journal*
SFM	*Santa Fe Magazine*
SJ	*Switchmen's Journal*
SMAA	Switchmen's Mutual Aid Association

Preface

1. Alfred D.Chandler, Jr., *The Visible Hand*, p.204; U.S. Department of the Interior, Census Office, *Report on the Agencies of Transportation in the United States*, 47th Cong., 2d sess., 1883, p. 13; Albert Fishlow, "Productivity and Technological Change in the Railroad Sector, 1840– 1910," p. 613; U.S. Department of the Interior, Bureau of the Census, *Compendium of the Tenth Census*, 1378–89.

Chapter 1

1. Useful general histories of the company are James Marshall, *Santa Fe: The Railroad That Built an Empire*; L.L.Waters, *Steel Trails to Santa Fe*; and Keith L.Bryant, Jr., *History of the Atchison, Topeka and Santa Fe Railway*.

2. *Topeka Commonwealth*, August 21, 1869; William S.Hinckley, *The Early Days of the Santa Fe*, p.45; Payrolls, 1874, AT & SF Collection, Kansas State Historical Society, Topeka, Kansas; U.S. Department of the Interior, *Agencies of Transportation*, p. 13; *Newton Kansan*, August 22, 1922; List of Buildings, 1884, Microbox 727, AT&SF; *La Junta, Colorado*, p.2; Tom Macrae, "The Development of La Junta," *SFM* 4 (November 1911): 52; Jim F.Heath, "A Study of the Influence of the Atchison, Topeka & Santa Fe Railroad Upon the Economy of New Mexico, 1878 to 1900," pp.56–57; Kansas BL & IS, *Report, 1886*, p.421; *Las Vegas [New Mexico] Daily Optic*, October 22, 1897.

3. *Raton News and Press*, January 21, 1882; *Topeka State Record*, March 24, 1874; *Topeka Daily Capital*, October 17, 1885; *Emporia Gazette*, October 14, 1898.

4. AT & SF, *Rules and Instructions Governing Employes of the Department of Track, Bridges and Buildings* (1883), pp. 3–93, passim (hereafter cited as AT & SF, *Track and B & B Rules 1883*); Joseph Kindelan, *The Trackman's Helper*, pp. 32–210, passim; William J. Pinkerton, *His Personal Record*, pp. 72–73, 215; AT & SF, *Track and B & B Rules, 1892* pp. 5–31, passim.

5. Payrolls, June 1895, AT & SF Collection; *Railway Gazette*, June 1, 1883; *LEJ* 15 (February 1887): 118–20; AT & SF, Accounting Department, *Instructions to Station Freight Agents in Effect August 1st, 1890*, 3–47, passim.

6. *Las Vegas Daily Optic*, May 14, 1885, May 14, 1886; Angus Sinclair, *Locomotive Engine Running and Management*, p. 18; Albuquerque *Daily Citizen*, July 19, 1893; AT & SF, *Rules and Regulations of the Operating Department*, pp. 45–65. Until 1885 on the Atlantic & Pacific and 1891 on the Santa Fe proper, baggagemen also rode in the

train, but in those years management eliminated this class of trainmen when the companies reached contracts with Wells Fargo to have their messengers perform the duty. *Las Vegas Daily Optic*, October 9, 1885; *Raton Range*, August 9, 1891.

7. Payrolls, June 1895, AT & SF, Collection; *Las Vegas Daily Optic*, October 16, 1895; *Topeka Daily Capital*, October 1, 1899. By the end of the century the company also had a tie treatment plant at Purcell, Oklahoma. *Emporia Gazette*, April 8, 1899.

8. BL & IS, *Report, 1886*, p. 421; BL & IS, *Report, 1887*, p. 290; BL & IS, *Report, 1888*, pp. 267–92; Henry Cabot Lodge, "A Perilous Business and the Remedy," p. 190.

9. BL & IS, *Report, 1897*, tables 1 and 6; Stanley Vestal, *Queen of Cowtowns*, pp. 111–14; *Las Vegas Daily Optic*, December 22, 1888.

10. *North Topeka Mail*, January 18, 1883; BL & IS, *Report, 1897*, tables 8 and 9; *Las Vegas Daily Optic*, January 3, 1882, December 26, 1882, November 2, 1896; *R.R. Employes' Companion*, March 1, 1890; *Topeka Daily Capital*, October 17, 1885, July 28, 1892; *La Junta Tribune*, August 3, 1898, February 9, 1898, February 12, 1898; *Emporia Gazette*, April 24, 1894; Benjamin Johnson to Mary C. Johnson, January 3, 1884, Johnson Family Papers, Collection of Regional History, Cornell University, Ithaca, New York; W. Fred Cottrell, *The Railroader*, p. 25.

11. BL & IS, *Report, 1897*, tables 3, 4, 5, 6, and 18; E. D. Worley, *Iron Horses of the Santa Fe Trail*, p. 18; Hinckley, *Early Days*, pp. 23–24; Mrs. Avery Turner, *Avery Turner*, p. 8; *SFM* 8 (December 1913): 29–30; Chauncey Del French, *Railroadman*, p. 38.

12. *Las Vegas Daily Optic*, October 12, 1882, February 12, 1881, March 25, 1882, June 23, 1881, March 24, 1885.

13. Heath, "Influence of the AT & SF," p. 28; *RC* 3 (May 1886): 307; *Newton Evening Kansan*, September 14, 1900, quoting *Topeka Journal*; French, *Railroadman*, pp. 27, 37; *Las Vegas Daily Optic*, November 28, 1898; C. M. Chase, *The Editor's Run in New Mexico and Colorado*, p. 130; *Albuquerque Morning Democrat*, March 12, 1891; Richard Patterson, "Train Robbery," 48–53; *Railway Gazette*, April 20, 1898, May 27, 1898, June 17, 1898, July 29, 1898, August 19, 1898, November 25, 1898.

14. *Albuquerque Evening Democrat*, November 19, 1885; *LFM* 8 (October 1884): 613; *Railway Gazette*, August 15, 1884; *Coolidge Citizen*, April 26, 1889; *Las Vegas Daily Optic*, December 8, 1884, February 20, 1885, May 29, 1885, May 17, 1881; *Newton Evening Kansan*, June 10, 1898, June 22, 1900, July 3, 1899.

15. *Emporia News*, November 16, 1882; Voucher #6249, AT & SF Collection; J. Torr Harmer, "A.T. & S.F. and Leased Lines and Sundry Memos: No. 1," see notes under "Westinghouse Air Brake Co.," J. Torr

Harmer Papers, Baker Library, Harvard University, Boston, Massachusetts; Worley, *Iron Horses*, pp. 23–24; *LEJ* 31 (December 1897): 1076; *Railroad Register* (Topeka), April 30, 1894; *Newton Evening Kansan*, December 17, 1897.

16. Payrolls, June 1895, AT & SF Collection; *Emporia News*, July 28, 1888; *Raton Range*, July 10, 1891.

17. Edward Parson, "Recollections of My Life in New Mexico During the Eighties," *SFM* 14 (May 1920): 26; Heath, "Influence of the AT & SF," pp. 65–67; letter of R. L. Ellzey (Prescott Junction, Arizona) in *RT* 8 (December 1, 1892): 536.

18. *Emporia Gazette*, January 16, 1895; *Argentine Republic*, May 21, 1891; *Railway Gazette*, February 10, 1893; William Pinkerton, *Personal Record*, pp. 116–17; Heath, "Influence of AT & SF," p. 73; *Coolidge Times*, September 20, 1888.

19. French, *Railroadman*, p. 37; *Topeka Commonwealth*, September 3, 1874; *Chanute Blade*, October 28, 1893; *Chanute Daily Tribune*, January 16, 1894; *Capital*, December 23, 1893; *Emporia Gazette*, December 25, 1893.

20. *SFM* 5 (August 1911): 29–32.

21. BL & IS, *Report, 1895*, p. 119; *Albuquerque Daily Citizen*, June 24, 1893; BL & IS, *Report, 1887*, pp. 188–90; BL & IS, *Report, 1888*, pp. 189–90; BL & IS, *Report, 1889*, pp. 8–9; BL & IS, *Report, 1897*, pp. 224–36.

22. Paul V. Black, "Management Personnel Policies on the Burlington Railroad: 1860–1900," pp. 269–313; David Lightner, "Labor on the Illinois Central Railroad, 1852–1900," pp. 156, 158, 220–24, 230, 303, 307–8; BL & IS, *Report, 1898*, p. 170; Payrolls, June 1874, AT & SF, Collection; BL & IS, *Report, 1886*, pp. 116, 352, 355, 432–34; BL & IS, *Report, 1899*, pp. 15–19, 64–66, 102–9, 165–77; U.S. Department of Labor, *Fifteenth Annual Report of the Commissioner of Labor, 1900*, pp. 674, 1283, 1479; U.S. Department of Labor, Bureau of Labor Statistics, *Bulletin #499*, pp. 430–42; *RTJ* 7 (October 1890): 532–33; *RT* 15 (April 1899): 269–71.

23. BL & IS, *Report, 1886*, p. 355; *Emporia News*, July 27, 1877.

24. *Railway Gazette*, November 16, 1888; August 22, 1890; BL & IS, *Report, 1892*, pp. 9–10; BLE, *Official Report of Agreements Made Between the Officials of the Roads Represented and the Committees Representing the Engineers Employed Thereon, as reported prior to April 1st, 1898*, pp. 34–35; Payrolls, 1893–1898, AT & SF Collection.

25. Pension lists and "Employes Long in the Service" columns in *SFM* 1–10 (1906–16).

26. *Newton Evening Kansan*, September 28, 1897, quoting *Sterling Bulletin*; *SFM* 8 (March 1914): 63.

27. Pension lists and "Employes Long in the Service" columns in *SFM* 1–10 (1906–16).

28. *SFM* 8 (November 1914): 52 and 10 (August 1916): 47–48; Frank Cunningham, *Big Dan,* p. 167.

29. *R.R. Employees' Companion,* November 30, 1889; *Hamilton County Bulletin,* October 10, 1890; *Newton Evening Kansan,* July 9, 1900; *Emporia Gazette,* January 5, 1893; *Newton Kansan,* August 22, 1922.

30. *Las Vegas Daily Optic,* June 23, 1896, March 25, 1898; *Raton Gazette,* May 19, 1898, November 22, 1900.

31. *Las Vegas Daily Optic,* June 30, 1886, May 13, 1886, June 19, 1886; *Newton Evening Kansan,* December 5, 1899, May 6, 1900, May 7, 1900; *Emporia Gazette,* May 29, 1900.

32. *Las Vegas Daily Optic,* June 29, 1892; Cunningham, *Big Dan,* p. 167; *SFM* 8 (March 1914): 63. The survey of the two columns in *SFM* reveals the pull of California, especially among stationmen and shopmen.

33. BL & IS, *Report, 1885,* p. 262; BL & IS, *Report, 1899,* pp. 15–19, 60–63; *RT* 16 (April 1899): 269–71.

34. Heath, "Influence of the AT & SF," pp. 60–61; *Las Vegas Daily Optic,* October 18, 1889, March 21, 1896; William J. Cunningham, "Scientific Management in the Operation of Railroads," p. 553.

35. BL & IS, *Report, 1891,* p. 42.

36. *Las Vegas Daily Optic,* January 5, 1886; BL & IS, *Report, 1891,* p. 48; AT & SF, *Rules and Regulations of the Operating Department,* pp. 46, 60, 64.

37. *Newton Evening Kansan,* August 10, 1897, June 4, 1897; *Topeka Daily Capital,* October 5, 1899; *Las Vegas Daily Optic,* September 28, 1887, May 21, 1895, May 11, 1897; *Newton Kansan,* December 2, 1897, citing *Wellington Journal;* letter of "Handy Andy" (Arkansas City) in *Neodesha Register,* February 10, 1893; letter of Irene J. (Arkansas City) in *LFM* 15 (November 1891): 1001.

38. Cottrell, *Railroader,* pp. 71–72; *Las Vegas Daily Optic,* January 5, 1886; letter of "Chio" (Topeka) in *RTJ* 5 (June 1888): 304; letter of C.C. Reynolds (Raton) in *LEJ* 20 (May 1892): 420–21.

39. BL & IS, *Report, 1897,* pp. 224–36; *Newton Evening Kansan,* March 19, 1898, April 30, 1898; *Las Vegas Daily Optic,* March 23, 1898.

40. *Newton Evening Kansan,* March 25, 1898, quoting the *Topeka Journal;* Hinckley, *Early Days,* p. 30; *Railway Gazette,* November 16, 1888; *Raton Range,* November 9, 1888; *Las Vegas Daily Optic,* October 14, 1889; James E. Wright, *The Politics of Populism,* pp. 166–67; *Railroad Register,* May 12, 1893, July 7, 1893; *Topeka Daily Capital,* July 2, 1893; Payrolls, 1893 and 1895, AT & SF Collection.

41. *Topeka Daily Capital*, September 16, 1892; M. J. Drury, "Reminiscences of an Old-Timer in the Mechanical Department," *SFM* 11 (March 1917): 21; Worley, *Iron Horses*, p. 20; *Optic*, March 23, 1885; letter of "A New Spark Arrester," (Topeka) in *Railroad Register*, May 26, 1893; BL & IS, *Report, 1890*, p. 134; BL & IS, *Report, 1891*, pp. 48–49.

42. *Newton Evening Kansan*, July 5, 1898, July 25, 1898, January 9, 1899, February 3, 1899; *Emporia Gazette*, January 8, 1892; BL & IS, *Report, 1899*, pp. 15–19, 60–63; Heath, "Influence of the AT & SF," pp. 67–68.

43. *Las Vegas Daily Optic*, July 7, 1884, July 11, 1884, July 29, 1884, August 21, 1880, August 5, 1886, January 19, 1886, January 22, 1891; anonymous letter from Woodward, I.T. in *Neodesha Register*, May 27, 1892; Vestal, *Queen of Cowtowns*, p. 263; *Emporia News*, January 11, 1886.

44. Kindelan, *Trackman's Helper*, pp. 32–33, 60–61, 168–69; 177–78; *Argentine Republic*, July 11, 1889; *Las Vegas Daily Optic*, May 7, 1888, November 22, 1896; *Newton Evening Kansan*, March 22, 1900. Measures of seasonality are calculated from an analysis of the gross pay by month, department, and division recorded in the payrolls for 1895 and 1900 and for the engineers for the period September 1878 to August 1879.

45. AT & SF, *Annual Report (1876)*, p. 29; AT & SF, *Fifth Annual Report*, p. 36. Spring cattle rush traffic level is estimated on the basis of engine and train service payroll figures for the effected divisions.

46. Seasonality data (see n. 44); *Las Vegas Daily Optic*, October 26, 1896.

47. *Railway Gazette*, October 19, 1888; *Topeka Daily Capital*, January 7, 1891, February 7, 1892; *Raton Range*, May 7, 1896; *Las Vegas Daily Optic*, March 11, 1898; seasonality data (see n. 44).

48. *Chanute Blade*, July 16, 1891; seasonality data (see n. 44); letter of Mike Considine (Newton) in *Railroad Register*, January 12, 1894; *Newton Evening Kansan*, October 26, 1900; *Albuquerque Morning Democrat*, June 13, 1891.

49. U.S. Department of the Interior, *Statistics of the Population of the United States: Tenth Census*, pp. 735, 737; U.S. Department of the Interior, Census Office, *Eleventh Census of the United States*, 1890, 1:312–15, 324–37.

Chapter 2

1. *RTJ* 12 (May 1895): 418–19; AT & SF, *Track and B & B Rules, 1883*, p. 72; Walter M. Licht, "Nineteenth Century Railwaymen," pp. 59–60.

2. Hinckley, *Early Days*, pp. 15, 34, 44; *Topeka State Record*, August 2, 1871; Bryant, *History of the AT & SF*, p. 14; Henry V. Poor, *Manual of the Railroads of the United States: 1869–70*, p. 416.

3. Hinckley, *Early Days*, p. 15; *SFM* 2 (February 1908): 150; *Topeka Commonwealth*, August 21, 1869; Payrolls, June 1874, June 1879, June 1895 (middle division only), June 1896, AT & SF Collection.

4. Black, "Personnel Policies," p. 193; Licht, "Nineteenth Century Railwaymen," pp. 80–94; Anthony to W. B. Strong, April 11, 1878, Governor George T. Anthony Papers, Kansas State Historical Society.

5. *Albuquerque Evening Democrat*, October 21, 1885, October 22, 1885, November 5, 1885; *The Biographical Directory of the Railway Officials of America for 1887*, pp. 276–77.

6. *Newton Evening Kansan*, January 18, 1900; *Topeka Daily Capital*, January 18, 1900, January 19, 1900; Cunningham, *Big Dan*, pp. 161–63, 179.

7. *Argentine Republic*, May 3, 1888, quoting *Galesburg [Illinois] Republican*; *Las Vegas Daily Optic*, May 10, 1888.

8. M. J. Drury, "Reminiscences," p. 19; *Las Vegas Daily Optic*, January 12, 1891; *Railway Gazette*, December 21, 1900; Cunningham, *Big Dan*, p. 181.

9. *Optic*, October 7, 1882; February 7, 1899; Payrolls, June 1900, AT & SF Collection; J. C. Rockhold, "Passing of the Indian Sectionman," *SFM* 3 (June 1909): 743–49; *Raton Range*, June 28, 1900.

10. *Lebo Courier*, July 12, 1889; *SFM* 18 (June 1924): 40 and 20 (February 1926): 32; *Las Vegas Daily Optic*, May 7, 1888, May 10, 1888, May 31, 1888; *Newton Evening Kansan*, September 8, 1900. For the Italian worker recruitment system, see Humbert S. Nelli's *Italians in Chicago 1830–1930*, pp. 56–66.

11. BL & IS, *Report, 1900*, p. 27; William Pinkerton, *Personal Record*, p. 147; *Railroad Register*, March 24, 1893; *Neodesha Register*, February 12, 1892; *Newton Evening Kansan*, June 8, 1898.

12. *Atchison Daily Champion*, April 5, 1878; *Las Vegas Daily Optic*, August 15, 1890; *Topeka Daily Capital*, April 20, 1893, April 21, 1893, April 22, 1893, April 23, 1893; Donald L. McMurry, "Labor Policies of the General Managers' Association of Chicago, 1886–1894," p. 171; *Albuquerque Daily Citizen*, August 7, 1894.

13. *Albuquerque Daily Citizen*, August 18, 1890, August 26, 1890; *Las Vegas Daily Optic*, August 16, 1890; *Topeka Daily Capital*, April 22, 1893.

14. *Emporia News*, July 28, 1888; *Chanute Blade*, April 27, 1893; *Emporia Daily Republican*, July 7, 1894.

15. *Las Vegas Daily Optic*, July 25, 1894; *Raton Range*, July 6, 1894.

16. Timetable 1868, AT & SF Collection; AT & SF, *Rules and Reg-*

ulations for Conductors; AT & SF, Rules and Instructions for the Information and guidance of Employes in the Telegraph Department, (hereafter cited as Telegraph Rules); Track and B & B Rules 1883, AT & SF, Accounting Department, Instructions to Station Freight Agents. Three dissertations on American railroads and their laborers contain discussions of discipline policies similar to those of the Santa Fe: Lightner, "Labor on the Illinois Central," pp. 102–18, 161–62, 183–86, 246–52, 349–55; Black, "Personnel Policies," pp. 429–525; Licht, "Nineteenth Century Railwaymen," pp. 109–75.

17. AT & SF, Track and B & B Rules 1883, pp. 8–9; Time Table No. 37, AT & SF; AT & SF, Rules and Regulations of the Operating Department, p. 44.

18. AT & SF, Telegraph Rules, pp. 7, 11; Time Table No. 37, AT & SF Collection; Las Vegas Daily Optic, July 23, 1888, June 1, 1885; AT & SF, Rules and Regulations of the Operating Department, pp. 48–51, 54.

19. AT & SF, Telegraph Rules, p. 23; AT & SF, Track and B & B Rules 1892, pp. 13–25; Albuquerque Daily Citizen, February 20, 1892.

20. Albuquerque Evening Democrat, March 3, 1886; U.S. Interstate Commerce Commission, Evidence Taken by the Interstate Commerce Commission in the Matter of Proposed Advances in Freight Rates by Carriers, 61st Cong., 3d sess., 1911, pp. 2626–29; Cunningham, "Scientific Management," pp. 553–55; AT & SF, Track and B & B Rules 1892, pp. 5, 11–12, 22; Harvey County News, April 11, 1878; Topeka Daily Capital, October 17, 1885, June 4, 1911.

21. Las Vegas Daily Optic, January 7, 1895, August 7, 1890, January 15, 1891, October 7, 1884, March 23, 1886, June 21, 1888; Railway Gazette, June 26, 1891; RTJ 7 (October 1890): 553; Raton Range, February 21, 1895; Argentine Republic, December 20, 1894; Emporia Gazette, April 9, 1895; Heath, "Influence of the AT & SF," p. 75.

22. Topeka Daily State Journal, April 22, 1884; Albuquerque Morning Democrat, November 17, 1891; Heath, "Influence of the AT & SF," pp. 60–61; LEJ 31 (October 1897): 895.

23. Las Vegas Daily Optic, May 17, 1886; French, Railroadman, p. 46; SFM 2 (April 1908): 308.

24. Railway Gazette, December 16, 1881, July 28, 1893; Las Vegas Daily Optic, September 2, 1896; Raton Range, July 22, 1897.

25. Albuquerque Morning Journal, October 5, 1882; Newton Evening Kansan, July 15, 1899; Topeka Daily Capital, September 29, 1897, December 17, 1899; Las Vegas Daily Optic, January 31, 1893; Albuquerque Daily Citizen, August 19, 1892; Raton Range, February 2, 1893, February 16, 1893; Trinidad Daily News, April 29, 1893, September 29, 1893; Railway Gazette, February 3, 1893, February 10, 1893, October 6, 1893; Colorado v. Perry D. Ageter and William Gossett, Criminal Ac-

tions Nos. 2517–21, Las Animas Co. Court Records; *Colorado v. N. T. West*, Criminal Actions No. 2525, Las Animas Co. Court Records; *Colorado v. K. R. Goff and wife*, Criminal Actions No. 2526, Las Animas Co. Court Records.

26. *Las Vegas Daily Optic*, November 2, 1887, June 12, 1888, June 22, 1888, February 5, 1889; *Emporia News*, December 30, 1886; *Argentine Republic*, February 9, 1888; *Railway Gazette*, February 1, 1889, July 17, 1891; *RC* 4 (March 1887): 154 and 8 (November 1891): 607.

27. *Las Vegas Daily Optic*, December 14, 1888; May 8, 1891, January 28, 1895; Allan Pinkerton, *Tests on Passenger Conductors Made by the National Detective Agency*, p. 4; A. R. Glazier, "Reminiscences of an Old-Timer," *SFM* 11 (July 1917): 44; *Emporia Gazette*, April 19, 1895; *RC* 17 (October 1900): 717; *Newton Evening Kansan*, July 5, 1897, February 2, 1899; *Albuquerque Morning Journal*, March 24, 1882.

28. William Higgins to Hubbell, November 29, 1884; Barr to Hubbell, December 1, 1884, December 31, 1884, William O. Hubbell Papers, Kansas State Historical Society, Topeka, Kansas.

29. Hubbell to Barr, December 10, 1884; Hubbell to Barr, December 12, 1884; Hubbell to Barr, December 16, 1884; Hubbell to Barr, December 27, 1884, Hubbell Papers. All letters by Hubbell are drafts of letters that he presumably sent.

30. Letter of C (Dodge City) in *RC* 16 (February 1899): 156; *Las Vegas Daily Optic*, October 21, 1881, April 3, 1891, September 14, 1897; *Railway Gazette*, December 3, 1870, April 10, 1891; *Newton Kansan*, October 28, 1897; BL & IS, *Report, 1900*, p. 51; *Topeka Daily State Journal*, November 3, 1883.

31. French, *Railroadman*, p. 47; letter of "An Employee" (Nickerson) in *RTJ* 4 (October 1887): 512. The payrolls of the 1890s contain many cases of "mail failure" among stationmen.

32. *Railway Gazette*, August 22, 1890; *Argentine Republic*, December 20, 1894; *Las Vegas Daily Optic*, January 11, 1886, January 15, 1891, June 5, 1895, May 14, 1896.

33. "Circular of July 20, 1897," in possession of author; *Railway Gazette*, October 18, 1895.

34. *Newton Evening Kansan*, July 13, 1897, August 12, 1897, February 14, 1898, February 15, 1898, February 22, 1898; BL & IS, *Report, 1899*, pp. 38, 51; U.S. Industrial Commission, *Report* 17:808.

35. *RC* 14 (August 1897): 565; *RTJ* 14 (November 1897): 998; BL & IS, *Report, 1899*, pp. 8–12, 38, 44, 48, 51.

36. "Circular of July 20, 1897"; *Newton Evening Kansan*, March 17, 1898.

37. AT & SF, *Track and B & B Rules 1883*, p. 10; *RTJ* 7 (January 1890): 25; *Albuquerque Morning Democrat*, January 20, 1891; *Al-*

buquerque *Daily Citizen*, January 19, 1891, February 2, 1891, May 21, 1891.

38. *Topeka Daily Blade*, April 9, 1878; *RTJ* 7 (October 1890): 532–33; *RT* 16 (June 1899): 515, BL & IS, *Report*, *1892*, p. 7; *Capital*, April 25, 1893.

39. BLE, *Report of Agreements*, pp. 30–31; *Las Vegas Daily Optic*, June 7, 1897.

40. Letter of Don Ventura (Winslow) in *RTJ* 9 (October 1892): 722; *Las Vegas Daily Optic*, June 7, 1897; *Albuquerque Daily Citizen*, April 8, 1892; *Newton Evening Kansan*, February 2, 1899; ORC, *Proceedings*, 1891, p. 18; ORC, *Proceedings*, 1893, pp. 23, 32, 35; ORC, *Proceedings*, 1897, p. 18.

41. *Las Vegas Daily Optic*, May 4, 1888; Henry Pelling, *Popular Politics and Society in Late Victorian Britain*, pp. 37–61.

42. *Las Vegas Daily Optic*, July 23, 1892; *Harvey County News*, June 20, 1878, quoting *Sterling [Kansas] Gazette*; *Railway Gazette*, September 10, 1897; *Topeka Daily Capital*, August 11, 1879; *Railroad Register*, July 7, 1893.

43. Lawrence M. Friedman, *A History of American Law*, pp. 412–14; Swarts to Lewelling, July 26, 1894, Governor Lorenzo Lewelling Papers, Kansas State Historical Society, Topeka, Kansas. For a similar study of injury, health, and age-related paternalism, see Licht, "Nineteenth Century Railwaymen," pp. 288–309.

44. *Las Vegas Daily Optic*, January 23, 1889, October 12, 1897.

45. *Argentine Republic*, March 28, 1889; *Kansas City [Kansas] Labor Record*, August 31, 1894; *SFM* 18 (June 1924): 40.

46. *Albuquerque Daily Citizen*, June 23, 1893; *Newton Evening Kansan*, February 9, 1898; *SFM* 8 (February 1914): 55 and 1 (May 1907): 232. Some Santa Fe employees continued in their primary occupations into their seventies. *SFM* 1 (May 1907): 231 and 1 (August 1907): 333.

47. *Raton Guard*, January 27, 1882; *Emporia News*, November 16, 1882.

48. Payrolls, August and September, 1877, AT & SF Collection; *Topeka Daily State Journal*, October 26, 1883, January 30, 1884; *Railway Gazette*, January 11, 1883, March 21, 1884; *Las Vegas Daily Optic*, May 17, 1881; *Albuquerque Morning Journal*, May 18, 1882.

49. *Railway Gazette*, March 30, 1883, January 13, 1893, March 21, 1884; Atchison Railroad Employes' Association, *Charter and By-Laws, and Rules and Regulations*, p. 7; J. M. Meade, "History of the Santa Fe," pp. 19–21, Microbox 372, AT & SF Collection.

50. Atchison Railroad Employes' Association, *Charter*, pp. 4–12; Meade, "History of the Santa Fe," pp. 19–28, AT & SF Collection; *Railroad Register*, April 27, 1894.

51. *RTJ* 13 (March 1896): 178; BL & IS, *Report, 1887,* pp. 179, 189; BL & IS, *Report, 1890,* p. 135; Atchison Railroad Employes' Association, *Charter,* p. 10; BL & IS, *Report, 1886,* p. 368; *Topeka Daily Capital,* March 6, 1892, April 6, 1892; *LFM* 20 (May 1896): 693.

52. *Las Vegas Daily Optic,* October 9, 1885, May 9, 1884, December 1, 1885, December 26, 1885; *San Marcial Reporter,* January 2, 1892; *Albuquerque Daily Citizen,* July 1, 1891; *Topeka Daily Capital,* June 14, 1891; *Newton Evening Kansan,* July 25, 1898; letter of Mrs. C. B. Wellman (Needles) in *LFM* 27 (May 1899): 494.

53. *LEJ* 20 (October 1886): 724; letter of committee of lodge Number 251 (Raton) in *LEJ* 28 (March 1894): 270; *Las Vegas Daily Optic,* January 5, 1886; *Railroad Register,* August 3, 1894; *Railway Gazette,* July 30, 1897; *Emporia Gazette,* May 17, 1899.

54. AT & SF, *Annual Report, 1873,* p. 12; *Las Vegas Daily Optic,* October 27, 1882, May 1, 1882; Edward Parsons, "Recollections of My Life," p. 26; *Raton News and Press,* November 19, 1881.

55. *Raton News and Press,* October 22, 1891, January 21, 1882.

56. *Albuquerque Morning Journal,* June 9, 1882; Dils, *Horny Toad Man,* pp. 22, 42; *Las Vegas Daily Optic,* May 1 1894; *Raton Range,* February 15, 1889; *Albuquerque Morning Democrat,* February 2, 1895; *Raton Gazette,* March 16, 1899.

57. *Raton News and Press,* January 21, 1882; Harmer, "A.T. and S.F. and Leased Lines and Sundry Memos: No. 1," see notes under "Reading Rooms," Harmer Papers; *Railway Gazette,* March 13, 1896; *Las Vegas Daily Optic,* April 3, 1888; *Otero County Eagle,* November 22, 1889; *Argentine Republic,* December 12, 1889.

58. *Emporia Gazette,* April 9, 1900; BL & IS, *Report, 1885,* p. 120; *Emporia Democrat,* March 5, 1884; *Albuquerque Daily Citizen,* June 23, 1893, May 23, 1891; *Argentine Republic,* February 9, 1888; U.S. Department of Labor, *Annual Report of the Commissioner of Labor, 1889,* p. 342; *Las Vegas Daily Optic,* January 30, 1885; S. E. Busser, *The Santa Fe Reading-room System,* p. 4; *LEJ* 34 (December 1900): 799, quoting *Topeka Daily Capital; Otero County Eagle,* November 29, 1889; *R.R. Employes' Companion,* May 18, 1889.

59. *North Topeka Mail,* February 8, 1883; *Railroad Register,* April 7, 1893, June 19, 1893; *Railway Gazette,* November 16, 1883, May 12, 1899.

Chapter 3

1. *San Marcial Reporter,* May 16, 1891, September 7, 1889; *Argentine Republic,* April 9, 1891; Glazier, "Reminiscences," p. 41; Dils,

Horny Toad Man, p. 103; *Emporia Gazette*, February 14, 1900, quoting *Kansas City Journal*.

2. *Railway Gazette*, February 10, 1893; Charles B. George, *Forty Years on the Rail*, pp. 188–94; Frank P. Donovan, Jr., *The Railroad in Literature*, pp. 5–6.

3. BL & IS, *Report, 1897*, p. 223; George, *Forty Years*, p. 164.

4. *Argentine Republic*, April 9, 1891; *Railway Gazette*, March 6, 1885, citing *Medical and Surgical Reporter; Raton News and Press*, January 21, 1882, quoting *St. Louis Republican; Las Vegas Daily Optic*, November 4, 1898, November 4, 1895; *Emporia Gazette*, November 22, 1890, August 8, 1898.

5. *Newton Evening Kansan*, March 12, 1898; *Las Vegas Daily Optic*, March 3, 1891, May 14, 1898; letter of S (Dodge City) in *LFM* 11 (November 1897): 655.

6. *Las Vegas Daily Optic*, February 27, 1891, May 5, 1886; *Emporia Gazette*, July 5, 1895; *Chanute Blade*, January 9, 1891.

7. *Topeka Daily State Journal*, April 30, 1897; *Emporia Gazette*, March 3, 1899, May 5, 1899; *Topeka Daily Capital*, April 14, 1892; *Las Vegas Daily Optic*, May 13, 1897, June 24, 1898; *La Junta Tribune*, August 20, 1898; *Newton Evening Kansan*, September 1, 1898; *Raton Gazette*, May 19, 1898.

8. *R.R. Employes' Companion*, November 9, 1889; Richard Ulric Miller, "American Railroad Unions and the National Railways of Mexico," p. 241; *Las Vegas Daily Optic*, June 17, 1880, May 29, 1897; letter of Teddy (Cleburne) in *RC* 13 (February 1896): 116.

9. Letter of Mark (Kansas City, Missouri) in *SJ* 6 (April 1892): 913; letter of George F. Koote (Trinidad) in *RT* 6 (March 15, 1890): 146; *Albuquerque Daily Citizen*, February 6, 1891; Cunningham, *Big Dan*, p. 181; letter of "Needles" (Needles) in *LFM* 9 (January 1885): 46; *Raton News and Press*, October 29, 1881; E. S. Davis, *Emporia City Directory 1896*. Using the company's payrolls, calculations of persistence have been made for the periods June 1874 to June 1879 for all employees and from June 1895 to June 1900 for all middle division and selected groups of Rio Grande division workers. Some of the middle and Rio Grande divisions' employees of the 1890s who are counted as nonpersisters did remain with the Santa Fe but had changed divisions. However, the number of such persons was very small. None of the workers studied from the middle and Rio Grande divisions' payroll of June 1895 appear to have moved to the other division as of 1900.

10. Letter of "Klondike" (New Mexico) in *RT* 15 (February 1898): 165.

11. Besides the payroll persistence data (see n. 9), two sets of data are

used to derive these statistics. One is based on a linkage of the 1895 and 1900 middle division payrolls. This payroll information is combined with 1895 census data for Nickerson, Dodge, and Emporia, and the 1895 Emporia real estate tax records and city directory. The other data set covers the period 1880 to 1884 and is less reliable since it is more accurately a measure of geographic mobility than of turnover of the company's labor force. In it the 1880 census of Emporia is linked with the city's real estate assessment rolls of that year and the city directory compiled four years later.

12. "Letter of a Station Agent" by "Rox" in *Neodesha Register*, April 29, 1893; *R.R. Employes' Companion*, November 9, 1889.

13. *Albuquerque Daily Citizen*, June 6, 1891; *Las Vegas Daily Optic*, April 27, 1893.

14. Ben Johnson to Mary C. Johnson, January 21, 1885, Johnson Family Papers; National Women's Christian Temperance Union, *Minutes, 1882*, pp. 3, lviii–lxi.

15. Letter of "Hot Springs" (East Las Vegas) in *SJ* 6 (April 1892): 902; *La Junta Tribune*, February 26, 1898.

16. Letter of "Sobriety" (Osawatomie, Kansas) in *LEJ* 24 (April 1890): 275; *Las Vegas Daily Optic*, May 26, 1884.

17. *Topeka Daily State Journal*, November 14, 1883; *Albuquerque Morning Journal*, November 24, 1882; Drury, "Reminiscences," p. 19; French, *Railroadman*, pp. 23–51.

18. Ben Johnson to Charles D. Johnson, September 21, 1884, Johnson Family Papers; *Trinidad Daily News*, January 5, 1881; *Albuquerque Morning Journal*, March 22, 1882, April 12, 1882.

19. Letter of "Three Bachelor Trainmen" in *Albuquerque Daily Citizen*, June 6, 1891; letter of Mrs. M (Chanute) and following note by editor in *RTJ* 15 (December 1891): 1092; *Emporia Gazette*, April 7, 1899; *Albuquerque Daily Citizen*, October 12, 1894; Cunningham, *Big Dan*, p. 171; *Albuquerque Evening Democrat*, October 23, 1885; J. Harvey Reed, *Forty Years a Locomotive Engineer*, passim.

20. *SFM* 2 (October 1907): 419 and 18 (May 1924): 41; *Newton Evening Kansan*, March 22, 1897, September 14, 1900; *La Junta Tribune*, January 5, 1898.

21. *Newton Evening Kansan*, July 7, 1897, quoting *Chanute Tribune*; BL & IS, *Report, 1900*, p. 27.

22. BL & IS, *Report, 1887*, p. 177; BL & IS, *Report, 1897*, pp. 256–337; BL & IS, *Report, 1899*, pp. 14–37.

23. *Emporia Gazette*, June 17, 1895; Ben Johnson to Charles D. Johnson, March 25, 1883, Johnson Family Papers.

24. *Topeka Daily Capital*, August 7, 1879; John Ripley to author, September 4, 1979; *Newton Evening Kansan*, May 6, 1898, May 26,

1898, November 11, 1898, March 30, 1900; *Railroad Register*, June 29, 1894; Cottrell, *Railroader*, p. 73; *Emporia Gazette*, March 15, 1899, May 31, 1899, October 25, 1899.

25. Letter of T. E. D. (Arkansas City) in *LFM* 5 (May 1891): 437; *LFM* 10 (January 1896): 60; *Newton Evening Kansan*, June 12, 1898; *Emporia Gazette*, July 11, 1895; *Las Vegas Daily Optic*, January 15, 1897.

26. *Emporia Gazette*, December 23, 1892, February 8, 1900; letter of L. M. Johnson (Wichita) in *LEJ* 27 (May 1893): 418; letter of Cal Wimberly (Dodge City) in *RC* 15 (October 1898): 706; *Topeka Daily Capital*, January 31, 1900, February 11, 1900; *Newton Evening Kansan*, January 24, 1900, citing *Topeka Daily Capital*.

27. *Las Vegas Daily Optic*, April 4, 1889, April 26, 1889; *Emporia News*, April 8, 1889, June 7, 1889; Carl Coke Rister, *Land Hunger*, pp. 121, 135, 140, 142, 163–64, 213.

28. French, *Railroadman*, p. 24; *Las Vegas Daily Optic*, February 11, 1898, citing *Topeka Journal*; letter of "Pa" (Winslow) in *RC* 17 (June 1900): 428.

29. *Raton Range*, June 7, 1889; A. T. Andreas, *History of the State of Kansas*, p. 779; *Topeka Commonwealth*, May 11, 1876; payroll-census persistence data (see n. 11).

30. *Las Vegas Daily Optic*, December 31, 1879, March 1, 1882, October 27, 1884; *Albuquerque Daily Citizen*, March 7, 1891; *LEJ* 15 (June 1881): 257; *History of the Arkansas Valley, Colorado*, p. 819; letter of "Shack" (Winslow) in *RC* 4 (September 1887): 409; *Emporia Gazette*, April 29, 1899, May 21, 1900; *Emporia News*, January 12, 1879, June 1, 1889; linkage of 1880 census of Emporia with the 1885 city directory.

31. *Las Vegas Daily Optic*, May 27, 1882, March 15, 1884, August 24, 1891; *North Topeka Mail*, January 25, 1883; *Albuquerque Daily Citizen*, December 23, 1891, January 3, 1892; advertisement, *LEJ* 18 (February 1884): 114.

32. *RT* 16 (July 1899): 604–5 and 16 (August 1899): 714; *Las Vegas Daily Optic*, April 13, 1893, September 22, 1893, June 1, 1881, February 1, 1894, May 15, 1894, October 23, 1896, September 3, 1897; *Railroad Register*, June 30, 1893; letter of C. W. B. (Raton) in *RC* 13 (August 1896): 503.

33. *Newton Evening Kansan*, February 28, 1898, citing *Florence Bulletin*; Turner, *Avery Turner*, p. 8; *Railroad Register*, March 24, 1893; *Santa Fe* 1 (March 1899): 3; *Las Vegas Daily Optic*, March 11, 1884, February 23, 1885, December 28, 1887; *Raton Range*, January 30, 1891; *SFM* 2 (April 1908): 308 and 7 (November 1913): 40–41; Andreas, *History of Kansas*, p. 854; *Emporia Gazette*, June 19, 1895, May 17, 1899; *Coolidge Citizen*, June 15, 1888, August 24, 1888; *Newton Evening Kansan*, May 28, 1898, December 5, 1899, May 6, 1900, May 7, 1900.

Chapter 4

1. Coulter and Ramaley, *Historical and Business Review of Emporia, 1880,* pp. 28–29; *A History of the State Normal School of Kansas for the First Twenty-Five Years,* pp. 64–70.

2. U.S. Census 1880 for Emporia, Dodge City, Nickerson; U.S. Special Census 1885 for Las Vegas, San Marcial; Kansas Census 1885 for Emporia, Nickerson; Kansas Census 1895 for Emporia, Arkansas City, Nickerson; U.S. Census 1900 for Emporia, Dodge City, Las Vegas, Raton, San Marcial.

3. *Arkansas City Evening Dispatch,* May 17, 1887; *Raton Guard,* February 17, 1882; *Raton Range,* July 26, 1894.

4. *Coolidge Citizen,* August 1, 1890, December 10, 1886; *Kansas State Gazette and Business Directory: 1878,* p. 586; *Topeka Commonwealth,* October 31, 1878; *Nickerson Argosy,* December 7, 1878, June 21, 1879; *Hamilton County Bulletin,* March 27, 1891, April 3, 1891, May 7, 1891; William E. Connelley, *History of Kansas Newspapers,* p. 201.

5. *Annals of Emporia and Lyon County,* pp. 5, 8, 30–31, 64–65; Kansas State Board of Agriculture, *Report, 1875,* p. 182.

6. *Emporia City Directory, 1877,* passim; *Emporia Gazette,* July 28, 1900; *Emporia News,* November 24, 1879, March 29, 1880, June 23, 1880; *Newton Kansan,* October 7, 1897; Kansas Board of Agriculture, *Report, 1875,* p. 182; U.S. Census 1880 for Emporia.

7. The censuses of 1880, 1885, 1895, and 1900 in conjunction with taxrolls and city directories form the basis for the following demographic study. Data for all working males in Emporia has been gathered for 1880. For 1885 and 1895 all the town's railroaders and all working males in the Third Ward have been recorded, while a sample of about one in five nonrailroaders has been taken from each other ward. For 1900 all railroaders again have been recorded and samples taken of nonrailroaders. Weighting has been used for all the samples to reflect the total employed male population in each ward.

8. Payrolls, June 1874, 1879, 1895, and 1900, AT & SF Collection; BL & IS, *Report, 1889,* p. 326; *Las Vegas Daily Optic,* July 26, 1892; letter of "Klondike" (New Mexico Division) in *RT* 15 (February 1898): 165; letter of an anonymous New Mexico Division Order of Railway Telegrapher member in *RT* 15 (October 1898): 860; letter of N.P.J.(Denver) in *RT* 15 (May 1898): 410; letter of "Cert. 236" (Western Division) in *RT* 15 (December 1898): 1040; *Emporia Gazette,* June 16, 1899.

9. Emporia data (see n. 7).

10. BL & IS, *Report, 1890,* p. 6; BL & IS, *Report, 1886,* p. 421; BL & IS, *Report, 1887,* p. 268; BL & IS, *Report, 1888,* p. 267; BL & IS, *Report, 1889,* p. 337.

11. Merle Curti, *The Making of an American Community*, pp. 55–56.

12. Emporia data (see n. 7).

13. Ibid.

14. Ibid.

15. Ibid., Payrolls, June 1874 and 1879, AT & SF.

16. Emporia data (see n. 7).

17. Anonymous, *RTJ* 8 (Jan. 1891): 14–15; Emporia data (see n. 7).

18. Emporia data (see n. 7).

19. Perlee Burton article from *College Life* in *Emporia Gazette*, March 13, 1897.

20. Ethel Stafford in *Emporia Gazette*, March 27, 1897; "A Railroader's Wife" in *Emporia Gazette*, March 17, 1897; "Engineer's Wife" in *Emporia Gazette*, March 27, 1897; "A Railroad Man's Mother" in *Emporia Gazette*, March 19, 1897; "Ex-RR Man" in *Emporia Gazette*, March 19, 1897.

21. *Emporia City Directory, 1877*, passim; Emporia data (see n. 7).

22. Emporia data (see n. 7).

23. *Annals of Emporia*, p. 99; Emporia data (see n. 7); J. W. Truitt *General City Directory of Emporia, Kansas, 1883*, p. 91.

24. Emporia data (see n. 7).

25. *Emporia News*, February 13, 1883; *Emporia Daily Republican*, February 6, 1885; J. W. Truitt, *General City Directory*, passim; Hosterman and Garner, *The Emporia City Directory for 1885–86*, passim; *Emporia Daily Republican*, December 6, 1884, January 15, 1885; *Emporia News*, December 8, 1885; *Emporia Gazette*, June 1, 1894, March 30, 1895, November 29, 1895; E. S. Davis, *Emporia City Directory 1896*, passim.

26. Thomas Bender, *Community and Social Change in America*, p. 7.

27. Letter of S. E. D. (address not given) in *LEJ* 10 (January 1876): 21–22; Emporia data (see n. 7).

28. See n. 25. The class division in fraternal society membership noted here is in sharp contrast to the contention of Don H. Doyle and Stuart Blumin that voluntary associations served to increase community cohesion. Don Harrison Doyle, *The Social Order of a Frontier Community*, pp. 178–93; Stuart M. Blumin, *The Urban Threshold*, pp. 160–65.

29. The pioneering work pointing to the disintegration of community in the late nineteenth century is Robert H. Wiebe's *The Search for Order, 1877–1920*. More recent important works on community include: Robert H. Wiebe, *The Segmented Society*, and Thomas Bender, *Community and Social Change in America*.

Chapter 5

1. Lewis Atherton, *Main Street on the Middle Border*, pp. 212–14.

2. *Las Vegas Daily Optic*, October 12, 1892, December 9, 1893; *Coolidge Citizen*, April 5, 1889; *Railroad Register*, April 21, 1893; *Albuquerque Morning Democrat*, May 1, 1891; *Raton Range*, April 5, 1894; *Emporia Gazette*, April 5, 1899; *Albuquerque Daily Citizen*, November 25, 1893; *Kansas City Labor Record*, August 31, 1894.

3. *Topeka Daily Capital*, August 7, 1892, November 10, 1892; *Emporia Daily Republican*, November 9, 1892; *Emporia Gazette*, November 6, 1893, April 10, 1897, April 5, 1899.

4. Robert R. Dykstra, *The Cattle Towns*, pp. 361–64; *Emporia Daily Republican*, July 3, 1894; affidavit of John Wallace in *Union Trust Co. of N.Y. (Trustee)* v. *AT & SF RR Co.*, file No. 829, U.S. District Court, New Mexico Territory, 1st Judicial District, Federal Archives and Record Center, Denver.

5. *Topeka Commonwealth*, August 16, 1877, August 23, 1877, September 6, 1877, November 8, 1877.

6. Edith Walker and Dorothy Leibengood, "Labor Organization in Kansas," p. 286; Ben Johnson to Catherine M. Johnson, May 10, 1886, Johnson Family Papers; *Emporia News*, March 23, 1886; Leon R. Fisk, "Workingman's Democracy," pp. 5–10, 282–86, 290–91; William F. Zornow, *Kansas*, pp. 196–97; *Emporia Daily Republican*, May 23, 1886, May 27, 1886; *Emporia News*, May 24, 1886.

7. *Topeka Daily Capital*, February 15, 1891; *LEJ* 25 (June 1891): 544, and 25 (October 1891): 946.

8. *Topeka Daily Capital*, January 13, 1891.

9. *Topeka Daily Capital*, February 7, 1891, February 4, 1891, February 5, 1891, February 6, 1891; letter of W. M. Mitchell in *RC* 8 (December 1891): 645.

10. Kansas Senate, *Journal*, 6th biennial legislature, 1889, passim; Kansas Senate, *Journal*, 7th biennial legislature, 1891, pp. 1, 268, 373, 400, 486, 596, 656, 806, 894; *Topeka Daily Capital*, February 12, 1891, March 6, 1891.

11. *Topeka Daily Capital*, March 6, 1891; *Emporia Gazette*, March 25, 1891; *Neodesha Register*, October 16, 1891; letter of W. M. Mitchell in *RC* 8 (December 1891): 645–46; *LEJ* 25 (May 1891): 461–62.

12. Letter of W. M. Mitchell in *RC* 8 (December 1891): 645; Kansas House, *Journal*, 7th biennial legislature, 1891, pp. 90, 167–68, 216, 623, 713; letter of R. B. Tration (no address given) in *LEJ* 25 (March 1891): 226; *Topeka Daily Capital*, February 4, 1891, February 5, 1891; *RC* 8 (February 15, 1891): 183; *Neodesha Register*, March 13, 1891.

13. Robert Richmond, *Kansas*, pp. 178–79.

14. Kansas Senate, *Journal*, 8th biennial legislature, 1893, pp. 340—42, 499, 555, 924.

15. BL & IS, *Report, 1895*, p. 119; BL & IS, *Report, 1889*, pp. 8—9; BI & IS, *Report 1897*, pp. 224—36; *Topeka Daily Capital*, March 4, 1893, February 13, 1891.

16. *Topeka Daily Capital*, February 9, 1893, February 15, 1893, March 4, 1893.

17. Kansas House, *Journal*, 8th biennial legislature, 1893, pp. 492—96.

18. Kansas House, *Journal*, 9th biennial legislature, 1895; Kansas Senate, *Journal*, 9th biennial legislature, 1895; Kansas House, *Journal*, 10th biennial legislature, 1897; Kansas Senate, *Journal*, 10th biennial legislature, 1897; *LEJ* 31 (May 1897): 428—29.

19. Howard R. Lamar, *The Far Southwest 1846—1912*, pp. 147—48, 176—201.

20. *Weekly New Mexican Review* (Santa Fe), February 9, 1893; *Albuquerque Daily Citizen*, January 20, 1893; New Mexico House, *Journal*, 30th sess., 1893, pp. 84, 219, 247, 300, 304—5; New Mexico Council, *Journal*, 30th sess., 1893, pp. 46, 143, 247; *Las Vegas Daily Optic*, February 1, 1893; *Raton Range*, January 12, 1893, February 9, 1893.

21. *Las Vegas Daily Optic*, February 1, 1893; New Mexico House, *Journal*, 30th sess., 1893, pp. 7—8, 84, 219, 300, 304—5; New Mexico Council, *Journal*, 30th sess., 1893, 7—8, 46, 143.

22. Editorial, *RC* 8 (July 1891): 428; *RTJ* 8 (November 1891): 794—95.

23. *Railroad Register*, July 27, 1894; September 8, 1894; *Emporia Gazette*, June 12, 1894.

24. *Neodesha Register*, 1891—92.

25. *Monthly Balance* 1 (October 1891): 34 and 1 (August 1891): 12.

26. Letter of W. M. Mitchell in *RC* 8 (December 1891): 646.

27. Statement of Newton committee in *RC* 8 (November 1891): 587; *Neodesha Register*, October 16, 1891; *Topeka Daily Capital*, December 7, 1892.

28. *Neodesha Register*, September 2, 1892, May 27, 1892, May 13, 1892, October 14, 1892; *RC* 9 (May 1892): 203; *Las Vegas Daily Optic*, November 30, 1888; *Newton Kansan*, November 1, 1894; *Emporia Gazette*, November 3, 1892; *Chanute Blade*, October 6, 1892; Kansas Board of Railroad Commissioners, *Report, 1892*, pp. 236—38; *Railway Gazette*, May 25, 1894; letter of W. N. Breen (Emporia) in *LFM* 27 (October 1899): 473.

29. U.S. Census 1895 for Emporia, Arkansas City, Peabody, and Nickerson. Because they do not give place of parents' birth, Kansas censuses were not very good indicators of ethnicity. Yet, the birthplace

figures they do give showed no evidence of glaring demographic differences between Nickerson and Peabody or between the railroader wards and the rest of Emporia and Arkansas City.

30. Gubernatorial vote totals cited in: *Emporia Daily Republican,* November 8, 1888, November 5, 1890, November 9, 1892; *Emporia Gazette,* November 9, 1894, November 4, 1896; *Arkansas City Republican Traveler,* November 15, 1888, November 6, 1890, November 10, 1892, November 8, 1894, November 5, 1896; *Hutchinson Democrat,* November 17, 1888; *Nickerson Argosy,* November 6, 1890, November 10, 1892, November 8, 1894, November 5, 1896; *Peabody Gazette,* November 13, 1888, November 13, 1890, November 10, 1892, November 15, 1894, November 12, 1896. Statements on railroader voting must be guarded because there is an "ecological fallacy" in concluding that because certain areas had many railroaders and voted a certain way, the railroaders therefore voted in the majority. However, this study accepts the ward voting data as rough indicators of railroader and nonrailroader partisan preferences. W. S. Robinson, "Ecological Correlations and the Behavior of Individuals," pp. 351–57.

31. Letter of W. M. Mitchell in *RC* 8 (December 1891): 645; gubernatorial vote totals (see n. 30).

32. Louise E. Rickard, "The Impact of Populism on Electoral Patterns in Kansas, 1880–1900," p. 59; gubernatorial vote totals (see n. 30).

33. Rickard, "Impact of Populism," pp. 112, 115; gubernatorial vote totals (see n. 30).

34. Rickard, "Impact of Populism," pp. 112–13; gubernatorial vote totals (see n. 30).

35. Letter of B. B. (Newton) in *LFM* 19 (April 1895): 353–54; letter of "No. 276" (Chanute) in *RTJ* 15 (February 1898): 189.

36. Ibid.; *LFM* 29 (September 1900): 216–18; letter of "Hooker" (Emporia) in *LFM* 27 (October 1899): 675.

37. Letter of J. R. Scates (Arkansas City) in *RC* 16 (November 1899): 891; letter of W. N. Breen (Emporia) in *LFM* 27 (October 1899): 474; letter of "Gas Belt" (Chanute) in *RTJ* 17 (December 1900): 1035; ORC, *Proceedings, 1899,* pp. 29, 36.

Chapter 6

1. Letter of a committee of lodge No. 130 (Topeka) in *LEJ* 10 (March 1876): 132; BL & IS, *Report, 1890,* pp. 79, 137; *Railway Carmen's Journal* 3 (November 1893): 559–68; Leonard Painter, *Brotherhood of Railway Carmen of America,* pp. 40–41; *Railroad Register,* Sept. 8, 1893.

2. *Las Vegas Daily Optic,* March 20, 1885; *Emporia News,* July 27, 1877; *Topeka Commonwealth,* July 27, 1877; *Emporia Ledger,* July 26,

1877; *Neodesha Register,* April 29, 1892; *Railroad Register,* June 30, 1893.

3. *Las Vegas Daily Optic,* February 3, 1886.

4. *Emporia News,* October 30, 1883; *Topeka Daily Capital,* August 6, 1891, August 9, 1891.

5. U.S. Industrial Commission, *Report* 17:822–42; D.W. Hertel, *The History of the Brotherhood of Maintenance of Way Employes,* pp. 24–25; BL & IS, *Report, 1890,* p. 118; BL & IS, *Report, 1897,* pp. 224–35.

6. BLE, *Report of Agreements,* pp. 30–34; *RTJ* 7 (October 1890): 533; *RC* 9 (June 1892): 227; Mark Perlman, *Machinists,* pp. 247–48; *RT* 16 (April 1899): 269–71 and 16 (June 1899): 515.

7. *SJ* 8 (June 1893): 89; *Neodesha Register,* January 27, 1893; letter of a committee of lodge No. 130 (Topeka) in *LEJ* 10 (March 1876): 132; letter of "Correspondent" (Newton) in *RC* 8 (July 1892): 405; *RC* 1 (September 1884): 459; *Emporia Gazette,* November 9, 1900, November 26, 1900; *LEJ* 25 (May 1891): 463 and 25 (October 1891): 958; *Railway Carmen's Journal* 5 (February 1900): 26.

8. Reed C. Richardson, *The Locomotive Engineer, 1863*–1963, p. 196; Dan Mater, "The Development and Operation of the Railroad Seniority System," p. 395; Archibald M. McIsaac, *The Order of Railroad Telegraphers,* p. 7; *Albuquerque Morning Democrat,* December 17, 1891; *Railway Gazette,* December 25, 1891; *Galveston Daily News,* October 20, 1892; Painter, *Brotherhood of Railway Carmen of America,* pp. 40–41.

9. *Emporia Gazette,* May 25, 1898; *Las Vegas Daily Optic,* January 12, 1891; letter of "Hot Springs" (Las Vegas) in *RT* 6 (April 1892): 902.

10. *Emporia Gazette,* October 18, 1892; *Emporia News,* April 12, 1878; *Topeka Daily Blade,* April 9, 1878; *LEJ* 12 (June 1878): 274; BLE, *Report of Agreements,* p. 33.

11. *Railroad Register,* April 28, 1893; BL & IS, *Report, 1892,* p. 150; Payrolls, March–April 1893, AT & SF Collection; *Emporia Gazette,* November 14, 1900.

12. U.S. Bureau of the Census, *Historical Statistics of the United States,* 1:212. In the case of the yardmen, the union may have been more instrumental in maintaining, rather than increasing, wages since most of the hike in switchmen's wages occurred before the formation of the SMAA in 1886. On the other hand the IAM, IBB, and NBBM may have accomplished more for their members than the above indicates because, though their wages dropped in the two-decade period, Kansas survey data indicates that the eight to ten years before 1895, which included the peak of their union activity, saw a rise in average daily pay. BL & IS, *Report, 1885,* p. 262; BL & IS, *Report, 1886,* p. 421; BL & IS, *Report,*

1887, p. 268; BL & IS, *Report, 1888*, p. 267; BL & IS, *Report, 1889*, pp. 336–37.

13. *Harvey County News*, July 26, 1877; *Emporia News*, July 27, 1877; *Emporia Ledger*, April 18, 1878; *Railway Gazette*, November 16, 1888.

14. Mater, "Railroad Seniority," pp. 387, 393–94; *Las Vegas Daily Optic*, November 3, 1888; Chalmers L. Pancoast, "Old Timers of the New Mexico Division," *SFM* 4 (May 1910): 35.

15. *Las Vegas Daily Optic*, December 5, 1889, December 20, 1889, December 21, 1889; letter of "X.Y.Z." in *RC* 13 (April 1896): 269.

16. *RC* 9 (June 1892): 227 and 11 (April 1894): 190) *Las Vegas Daily Optic*, November 7, 1893; *Argentine Republic*, May 3, 1894.

17. Walter Licht, "The Dialectics of Bureaucratization: The Case of Nineteenth-Century American Railwaymen, 1830–1877," paper given at the Convention of the Organization of American Historians, New York City, April 12, 1978, pp. 19–20.

18. *RT* 16 (April 1899): 270–71; Perlman, *Machinists*, p. 254; *RC* 9 (June 1892): 226; ORC, Proceedings, 1897, pp. 11, 16.

19. Letter of "Mikado" (Topeka) in *LEJ* 20 (July 1886): 467.

20. *LFM* 13 (April 1889): 337; William H. Buckler, "The Minimum Wage in the Machinists' Union," in *Studies in American Trade Unionism*, ed. by Jacob H. Hollander and George E. Barnett, p. 134; *RTJ* 10 (September 1893): 751.

21. McIsaac, *Railroad Telegraphers*, pp. 16, 34.

22. Bryant, *History of the AT & SF*, pp. 168–69; AT & SF, *Fifth Annual Report*, pp. 11–13; Albro Martin, *Enterprise Denied*, pp. 59, 94–95.

23. Letter of W. L. G. (Temple) in *LFM* 26 (June 1899): 688; Licht, "Nineteenth Century Railwaymen," pp. 241–42; *La Junta Tribune*, July 13, 1898; letter of "Bon Ami" (East Las Vegas) in *LFM* 27 (October 1899): 446–47.

24. *Emporia Gazette*, February 24, 1899, June 30, 1899, September 11, 1900; *Las Vegas Daily Optic*, January 14, 1899; letter of "Headlight" (Winslow) in *LFM* 27 (July 1899): 110.

25. *Raton Gazette*, July 7, 1898; Bryant, *History of the AT & SF*, pp. 220, 224–25.

26. Letter of "Member" (Needles) in *LFM* 28 (January 1900): 85; *Albuquerque Daily Citizen*, July 19, 1893; *Las Vegas Daily Optic*, April 2, 1897.

27. BL & IS, *Report, 1899*, p. 43; *Las Vegas Daily Optic*, August 12, 1885; *Raton Range*, August 18, 1898, citing *San Marcial Bee*.

28. BL & IS, *Report, 1899*, pp. 38, 44, 48, 51, 54–55; *Emporia*

Gazette, February 1, 1900, March 12, 1900; Newton Evening Kansan, September 10, 1900.

29. Railway Gazette, November 8, 1882, quoting New Orleans Times-Democrat; Paul V. Black, "Personnel Policies," p. 253; William Pinkerton, Personal Record, pp. 15–16.

30. Newton Evening Kansan, February 20, 1899, March 4, 1899; Las Vegas Daily Optic, February 10, 1899.

31. RTJ 16 (April 1899): 371–72; John Stover, The Life and Decline of the American Railroad, p. 71.

32. Emporia Gazette, August 27, 1900; Railway Gazette, November 17, 1899.

33. Newton Evening Kansan, December 6, 1899; letter of "Packing Hook" (Topeka) in Railway Carmen's Journal 6 (May 1901): 121; Topeka Daily Capital, November 22, 1899, December 13, 1899, December 31, 1899; Newton Evening Kansan, November 22, 1899, April 5, 1900; Railway Carmen's Journal 5 (July 1900): 133–35; Monthly Journal 9 (May 1897): 139–40; Carl Russell Graves, "Scientific Management and the Santa Fe Railway Shopmen of Topeka, Kansas, 1900–1925," pp. 66–67, 128–32.

34. Albuquerque Morning Democrat, July 4, 1891.

35. Letter of "Pa" (Winslow) in RC 17 (June 1900): 429; RTJ 17 (November 1900): 959–63; BL & IS, Report, 1899, pp. 43, 54; letter of W. W. Beebe (Las Vegas) in RTJ 17 (July 1900): 595; RC 17 (March 1900): 192 and 17 (June 1900): 415.

Chapter 7

1. Philip Taft, "Theories of the Labor Movement"; Mark Perlman, Labor Union Theories in America; Thomas A. Kreuger, "American Labor Historiography, Old and New"; Melvyn Dubofsky, Industrialism and the American Worker, 1865–1920; David Brody, "The Old Labor History and the New." The social and psychological importance of unions emphasized in this chapter have been explored by Robert H. Hoxie in A History of Trade Unionism in the United States, Frank Tannenbaum in The Labor Movement: Its Conservative Functions and Social Consequences and A Philosophy of Labor, E. P. Thompson in The Making of the English Working Class, and Herbert Gutman in "Work, Culture and Society in Industrializing America, 1815–1919."

2. BL & IS, Report, 1890, pp. 132–36; BL & IS, Report, 1898, pp. 101, 113, 118, 124, 133, 144–45; BL & IS, Report, 1899, pp. 41, 46, 50, 53–54, 57, 80, 82, 88; BL & IS, Report, 1900, pp. 23, 26, 29, 32, 51–52, 54–55, 58. The social functions of railroad brotherhoods portrayed here closely

parallel those of late nineteenth-and early twentieth-century Lynn, Massachusetts, unions examined by John T. Cumbler and of nonunion fraternal lodges described both by Cumbler and Don Doyle. John T. Cumbler, *Working-Class Community in Industrial America*, pp. 37–41, 44–53, 58–59, 68–69; Doyle, *The Social Order of a Frontier Community*, pp. 184–91.

3. U.S. Industrial Commission, *Report* 17:848.

4. Letter of "C." (Dodge) in *RC* 15 (May 1898): 366; BL & IS, *Report*, *1898*, p. 124; letter of P. J. Conlon (Kansas City, Kansas) in *Monthly Journal* 9 (May 1897): 156.

5. Letter of C. Yendys Retlaw (Kansas City) in *SJ* 1 (January 1887): 421; letter of "Extra Man" (Emporia) in *SJ* 8 (September 1893): 372; ORC, *Proceedings*, *1888*, pp. 164–65; ORC, *Proceedings*, *1893*, p. 262; letter of "Try It Again" (Winslow) in *RTJ* 5 (August 1888): 411.

6. This assessment is deduced from lists of officers of the following lodges: BRT lodges at Topeka, Las Vegas, and San Marcial (1886–1900, except 1888); ORC lodges at Emporia and Las Vegas (1884–99); and BLE lodges at Emporia (1876–89) and Albuquerque (1882–89).

7. *Las Vegas Daily Optic*, December 28, 1881; letter of H. D. Fuller (Topeka) in *SJ* 2 (October 1887): 264; *Raton Range*, December 29, 1892; *Topeka Daily Capital*, April 24, 1891; *Albuquerque Daily Citizen*, March 17, 1894.

8. U.S. Industrial Commission, *Report* 17:847; *Railway Carmen's Journal* 4 (November 1899): 101; letter Mrs. Will H. Schillinger (Rock Island, Illinois) in *Monthly Journal* 8 (January 1897): 539; *Monthly Journal* 9 (June 1897): 223.

9. Letter of Flora (Topeka) to *RTJ* 9 (May 1892): 419; letter of "An O.R.C. Member's Wife" (Needles) in *RC* 12 (July 1895): 399; Lloyd Reynolds and Charles Killingsworth, *Trade Union Publications*.

10. *LEJ* 32 (May 1898): 341 and 29 (April 1895): 322; letter of Mrs. C. A. Switzer (Chanute) in *LFM* 19 (October 1895): 895; letter of Mrs. Anna M. Starr (Argentine) in *LFM* 24 (May 1898): 554.

11. Letter of Mrs. T. H. Schmutz (address not given) in *LFM* 21 (July 1896): 86–87; letter of Minnie Sherman (Topeka) in *LFM* 29 (July 1900): 89.

12. Letter of J.F.F. (Raton) in *RTJ* 16 (February 1899): 163–64.

13. Letter of "One Who Was There" (Emporia) in *LEJ* 17 (June 1883): 312–13; *LEJ* 18 (October 1884): 610; letter of committee of lodge No. 251 (Raton) in *LEJ* 19 (January 1885): 37; letter of "Trediserp" (Winslow) in *LEJ* 32 (April 1898): 261.

14. Letter of Mrs. Lucy Walden (Topeka) in *SJ* 2 (December 1887): 352; letter of Mrs. Albert L. Beardsley (Chanute) in *LEJ* 26 (March 1896): 218; *LEJ* 25 (December 1891): 1125.

15. *RC* 1 (September 1884): 460; letter of Milo (Albuquerque) in *SJ* 6 (June 1891): 109; BL & IS, *Report, 1890,* p. 136; *Topeka Daily Capital,* March 6, 1892; *Newton Evening Kansan,* December 31, 1898; letter of W. H. T. (Arkansas City) in *RTJ* 8 (May 1891): 248–49; *LEJ* 19 (February 1885): 103; letter of W. J. Ribley (San Marcial) in *LEJ* 19 (July 1885): 416.

16. Editorial, *LFM* 8 (May 1884): 279; letter of Milo (Albuquerque) in *SJ* 6 (June 1891): 109.

17. Editorial, *RTJ* 5 (August 1888): 371; BL & IS, *Report, 1890,* p. 73; the following correspondence in the *RTJ:* George F. Gillette (Albuquerque) 5 (August 1888): 407–8; Bertha (Needles) 9 (August 1892): 671; "Fitz" (Raton) 12 (February 1895): 147; J. S. McEwen (Chanute) 12 (November 1895): 1026; letter of "La Junta" (La Junta) in *SJ* 4 (February 1890): 463; *Albuquerque Morning Democrat,* March 22, 1893.

18. *Neodesha Register,* September 9, 1892.

19. Letter of Grant Cornelius (Winslow) in *RTJ* 17 (June 1900): 440; letter of "A Member of 206" (Temple) in *RTJ* 12 (March 1895): 263.

20. Letter of W. H. T. (Arkansas City) in *RTJ* 8 (May 1891): 248–49; *Raton Comet,* January 23, 1885.

21. BL & IS, *Report, 1890,* p. 132.

22. Ibid., pp. 118, 132; letter of "Slim" (Chanute) in *RTJ* 14 (April 1897): 327; letter of "B. of L.F." (Santa Fe) in *LFM* 13 (October 1889): 928; U.S. Department of Labor, *Report, 1889,* pp. 37–39.

23. See the following correspondence to the *SJ:* "Guess" (Topeka) 3 (July 1888): 113; Mrs. George H. Dice (Newton) 8 (February 1894): 769; "I Know" (Topeka) 2 (January 1888): 400; "Sure" (Topeka) 2 (February 1888): 444.

24. *LEJ* 16 (November 1882): 581; *North Topeka Mail,* April 12, 1883; *Santa Fe* 1 (April 1898): 5–6; letter of W. N. Breen (Emporia) in *LFM* 27 (July 1899): 103; BL & IS, *Report, 1890,* p. 142.

25. T. P. O'Rourke, "The Fireman's Fate," in *LFM* 3 (November 1879): 331; *Neodesha Register,* May 27, 1892; U.S. Industrial Commission, *Report* 17:825; J. B. Kennedy, "The Beneficiary Features of the Railway Unions," in *Studies in American Trade Unionism,* ed. Jacob H. Hollander and George E. Barnett.

26. Kennedy, "Beneficiary Features," pp. 324–30; letter of "Rough Neck" (Newton) in *SJ* 8 (March 1894): 846; letter of John A. Martin (La Junta) in *LFM* 18 (March 1894): 294; letter of W. R. McNeil (Newton) in *RTJ* 12 (May 1895): 433–34. Membership in the BLE's insurance was reported regularly in the *LEJ.*

27. Editorial, *Monthly Journal* 9 (June 1897): 201.

28. George E. Barnett, *The Printers,* 89–107; Ronald Conklin Brown, "Hard-Rock Miners of the Great Basin and Rocky Mountain West, 1860–1920," pp. 408–12.

29. It is noteworthy that the highly mobile switchmen, trainmen, and enginemen were among the earliest and most strongly unionized, while the relatively stationary shopmen were slow to organize and were less successful in their efforts. Lloyd Ulman observed that highly mobile carpenters and printers were among the first and most thoroughly unionized. Melvyn Dubofsky found that the IWW was able to unionize the transient "timber beasts, hobo harvesters, and itinerant construction workers." Those workers with the most fleeting contact with a community may well have found the social benefits of unions most attractive. Ulman, *Rise of the National Trade Union*, p. 50; Melvyn Dubofsky, *We Shall Be All*, p. 148; Cottrell, *Railroader*, pp. 6–7, 13, 33, 42–50.

Chapter 8

1. Research for this study revealed twenty-six strikes. However, considering that many were very localized, that some lasted a matter of hours, if not minutes, and that many newspapers—the only sources of information on minor walkouts—have not been surveyed, thirty strikes is a conservative estimate.

2. *Harvey County News*, July 26, 1877.

3. *Atchison Daily Champion*, April 5, 1878; *Albuquerque Daily Citizen*, March 24, 1893, November 19, 1890; *Coolidge Citizen*, October 26, 1888; *Las Vegas Daily Optic*, July 22, 1890, July 23, 1890; *Emporia News*, July 23, 1888, July 28, 1888; McIsaac, *Railroad Telegraphers*, pp. 16, 34.

4. *Newton Daily Republican*, July 6, 1894; *Topeka Daily Capital*, April 22, 1893.

5. Payrolls, March–April 1878, May 1879, June 1894, AT & SF Collection; Tax Assessment Rolls, City of Emporia 1894, Lyon County Courthouse, Emporia, Kansas.

6. *Chanute Vidette*, July 26, 1894; *Las Vegas Daily Optic*, July 13, 1894; *Railroad Register*, July 20, 1894.

7. *Raton Range*, July 19, 1894.

8. *Topeka Commonwealth*, April 11, 1878; *Albuquerque Daily Citizen*, January 20, 1893; *Kansas City Star*, June 30, 1894.

9. James H. Ducker, "Workers, Townsmen and the Governor," pp. 24–26.

10. Payrolls, July 1894, AT & SF Collection. Besides those given in Table 6 the towns examined were Ottawa, Florence, Dodge City, Arkansas City, Wichita, La Junta, Trinidad, and San Marcial.

11. Ibid.

12. Ibid.

13. Ibid.

14. Ibid.

15. *Chicago Tribune*, July 9, 1894; International Association of Machinists, *Proceedings, 1895*, p. vi; *Topeka Daily Press*, June 29, 1894.

16. *Kansas City Star*, July 7, 1894; *Newton Kansan*, July 12, 1894.

17. *Albuquerque Daily Citizen*, June 29, 1894; *Kansas City Star*, July 4, 1894, July 5, 1894.

18. ORC, *Proceedings, 1895*, p. 68; *LFM* 17 (December 1893): supplement, p. 25; 18 (December 1894): 1214 and 26 (January 1899): 126; *RTJ* 10 (June 1894): 562 and 10 (December 1894): 1147; *Kansas City Star*, June 30, 1894, July 6, 1894.

19. Bender, *Community and Social Change*, p. 74.

20. *Harvey County News*, July 26, 1877, August 2, 1877; *Newton Kansan*, July 26, 1877; *Kansas State Gazette and Business Directory: 1878*, p. 583.

21. *Emporia Ledger*, April 11, 1878; *Newton Kansan*, May 2, 1878, May 9, 1878; *Topeka Commonwealth*, April 7, 1878; Report of J.D.Gunn to Governor George T. Anthony, Correspondence Received, Box No. 5, "Railroads, 1877, 1878" file, Anthony Papers.

22. *Emporia Gazette*, July 6, 1894; *Strong City Derrick*, July 7, 1894.

23. For Kansas towns, see the 1895 state manuscript census; for other towns, see the 1900 U.S. manuscript census.

24. *Kansas City Star*, July 10, 1894, July 1, 1894, July 5, 1894, July 7, 1894; *Topeka Daily Press*, July 22, 1894.

25. *Kansas City Star*, July 6, 1894, June 29, 1894, July 8, 1894; *Railroad Register*, July 5, 1894; *Topeka Daily Press*, July 22, 1894.

26. *Argentine Republic*, July 19, 1894, August 30, 1894; *Kansas City Star*, July 13, 1894; *Nickerson Argosy*, July 26, 1894.

27. *Albuquerque Daily Citizen*, July 3, 1894; *Santa Fe New Mexican*, July 7, 1894, July 3, 1894, July 11, 1894; letters of Judge Edward P. Sands to Sheriff McCuistion and U.S. Marshal Edward L. Hall and affidavits of U.S. Marshals Hall and John Wallace in *Union Trust Co. of N.Y. (Trustee)* v. *AT & SF RR Co.*, file 829, U.S. District Court, New Mexico Territory, 1st Judicial District.

28. *Las Vegas Daily Optic*, June 28, 1894, June 30, 1894, July 2, 1894, July 5, 1894.

29. *Las Vegas Daily Optic*, July 9, 1894, July 11, 1894; *Raton Range*, July 19, 1894, July 26, 1894, August 2, 1894.

30. *Topeka Daily Blade*, April 9, 1878, April 10, 1878; *Topeka Commonwealth*, April 11, 1878; Andreas, *History of Kansas*, pp. 563, 572–74, 577, 581.

31. *Newton Daily Republican*, July 3, 1894, July 7, 1894.

32. *Emporia Daily Republican*, July 2, 1894, July 6, 1894.

33. *Emporia Daily Republican*, July 3, 1894; *Emporia Tidings*, July 3, 1894.

34. *Emporia Gazette*, July 3, 1894; *Arkansas City Republican Traveler*, July 5, 1894.

35. *Topeka Daily Press*, August 14, 1894; *Kansas City Star*, July 19, 1894; *Arkansas City Republican Traveler*, July 5, 1894; Ray Ginger, *Eugene V. Debs*, pp. 130–31.

36. *Arkansas City Evening Dispatch*, March 19, 1888; *Albuquerque Daily Citizen*, July 12, 1894.

37. *Harvey County News*, July 26, 1877; *Chanute Blade*, April 20, 1893; *Emporia Daily Republican*, July 2, 1894; *Railroad Register*, April 28, 1893, April 21, 1893; *Las Vegas Daily Optic*, June 29, 1894.

38. *Nickerson Argosy*, April 20, 1893; *Topeka Daily Capital*, April 27, 1893.

39. *Newton Daily Republican*, August 23, 1894; *LEJ* 28 (October 1894): 949.

40. *Las Vegas Daily Optic*, September 26, 1894, October 11, 1894, November 28, 1894; *Railroad Register*, October 26, 1894; *Albuquerque Daily Citizen*, August 10, 1894; *Arkansas Valley Democrat*, August 24, 1894; *Kansas City Star*, July 19, 1894; *Emporia Tidings*, August 16, 1894; *Newton Evening Kansan*, April 22, 1899.

41. *Railroad Register*, October 26, 1894; *Albuquerque Daily Citizen*, September 7, 1894; *Kansas City Star*, July 18, 1894; *Las Vegas Daily Optic*, April 19, 1895; *Raton Reporter*, February 23, 1895.

42. *Las Vegas Daily Optic*, January 12, 1895; note of assessor W. F. Hendry on page following census listing in Kansas Census 1895 for Nickerson; William Pinkerton, *Personal Record*, p. 145.

Conclusion

1. Marshall, *Santa Fe*, p. 279.

2. Useful comparisons of the two schools can be found in Krueger, "American Labor Historiography"; Dubofsky, *Industrialism and the American Worker*; Brody, "The Old Labor History and the New"; and David Montgomery, "To Study the People."

3. John R. Commons and Associates, *History of Labor in the United States*, and Selig Perlman, *A History of Trade Unionism in the United States*, are the two preeminent works of the old school. The antagonistic relations of management and labor on the railroads are evident in three major studies by labor historians of the old school—Robert V. Bruce, *1877: Year of Violence*; Donald L. McMurry, *The Great Burlington Strike of 1888*; and Almont Lindsey, *The Pullman Strike*.

4. A notable, if one-sided, exception to this is Philip Foner's *History of the Labor Movement in the United States*, which gives emphasis to left wing dissent in the A. F. of L.

5. Two recent works which recognize this variation are Peter N.

Stearns' *Lives of Labor* and Irwin Yellowitz's *Industrialization and the American Labor Movement, 1850–1900.*

6. Hoxie, *A History of Trade Unionism*; Tannenbaum, *The Labor Movement* and *A Philosophy of Labor*; Thompson, *English Working Class*; Hobsbawm, *Labouring Men*; Herbert Gutman, "Work, Culture, and Society."

7. Brown, *Hard-Rock Miners*, pp. 145–46; George A. Stevens, *New York Typographical Union No. 6*, pp. 472–510. Another recent work to give prominence to unions' social role is Cumbler's *Working-Class Community*, pp. 37–41, 44–53, 58–59, 68–69, 157.

8. Tannenbaum, *A Philosophy of Labor*, p. 60.

9. Andrew Dawson, "The Paradox of Dynamic Technological Change and the Labor Aristocracy in the United States, 1880–1914"; Stearns, *Lives of Labor*, esp. p. 196.

10. David Montgomery, "Workers' Control of Machine Production in the Nineteenth Century."

11. Stuart D. Brandes, *American Welfare Capitalism, 1880–1940.*

12. Nelson, *Managers and Workers*; David Montgomery, "To Study the People," 491–92. The deterioration of labor relations on the Santa Fe in the face of the introduction of scientific management is documented in Carl Graves's "Scientific Management and the Santa Fe Railway Shopmen of Topeka, Kansas, 1900–1925."

13. Perlman, *History of Trade Unionism*, p. 182; Martin, *Enterprise Denied*, pp. 124–28.

14. For a discussion of labor historiography giving emphasis to ethnicity, see Milton Cantor's introduction to his edited work, *American Workingclass Culture*, pp. 3–30.

15. *Albuquerque Morning Democrat*, March 21, 1893; *Albuquerque Daily Citizen*, June 30, 1894, July 12, 1894.

16. Bender, *Community and Social Change in America*; Blumin, *The Urban Threshold*; Atherton, *Main Street on the Middle Border*; Richard Alcorn, "Leadership and Stability in Mid-Nineteenth Century America."

17. Herbert Gutman, "Workers' Search for Power"; John T. Cumbler, "Labor, Capital, and Community"; Harry Jebsen Jr., "The Role of Blue Island in the Pullman Strike of 1894"; Jeremy W. Kilar, "Community and Authority Response to the Saginaw Valley Lumber Strike of 1885"; Shelton Stromquist, "Community Structure and Industrial Conflict in Nineteenth Century Railroad Towns," paper given at the Convention of the Organization of American Historians, New York City, April 12, 1978; Martin H. Dodd, "Marlboro, Massachusetts and the Shoeworkers' Strike of 1898–1899."

18. Herbert Gutman, "The Braidwood Lockout of 1874"; U.S. Census 1870 for Braidwood, Illinois.

Bibliography

Archival Sources

Boston. Baker Library, Harvard University. J. Torr Harmer Papers.

Denver, Colorado. Federal Archives and Record Center. U.S. District Court, New Mexico Territory, First Judicial District.

Emporia, Kansas. Lyon County Courthouse. Kansas Census 1894.

Emporia, Kansas. Lyon County Courthouse. Kansas Tax Assessments Rolls, Emporia 1880, 1885, 1894, 1895, 1900.

Ithaca, New York. Collection of Regional History, Cornell University. Johnson Family Papers.

Topeka, Kansas. Kansas State Historical Society. Atchison, Topeka & Santa Fe Railway Collection.

Topeka, Kansas. Kansas State Historical Society. Governor George T. Anthony Papers.

Topeka, Kansas. Kansas State Historical Society. Governor Lorenzo Lewelling Papers.

Topeka, Kansas. Kansas State Historical Society. Kansas Adjutant General's Correspondence.

Topeka, Kansas. Kansas State Historical Society. Kansas Census 1885, 1895.

Topeka, Kansas. Kansas State Historical Society. Kansas Secretary of State, "Incorporations" 1889–94.

Topeka, Kansas. Kansas State Historical Society. William O. Hubbell Papers.

Trinidad, Colorado. Las Animas County Courthouse. Las Animas County Colorado District Court, Criminal Actions.

Washington, D.C. National Archives. U.S. Census 1880, 1900.

Washington, D.C. National Archives. U.S. Special Census 1885.

Government Documents

Kansas Board of Railroad Commissioners. *Report, 1892.* Topeka: Hamilton Printing, 1892.

Kansas Bureau of Labor and Industrial Statistics. *Report 1885–1900.*

Kansas House. *Journal.* 1889–99.

Kansas Senate. *Journal.* 1889–99.

Kansas State Board of Agriculture. *Report.* 1875–94.

New Mexico Council. *Journal.* 1893.

New Mexico House. *Journal.* 1893.

Taylor, Paul S. "Migratory Laborers in the Wheat Belts of the Middle West and California: Second Half of the Nineteenth Century." *Subcommittee on Migratory Labor of the Senate Committee on Labor and Public Welfare on Migrant and Seasonal Farmworker Powerlessness.* 91st Cong., 1st and 2d sess., 1970.

U.S. Bureau of the Census. *Historical Statistics of the United States: Colonial Times to 1970.* Bicentennial ed. 2 vols. Washington, D.C.: Government Printing Office, 1975.

U.S. Department of the Interior. *Statistics of the Population of the United States: Tenth Census.*

U.S. Department of the Interior. Bureau of the Census. *Compendium of the Tenth Census.*

U.S. Department of the Interior. Census Office. *Eleventh Census of the United States, 1890.*

———. *Report on the Agencies of Transportation in the United States.* 47th Cong., 2d sess., 1883.

U.S. Department of Labor. *Annual Report of the Commissioner of Labor, 1889.* Washington, D.C.: Government Printing Office, 1890.

———. *Fifteenth Annual Report of the Commissioner of Labor, 1900.* 2 vols. Washington, D.C.: Government Printing Office, 1900.

U.S. Department of Labor. Bureau of Labor Statistics. *Bulletin #499.*

U.S. Industrial Commission. *Reports,* vol. 17.

U.S. Interstate Commerce Commission. *Evidence Taken by the Interstate Commerce Commission in the Matter of Proposed advances in Freight Rates by Carriers.* S. Doc. 725, 61st Cong., 3d sess., 1911.

Other Primary Sources

Adams, B. B., Jr. "The Every-Day Life of Railroad Men." In *The American Railway: Its Construction, Development, Management, and Appliances.* By Thomas C. Clark and others. New York: Charles Scribner's Sons, 1897.

Andreas, A. T. *History of the State of Kansas*. Chicago: A. T. Andreas, 1883.

Annals of Emporia and Lyon County. n.p., [1898].

Atchison Railroad Employes' Association. *Charter and By-Laws, and Rules and Regulations*. Topeka: Kansas Publishing House, 1884.

Atchison, Topeka & Santa Fe. *Annual Report*. 1873–1900.

———. *Rules and Instructions for the Information and Guidance of Employes in the Telegraph Department*. Topeka: Kansas Publishing House, 1882.

———. *Rules and Instructions Governing Employes of the Department of Track, Bridges and Buildings*. Topeka: Hall and O'Donald Litho., 1892.

———. *Rules and Instructions Governing Employes of the Department of Track, Bridges and Buildings*. Topeka: George W. Crane, 1883.

———. *Rules and Regulations for Conductors*. n.p., 1889.

———. *Rules and Regulations of the Operating Department*. n.p., 1901.

Atchison, Topeka & Santa Fe, Accounting Department.

———. *Instructions to Station Freight Agents in Effect August 1st, 1890*. n.p., n.d.

The Biographical Directory of the Railway Officials of America for 1887. Chicago: Railway Age Publishing, [1887].

Brotherhood of Locomotive Engineers. *Official Report of Agreements Made Between the Officials of the Roads Represented and the Committees Representing the Engineers Employed Thereon, as reported prior to April 1st, 1898*. Cleveland: Cleveland Printing and Publishing, 1898.

Busser, S. E. *The Santa Fe Reading-Room System*. n.p., n.d.

Chase, C.M. *The Editor's Run in New Mexico and Colorado*. Montpelier, Vt.: Argus and Patriot Steam Book and Job Printing House, 1882.

Chittenden Directory Company. *Chittenden's 1900–1 Emporia City Directory*. St. Louis: Chittenden Directory Co. 1900.

Colorado State Business Directory, 1882. Denver: J. A. Blake, 1882.

Colorado State Business Directory, 1887. Denver: James R. Ives, 1887.

Coulter and Ramaley. *Historical and Business Review of Emporia, 1880*. Emporia, Kans.: Ledger Printing House and Book Bindery, n.d.

Cunningham, Frank. *Big Dan: The Story of a Colorful Railroader*. Salt Lake City: Deseret News Press, 1946.

Cunningham, William J. "Scientific Management in the Operation of Railroads." *Quarterly Journal of Economics* 25:539–62.

Davis, E. S. *Emporia City Directory 1896*. Iola, Kans.: E. S. Davis, n.d.

Denham, Robert S. *The Emporia City Directory 1890–91*. Emporia, Kans.: Ezra Lamborn Printer and Binder, [1890].

Dils, Lenore. *Horny Toad Man*. El Paso: Boots and Saddle Press, 1966.

Eastman, Crystal. *Work-Accidents and the Law*. New York: Charities Publication Committee, 1910.

Emporia City Directory, 1877. n.p., n.d.

French, Chauncey Del. *Railroadman*. New York: Macmillan, 1938.

George, Charles B. *Forty Years on the Rail*. Chicago: R.R.Donnelley and Sons, 1887.

Gilman, Nicholas P. *A Dividend to Labor: A Study of Employers' Welfare Institutions*. Boston: Houghton, Mifflin, 1899.

History of the Arkansas Valley, Colorado. Chicago: O.L.Baskin and Co., 1881.

A History of the State Normal School of Kansas for the First Twenty-Five Years. Topeka: Kansas Publishing House, 1889.

Hosterman and Garver. *The Emporia City Directory for 1885–86*. Sioux City, Iowa: Tribune Press, 1884.

International Association of Machinists. *Proceedings*. 1889–99.

Journal (organ of the Brotherhood of Boilermakers and Iron Ship Builders of America). 1897–1900.

Kansas State Gazette and Business Directory: 1878. Detroit: R. L. Polk and Co. and A. C. Danser, n.d.

Kindelan, Joseph. *The Trackman's Helper*. Mitchell, Dakota: Joseph Kindelan, 1888.

Locomotive Engineers' Journal. 1873–1900.

Locomotive Firemen's Magazine. 1879–1900.

Lodge, Henry Cabot. "A Perilous Business and the Remedy." *North American Review* 423:189–95.

Monthly Balance (organ of the Brotherhood of Station Men). August-October 1891.

Monthly Journal (organ of the International Association of Machinists). 1896–1900.

National Women's Christian Temperance Union. *Minutes, 1882*. Brooklyn, 1882.

Order of Railway Conductors. *Proceedings*. 1888–99.

Pinkerton, Allan. *Tests on Passenger Conductors Made by the National Detective Agency*. Chicago: Beach and Barnard, 1870.

Pinkerton, William J. *His Personal Record: Stories of Railroad Life*. Kansas City, Mo.: Pinkerton Publishing, 1904.

Poor, Henry V. *Manual of the Railroads of the United States: 1869–70*. New York: H. V. and H. W. Poor, 1869.

Railroad Telegrapher. 1889–1901.

Railroad Trainmen's Journal. 1884–1900.

Railway Carmen's Journal. 1893–1900.

Railway Conductor. 1884–1900.

Railway Gazette. 1870–1900.

Railway Times (organ of the ARU). 1894–96.

Reed, J. Harvey. *Forty Years a Locomotive Engineer: Thrilling Tales of the Rail.* Prescott, Wash.: Charles H. O'Neil, 1912.

Santa Fe (organ of the Topeka RRYMCA). 1898–1900.

Santa Fe Magazine. 1906–26.

Sinclair, Angus. *Locomotive Engine Running and Management.* New York: J. Wiley and Sons, 1888.

Switchmen's Journal. 1886–94.

Truitt, J. W. *General City Directory of Emporia, Kansas, 1883.* Emporia: G. H. Rowland and Co., Steam Printers, 1883.

Turner, Mrs. Avery. *Avery Turner: Pioneer Railroad and Empire Builder of the Great Southwest.* Amarillo: Southwestern Printing, 1933.

Newspapers

Albuquerque Daily Citizen. 1885–95.

Albuquerque Evening Democrat. 1885–86.

Albuquerque Morning Democrat. 1882–89, 1891–95.

Albuquerque Morning Journal. 1882.

Argentine Republic. 1887–1900.

Arkansas City Daily Traveler. April–May 1893, June–August 1894.

Arkansas City Evening Dispatch. 1887–88, 1892.

Arkansas City Republican Traveler. November 1888–96.

Arkansas Valley Democrat (Arkansas City). June–August 1894.

Atchison Daily Champion. April 1878.

Chanute Blade. 1887–1900.

Chanute Daily Tribune. 1894.

Chanute Times. 1887–91.

Chanute Vidette. 1887–88, 1894.

Chronicle (Nickerson). 1894–97.

Coolidge Citizen. 1886–90.

Coolidge Times. 1887–90.

Dodge City Democrat. June 30–September 1, 1894.

Emporia Daily Republican. 1882, 1884–85, 1888, November 1890–92, 1894.

Emporia Democrat. 1882–85.

Emporia Gazette. 1890–1901.

Emporia Ledger. 1877–78.

Emporia News. 1870, 1877–89.

Emporia Tidings. June–August 1894.

Galveston Daily News. October 1892, November–December 1900.

Hamilton County Bulletin (Coolidge and Syracuse). September 1890–May 1891.

Harvey County News (Newton). 1876–79.

Kansas City Labor Record. 1894–1900.

Kansas City Star. 1883, 1894.

La Junta Tribune. 1898–99.

Las Vegas Daily Optic. 1880–1900.

Neodesha Register. 1891–93.

News and Press (Raton). October 1881–May 1882.

Newton Daily Republican. June–December 1894.

Newton Evening Kansan. 1897–1900.

Newton Kansan. 1877–79, 1894–97.

Nickerson Argosy. Dec. 1878–June 1879, Nov. 1890–92, 1893–97.

Nickerson Register. March 1888.

North Topeka Mail. October 1882–December 1883.

Otero County Eagle (La Junta). September 1889–June 1890.

Peabody Gazette. November 1888–96.

Pueblo Chieftain. July 1877–April 1878.

R.R. Employes' Companion (Topeka, Ottawa, Chanute, Wellington). 1888–90.

Railroad Register (Topeka). 1893–95.

Raton Comet. 1884–86.

Raton Gazette. 1898–1900.

Raton Guard. November 1881–July 1882.

Raton Range. 1888–1900.

Raton Reporter. 1894–1900.

San Marcial Reporter. 1888–92.

Santa Fe New Mexican. 1888, 1890, 1893–94.

Santa Fe Reporter. September 1892–February 1893.

Strong City Derrick. June–September 1894.

Topeka Commonwealth. 1869–70, 1876–78.

Topeka Daily Blade. 1877–78.

Topeka Daily Capital. 1879–80, 1885, 1890–94, 1900.

Topeka Daily Press. June–August 1894.

Topeka Daily State Journal. 1883–84, 1897.

Topeka State Record. 1869–75.

Trinidad Daily News. 1879–84, 1893.

Weekly New Mexican Review (Santa Fe). 1893.

Theses and Dissertations

Black, Paul V. "Management Personnel Policies on the Burlington Railroad: 1860–1900." Ph.D. dissertation, University of Wisconsin-Madison, 1972.

Brown, Ronald Conklin. "Hard-Rock Miners of the Great Basin and Rocky Mountain West, 1860–1920." Ph.D. dissertation, University of Illinois, 1975.

Fisk, Leon R. "Workingmen's Democracy: The Knights of Labor in Local Politics, 1886–1896." Ph.D. dissertation, University of Rochester, 1977.

Graves, Carl Russell. "Scientific Management and the Santa Fe Railway Shopmen of Topeka, Kansas, 1900–1925." Ph.D. dissertation, Harvard University, 1980.

Heath, Jim F. "A Study of the Influence of the Atchison, Topeka & Santa Fe Railroad Upon the Economy of New Mexico, 1878 to 1900." Master's Thesis, University of New Mexico, 1955.

Licht, Walter M. "Nineteenth Century American Railwaymen: A Study in the Nature and Organization of Work." Ph.D. dissertation, Princeton University, 1977.

Lightner, David. "Labor on the Illinois Central Railroad, 1852–1900." Ph.D. dissertation, Cornell University, 1969.

Rickard, Louise E. "The Impact of Populism on Electoral Patterns in Kansas, 1880–1900: A Quantitative Analysis." Ph.D. dissertation, University of Kansas, 1974.

Secondary Sources

Atherton, Lewis. *Main Street on the Middle Border.* 1st Quadrangle Paperback ed. Chicago: Quadrangle Paperbacks, 1966.

Barnett, Richard A. *The New Country: A Social History of the American Frontier, 1776–1890.* New York: Oxford University Press, 1974.

Bender, Thomas. *Community and Social Change in America.* New Brunswick, N.J.: Rutgers University Press, 1978.

Black, Paul V. "Experiment in Bureaucratic Centralization: Employee Blacklisting on the Burlington Railroad, 1877–1892." *Business History Review* 51:444–59.

Blumin, Stuart M. *The Urban Threshold: Growth and Change in a Nineteenth Century American Community.* Chicago: University of Chicago, 1976.

Bradley, Glenn D. *The Story of the Santa Fe.* Boston: Gorham Press, 1920.

Brody, David. "The Old Labor History and the New: In Search of an American Working Class." *Labor History* 20:111–26.

———. *Steelworkers in America: The Nonunion Era.* Cambridge: Harvard University Press, 1960.

Brown, Ronald C. *Hard-Rock Miners: The Intermountain West, 1860–1920*. College Station: Texas A & M University Press, 1979.

Bruce, Robert V. *1877: Year of Violence*. Indianapolis and New York: New Bobbs-Merrill, 1959.

Bryant, Keith L., Jr. *History of the Atchison, Topeka and Santa Fe Railway*. New York: Macmillan, 1974.

Chandler, Alfred D., Jr. *The Visible Hand: The Managerial Revolution in American Business*. Cambridge: Belknap Press of Harvard University Press, 1977.

Chudacoff, Howard P. *Mobile Americans: Residential and Social Mobility in Omaha 1880–1920*. New York: Oxford University Press, 1972.

Cochran, Thomas C. *Railroad Leaders, 1845–1890: The Business Mind in Action*. New York: Russell and Russell, 1965.

Connelley, William E. *History of Kansas Newspapers*. Topeka: Kansas State Printing Plant, 1916.

Cottrell, W. Fred. *The Railroader*. Stanford, Calif.: Stanford University Press, 1940.

Cumbler, John T. "Labor, Capital, and Community: The Struggle for Power." *Labor History* 15:395–415.

————. *Working-Class Community in Industrial America: Work, Leisure, and Struggle in Two Industrial Cities, 1880–1930*. Contributions in Labor History, No. 8. Westport, Conn.: Greenwood Press, 1979.

Curti, Merle. *The Making of an American Community: A Case Study of Democracy in a Frontier County*. Stanford, Calif.: Stanford University Press, 1959.

Dawson, Andrew. "The Paradox of Dynamic Technological Change and the Labor Aristocracy in the United States, 1880–1914." *Labor History* 20:325–51.

Dodd, Martin H. "Marlboro, Massachusetts and the Shoeworkers' Strike of 1898–1899." *Labor History* 20:376–97.

Donovan, Frank P., Jr. *The Railroad in Literature*. Boston: Railway and Locomotive Historical Society, 1940.

Doyle, Don Harrison. *The Social Order of a Frontier Community: Jacksonville, Illinois, 1825–70*. Urbana and Chicago: University of Illinois Press, 1978.

Dubofsky, Melvyn. *Industrialism and the American Worker, 1865–1920*. Arlington Heights, Ill.: AHM Publishing, 1975.

————. *We Shall Be All: A History of the Industrial Workers of the World*. Chicago: Quadrangle Books, 1969.

Ducker, James H. "Workers, Townsmen and the Governor: The Santa Fe Enginemen's Strike, 1878." *Kansas History*, 5:23–32.

Dykstra, Robert R. *The Cattle Towns.* New York: Atheneum 1973.

Fishlow, Albert. "Productivity and Technological Change in the Railroad Sector, 1840–1910." In *Output, Employment and Productivity in the United States After 1800.* National Bureau of Economic Research, Conference on Research in Income and Wealth, vol. 30. New York: National Bureau of Economic Research, 1966.

Friedman, Lawrence M. *A History of American Law.* New York: Simon and Schuster, 1973.

Ginger, Ray. *Eugene V. Debs: A Biography.* 1st Collier Books ed. New York: Collier Books, 1962.

Gitelman, Howard M. *Workingmen of Waltham: Mobility in American Urban Industrial Development 1850–1890.* Baltimore: Johns Hopkins University Press, 1974.

Griffen, Clyde, and Griffen, Sally. *Natives and Newcomers: The Ordering of Opportunity in Mid-Nineteenth-Century Poughkeepsie.* Cambridge: Harvard University Press, 1978.

Gutman, Herbert G. "The Braidwood Lockout of 1874." *Journal of the Illinois State Historical Society* 53:5–28.

———. "Work, Culture, and Society in Industrializing America, 1815–1919." *American Historical Review* 78:531–88.

———. "Workers' Search for Power: Labor in the Gilded Age." In *The Gilded Age: A Reappraisal.* Ed. H. Wayne Morgan. Syracuse, N.Y.: Syracuse University Press, 1963.

Harvey, Katherine A. *The Best-Dressed Miners: Life and Labor in the Maryland Coal Region, 1835–1910.* Ithaca, N.Y.: Cornell University Press, 1969.

Hertel, D. W. *The History of the Brotherhood of Maintenance of Way Employes: Its Birth and Growth.* Washington, D.C.: Ransdell, 1955.

Hiller, E. T. *The Strike: A Study in Collective Action.* Chicago: University of Chicago, 1928.

Hinckley, William S. *The Early Days of the Santa Fe.* Topeka: Crane and Co., n.d.

Hollander, Jacob H. and Barnett, George E., eds. *Studies in American Trade Unionism.* New York: Henry Holt and Co., 1907.

Hoxie, Robert H. *A History of Trade Unionism in the United States.* New York and London: D. Appleton and Company, 1917.

Jebsen, Harry, Jr. "The Role of Blue Island in the Pullman Strike of 1894." *Journal of the Illinois State Historical Society* 67:275–93.

Johnson, Arthur M. and Supple, Barry E. *Boston Capitalists and Western Railroads: A Study in the Nineteenth-Century Railroad Investment Process.* Cambridge: Harvard University Press, 1967.

Jones, Gareth Stedmen. *Outcast London: A Study in the Relationship Between Classes in Victorian Society.* Oxford: Clarendon, 1971.

Katz, Michael B. *The People of Hamilton, Canada West: Family and Class in a Mid-Nineteenth-Century City.* Cambridge: Harvard University Press, 1975.

Kilar, Jeremy W. "Community and Authority Response to the Saginaw Valley Lumber Strike of 1885." *Journal of Forest History* 20:67−79.

Korman, Gerd. *Industrialization, Immigration and Americanization: The View From Milwaukee, 1866−1921.* Madison: State Historical Society of Wisconsin, 1967.

Krueger, Thomas A. "American Labor Historiography, Old and New: A Review Essay." *Journal of Social History* 4:277−85.

Kuznets, Simon. *Seasonal Variation in Industry and Trade.* Publications of the National Bureau of Economic Research, Inc., No. 22. New York: National Bureau of Economic Research, 1933.

Lamar, Howard R. *The Far Southwest 1846−1912: A Territorial History.* New York: W. W. Norton and Co. 1970.

Lindsey, Almont. *The Pullman Strike: The Story of a Unique Experiment and of a Great Labor Upheaval.* Chicago: University of Chicago Press, 1942.

McIsaac, Archibald M. *The Order of Railroad Telegraphers: A Study in Trade Unionism and Collective Bargaining.* Princeton, N.J.: Princeton University Press, 1933.

McMurry, Donald L. "Labor Policies of the General Managers' Association of Chicago, 1886−1894." *Journal of Economic History* 13:160−78.

Marshall, James. *Santa Fe: The Railroad That Built an Empire.* New York: Random House, 1945.

Martin, Albro. *Enterprise Denied: Origins of the Decline of American Railroads, 1897−1917.* New York: Columbia University Press, 1911.

─────. *James J. Hill and the Opening of the Northwest.* New York: Oxford University Press, 1976.

Mater, Dan. "The Development and Operation of the Railroad Seniority System." *Journal of Business of the University of Chicago* 13:387−419.

Miller, Richard Ulric. "American Railroad Unions and the National Railways of Mexico: An Exercise in Nineteenth Century Proletarian Manifest Destiny." *Labor History* 15:239−60.

Montgomery, David. "Workers' Control of Machine Production in the Nineteenth Century." *Labor History* 17:485−96.

Nelli, Humbert S. *Italians in Chicago, 1880−1930: A Study in Ethnic Mobility.* New York: Oxford University Press, 1970.

Nelson, Daniel. *Managers and Workers: Origins of the New Factory*

System in the United States, 1880–1920. Madison: University of Wisconsin Press, 1975.

Ozanne, Robert. *A Century of Labor-Management Relations at McCormick and International Harvester.* Madison: University of Wisconsin Press, 1967.

Painter, Leonard. *Brotherhood of Railway Carmen of America.* Kansas City, Mo.: Brotherhood of Railway Carmen of America, 1941.

Patterson, Richard. "Train Robbery: The Birth, Flowering, & Decline of a Notorious Western Enterprise." *American West* 14:48–53.

Pelling, Henry. *Popular Politics and Society in Late Victorian Britain.* New York: St. Martin's Press, 1968.

Perlman, Mark. *Labor Union Theories in America: Background and Development.* Evanston, Ill.: Row, Peterson and Company, 1958.

———. *The Machinists: A New Study in American Trade Unionism.* Cambridge: Harvard University Press, 1961.

Pollack, Norman. *The Populist Response to Industrial America, Midwest Populist Thought.* Norton Library ed. New York: W. W. Norton and Co., 1966.

Rayback, Joseph George. *A History of American Labor.* 1966 ed. New York: Free Press; London: Collier-Macmillan, 1966.

Reynolds, Lloyd G. and Killingsworth, Charles C. *Trade Union Publications: The Official Journals, Convention Proceedings, and Constitutions of International Unions and Federations, 1850–1941.* 3 vols. Baltimore: Johns Hopkins Press, 1945.

Richardson, Reed C. *The Locomotive Engineer, 1863–1963: A Century of Railway Labor Relations and Work Rules.* Ann Arbor, Mich.: Bureau of Industrial Relations, Graduate School of Business Administration, University of Michigan, 1963.

Richmond, Robert W. *Kansas: A Land of Contrast.* St. Charles, Mo.: Forum Press, 1974.

Rister, Carl Coke. *Land Hunger: David L. Payne and the Oklahoma Boomers.* Norman: University of Oklahoma Press, 1942.

Robinson, W. S. "Ecological Correlations and the Behavior of Individuals." *American Sociological Review* 15:351–57.

Shannon, David A. "Eugene V. Debs: Conservative Labor Editor." *Indiana Magazine of History* 47:357–64.

Stearns, Peter N. "Measuring the Evolution of Strike Movements." *International Review of Social History* 19:1–27.

Stevens, George A. *New York Typographical Union No. 6: Study of a Modern Trade Union and Its Predecessors.* Albany, New York: J. B. Lyon, 1913.

Stover, John. *The Life and Decline of the American Railroad.* New York:

Oxford University Press, 1970.

Taft, Philip. "Theories of the Labor Movement." In *Interpreting the Labor Movement.* Ed. George W. Brooks, Milton Derber, David A. McCabe and Philip Taft. Champaign, Ill.: Industrial Relations Research Association, 1952.

Tannenbaum, Frank. *The Labor Movement: Its Conservative Functions and Social Consequences.* New York: G. P. Putnam's Sons, 1921.

———. *A Philosophy of Labor.* New York: Alfred A. Knopf, 1951.

Thernstrom, Stephan. *The Other Bostonians: Poverty and Progress in the American Metropolis: 1880–1970.* Cambridge: Harvard University Press, 1973.

———. *Poverty and Progress: Social Mobility in a Nineteenth Century City.* Cambridge: Harvard University Press, 1964.

Thompson, E. P. *The Making of the English Working Class.* 1966 ed. New York: Vintage Books, 1966.

Treble, J. H. "The Seasonal Demand for Adult Labour in Glasgow, 1890–1914." *Social History* 3:43–60.

Ulman, Lloyd. *The Rise of the National Trade Union.* Cambridge: Harvard University Press, 1955.

Vestal, Stanley. *Queen of Cowtowns: Dodge City.* New York: Harper and Brothers, 1952.

Walker, Edith and Leibengood, Dorothy. "Labor Organization in Kansas in the Early Eighties." *Kansas Historical Quarterly* 5:283–90.

Waters, L. L. *Steel Trails to Santa Fe.* Lawrence: University of Kansas Press, 1950.

Wiebe, Robert H. *The Search for Order, 1877–1920.* New York: Hill and Wang, 1967.

———. *The Segmented Society: An Introduction to the Meaning of America.* New York: Oxford University Press, 1975.

Worley, E. D. *Iron Horses of the Santa Fe Trail.* Dallas: Southwest Railroad Historical Society, 1965.

Wright, James E. *The Politics of Populism: Dissent in Colorado.* New Haven: Yale University Press, 1974.

Zornow, William F. *Kansas: A History of the Jayhawk State.* Norman: University of Oklahoma Press, 1957.

Index